INCENTIVE-BASED
INCOMES POLICIES

To the memory of
Abba Lerner, Arthur Okun, and Sidney Weintraub.

CONTENTS

LIST OF FIGURES

LIST OF TABLES

ACKNOWLEDGMENTS

This book is the second that Middlebury College has done on the topic of incentive anti-inflation plans; the first, done six years ago, introduced me to Middlebury. Both books are based on the proceedings of a Middlebury Conference on Economic Affairs, funded jointly by the Christian A. Johnson Endeavor Foundation and the Institute of Economic and Monetary Affairs. It is impossible to express how important those conferences have been to the intellectual atmosphere of Middlebury; because of them, Middlebury has become a center of economic policy discussions and one of the few undergraduate colleges where undergraduates interact with economics faculty from a variety of top universities, delving into the depths of theory and policy. The economic conference participants and other visitors have stimulated our students to consider issues beyond textbooks, and the entire school is enormously grateful to the Institute of Economic and Monetary Affairs, Julie Kidd, and the Christian A. Johnson Foundation for their support.

The book reflects the hard work of a great number of people, especially Sheila Cassin, secretary for the Middlebury College Economics Department, and Helen Reiff, president of Maxi Editorial Service. Helen not only helped coordinate the volume but also organized the bibliography and compiled the index.

I would like to thank all the individuals who attended the conference on which this volume is based and the members of my senior seminar at Middlebury who spent an entire semester working on these papers and the conference. I learned much from them and thank them. The papers all benefited from comments by the participants and students. I served as a conduit for the cross-fertilization of ideas, and added a few of my own. The authors showed amazing

xv

patience and good humor in the long revision process, and my appreciation is sincere.

This is the last book of mine for which Carol Franco will be the editor: not because she did not do an excellent job—she always does—but because she has deservedly moved up the corporate ladder and is now president of Ballinger Publishing Company. I thank her and also my new editor at Ballinger, Marjorie Williams, who took over responsibility for this book in midstream and did a wonderful job. Their good humor and *joie de vivre* makes working with them a pleasure. I thank them.

Others who played important roles in preparing this volume (and whose modesty almost prevented them from being profusely thanked—but I do thank them profusely) include Dave Barber, Barbara Roth, Gerry Galvin, and Wendy Wyatt.

FOREWORD

Our economy seems repeatedly to be on a tightrope, precariously negotiating a narrow passage between spiraling inflation and higher unemployment. Sometimes the fine line between them is called the NAIRU, for non-accelerating inflation rate of unemployment. The word is as unattractive as the condition, and the physical analogy it suggests is misplaced. But it has become part of the macroeconomists' vernacular.

No one can ever infallibly predict how the NAIRU will fluctuate. Expanding the economy in order to lower unemployment always entails some risk of generating faster inflation. The risk is greater as the actual unemployment rate is lower. But it is always hard to evaluate. Experts will disagree about the odds. Economists, and also politicians and the general public, will differ in their priorities, in how much risk of higher inflation they are willing to accept in the interest of reducing unemployment.

How do we as economists advise policymakers who are trying to steer the economy between the two hazards? Most conference attendees and most of the contributors to this volume have concluded that the predicament of conventional macroeconomic policy is intolerable. We believe that two or three extra points of unemployment—running the economy at seven or eight percent unemployment instead of four or five percent—is too costly a way of ensuring against crossing the NAIRU and triggering faster and faster inflation.

Our alternative is simple. We must find a less costly insurance policy, one that will greatly diminish the risk of accelerating prices at low unemployment rates. Of course, there are dissenters from this consensus, notably at this conference William Poole, recently a Member of the President's Council of Economic Advisers.

In my opinion, there is nothing *optimal* about the NAIRU. Indeed it is the connotation of optimality in the word "natural" that leads me to use the acronym in place of "natural rate of unemployment." By any name, it does not smell as sweet as a Walrasian equilibrium. It is not the result of intersections of marginal productivity schedules with labor supply curves. Whether you call it equilibrium or disequilibrium, it is not a situation in which prices have cleared markets but rather one in which excess supplies of labor and productive capacity persist.

Our economy is dominated by non-Walrasian institutions. Most wages and prices are decision variables determined by negotiation or administrative choice rather than by impersonal auction markets. Collective bargaining is not a way of life contemplated by Walras or by Arrow and Debreu. Even in the absence of unions, unemployed workers have very little of the influence on wages that they should and would have in competitive markets.

During the fall semester 1984–85, my own university was torn by a labor dispute between the administration and a newly organized union of clerical and technical workers. To me as an observing economist, it was striking that the supply/demand balance in the relevant labor markets was hardly ever mentioned by the two sides or by their partisans among faculty, students, and townspeople. It would have been considered "an inappropriate issue" for the university to raise, and it would have been unwise for the union to mention. At prevailing wages, benefits, and working conditions there seemed to be an excess supply of potential employees. In a Walrasian world, this would have led to a fall in wages. In the actual circumstances it was irrelevant. The existing employees had obtained the power to ignore such competition, and debates on the campus concerned the "justice" of their claims on the university's resources. The example is quite typical.

Our wage- and price-setting institutions respond asymmetrically to micro- and macroeconomic shocks. Prices and wages rise more readily and quickly than they fall, not only absolutely but relative to their ongoing inertial trends. The asymmetries apply over both time and space. Sectoral shifts of demand and supply, like the energy shocks of unhappy stagflationary memory, are on average inflationary, because they raise prices and/or wages more in excess-demand sectors than they lower them in excess-supply markets.

Given the institutions that generate these results, individual decisions to raise prices or wages damage third parties; they inflict, on society at large, costs that the price-makers or wage negotiators do not take into account. Just as markets fail to impose on those who pollute air and water the social costs of their acts, so inflation pollution is an externality neither felt nor considered by businesses and unions. Just as we seek by public intervention to internalize the costs of actions that damage the natural environment, so we can try to internalize the macroeconomic costs of decentralized price and wage decisions. That, too, will require government intervention.

Two general strategies of intervention are available. One is to make the world more Walrasian, more competitive. We can revamp our institutions toward the model Poole has in mind when he says, in effect: "Let the economy adjust to monetary and fiscal policies, rather than adapting those macro policies to the state of the economy. Accept as natural whatever unemployment rate comes out of those processes of adjustment." I don't think that dream can be made to come true. But I certainly do not exclude pro-competitive reforms from the agenda.

Every Council of Economic Advisers, Republican or Democratic, has had a list of pro-inflation "sacred cows" deserving of slaughter, much the same list year after year: Davis-Bacon, farm price supports, subsidies and restrictions of competition for the American merchant marine, vigorous antitrust enforcement, and on and on. Economists are virtually unanimous in favoring reforms of this kind, but they are politically difficult to obtain.

The second and more controversial approach is *incomes policy.* It is by no means inconsistent with the agenda of pro-competitive reform. This approach aims to create new institutions to offset the inflationary biases of existing price- and wage-setting institutions, recognizing that the latter are entrenched for many reasons, often for good social purposes. The tax- and market-based incomes policies proposed and discussed in this volume are designed precisely to restrain and correct the inflationary biases of existing institutions.

Advocates know that these measures inevitably entail administrative inefficiencies and inequities, and that they are bound to distort in some degree the allocation of resources among economic activities. However, we live in an imperfect world, and we have to make "second best" judgments. Ultimately the decisive consideration is that the macroeconomic losses of running the economy with chronic excess unemployment of labor and capacity are greater by orders of magnitude than the social costs of incomes policies.

For example, if the federal corporate and personal income tax codes are used to induce compliance with guideposts for wage and price increases, we have to expect and tolerate slippages of the same kind and degree that characterize other provisions of these codes. Despite these shortcomings, we know from experience that tax incentives and disincentives do work in the intended directions, even though they are administered and enforced largely by self-declaration and selective surveillance.

The design of incomes policies is still a worthy challenge to the imagination and ingenuity of economic architects, We need not rely exclusively on tax systems; we should be able to exploit other governmental programs and laws. Consider, for example, unemployment compensation. Some critics contend that its benefits increase the NAIRU by promoting voluntary unemployment. They probably exaggerate these effects, but reforms could diminish the disincentives for seeking and taking jobs without impairing benefits. A more important and unconventional reform of the unemployment compensation system would be to strengthen and extend the "merit rating" feature of its financing. Tax penalties could be levied on employers who have raised wages beyond guidepost ceilings during periods of high or rising unemployment.

In the current political and economic climate one cannot be optimistic about the prospects of reforms and innovations to diminish the inflationary risk of full employment. When the sun is shining no one cares to fix the leaky roof. Both inflation and unemployment are lower than they were early in the 1980s. Their relative improvement blinds the nation to the fact that on both counts we did much better in the 1950s and 1960s. Certainly we will never have effective incomes policies without presidential leadership of the highest order, and we cannot expect such a commitment in the present ideological mood of the country.

What is most disheartening is that the labor movement, which has the most to gain from full employment, has still learned nothing from the macroeconomic disappointments of the last fifteen years. Like business managers, labor leaders and their economists continue to discuss incomes policies myopically, in terms of burdens and sacrifices and their distribution. The larger picture is not one of sacrifice; from a national viewpoint there are immense gains to be achieved. Economy-wide restraints on *nominal* wages and prices will make nobody worse off. Labor will be better off because there will be more jobs.

This volume will be a helpful contribution to the public policy debate, especially if it attracts more economists to this important and challenging subject. The essays here collected cover the major proposals now on the table, specifically TIP and MAP. History tells us that intellectual, ideological, and political fashions change. The cruel unemployment/inflation dilemma is not going to disappear. Those who regard its resolution as the basic economic problem of modern capitalism must be ready with concrete remedies when the need and opportunity arise.

James Tobin
Yale University
July 19, 1985

INTRODUCTION

David C. Colander

Ideas and policies do not just come into existence; they evolve over time. Following that evolution is an interesting pastime, although more in the sense of watching a cricket than a soccer match. This book is one step in the evolution of an idea; it concerns what its advocates call incentive anti-inflation plans (tax and market-based incomes policies) but what are, in effect, supermodified wage and price controls. *Supermodified* is a significant modifier; the plans discussed here bear about as much resemblance to wage and price controls as a Model T does to a Mercedes 450 SL. Nonetheless they are a type of controls.

To understand the development of incentive anti-inflation plans, you must understand that economists don't like wage and price controls; for an economist, supporting wage and price controls is much like a civil libertarian supporting martial law. Economists' dislike of wage and price controls has kept them from studying the theory of controls (just as a civil libertarian is unlikely to study the theory of martial law): Most economists merely consider controls bad—something to be avoided. In fact, about the only book written on the theory of price controls is John Kenneth Galbraith's *A Theory of Price Control* (1952); soon thereafter Galbraith felt it necessary to "leave" the profession, and he started writing to a larger audience. (For a further discussion of this point see David C. Colander (1984).) The relevant object lesson was not lost on economists.

Using wage and price controls as a policy was another matter, and in the last fifty years various control programs have emerged (and died) in the U.S. During World War II, wage and price controls were generally agreed to be necessary; only the form of those controls was subject to debate. The World War II controls worked; with wage and price controls in place, unemployment fell from 14.6

1

percent in 1940 to 1.2 percent in 1944, GNP more than doubled during that same time period, and the economy provided the output necessary for the war effort.

Despite the success of the wartime controls, economists did not become advocates of controls. The success of the war effort was attributed to Keynesian economic policies and the stimulatory effect of expansionary fiscal policy. From a 1980s vantage point, it seems clear that Keynesian economic policies worked, at least in part, because wage and price controls were in effect, but the contribution of the wage and price controls to the expansion was quickly forgotten. After the war, everyone wanted the wage and price controls abandoned, and in 1946 they were.

The postwar period is interesting for both the theoretical and policy debates of the time. In that time period creeping, crawling inflation entered the picture. Before then, the economy either suffered galloping inflation or it didn't, and any inflation occurred simultaneously with increase in the money supply. After the war, the issue of inflation and its connection to money was not as clear. Inflation was there, but there was just a bit of it—not enough to convince everyone that it must be stopped. The U.S. government attempted to maintain aggregate demand at a high level; creeping inflation was merely an unpleasant side effect that many policymakers would rather have forgotten.

The question of whether creeping inflation was inherent in Keynesian policies provoked a theoretic debate on the usefulness of expansionary policies and whether it was possible to maintain a "high-pressure," rather than a "low-pressure," economy. Liberals argued that the government could maintain a high-pressure economy and that expansionary Keynesian policies could be instituted. Conservatives argued that the high-pressure economy could be only temporarily maintained and that soon the creeping inflation would overwhelm the economy. The debate took a variety of forms and was filtered down to the textbooks as a demand-pull/cost-push debate. Demand-pull inflation was "excess demand inflation," while cost-push inflation occurred because of monopoly, administered prices, or some similar nondemand-related phenomenon. Cost-push inflation was to be dealt with via controls; demand-pull inflation (the only type of inflation conservatives believed existed) was to be dealt with via contractionary policy. The debate was never really resolved; it eventually just died out. Good economists knew that the demand-pull/cost-push distinction didn't hold up, but once it was embodied in textbooks, it was too late.

CONTROLLING CREEPING INFLATION

The emergence of creeping inflation changed the nature of wage and price controls. Creeping inflation did not call for monstrous wage and price controls; rather, it called for what might be termed creeping controls—controls that reduced firms' and workers' tendencies to raise prices and wages but did not impose the strong compulsion inherent in administrative controls that created legal wage and price ceilings.

Since controls were so abhorred by the profession, it is not surprising that new words developed to describe these partial controls. Some of these include *guideposts, guidelines, incomes policies,* and *social contracts.* Conservatives gave a Shakespearian response to this evolutionary etymology: Controls by any other name are still controls.

The names given to the controls changed so frequently because none of the control programs, at least in the United States, were an enormous success. This is not to say that they were enormous failures; they were merely ambiguous. Even the criteria by which the controls were to be judged were subject to debate. In 1974, for example, a major summit conference on inflation was sponsored by the U.S. government. The transcripts of that conference reveal no agreement and little prospect for agreement on what inflation was, let alone on whether some type of an incomes policy would help combat it.

In Europe the experience with controls was better, and most European countries instituted some form of long-term wage and price policy. Austria provides probably the best example of a successful controls program. In Austria, government, business, and labor negotiate each year to determine the split of GNP. For most U.S. economists, the European experience is considered sui generis; European institutions are different, and the size of European economies is so much smaller than the U.S. economy that comparisons are not made. Moreover, the experience with European incomes policies is sufficiently unclear to allow opponents to claim that the policies were failures. Thus, the difference between the United States and Europe is a presumption: In Europe the incomes policies are presumed successes; in the United States they are presumed failures. The empirical work on these controls has not resolved the issue; this work has been inconclusive, since it is impossible to specify a meaningful noncontrol state.

Given the ambiguity of empirical tests and the sometimes purely political inclination for instituting the limited incomes policies (it seems to be a political maxim that it is better to look as if you are doing something to control inflation than actually to control inflation), it is not surprising that most U.S. economists reverted to their natural proclivities and opposed controls in any form.

THE EMERGENCE OF INCENTIVE
ANTI-INFLATION PLANS

In the evolution of controls, the attempt was to redesign controls so that they did as little harm to the market process as possible. Robert Solow's (1966) well-known justification for guidelines—that they offered a little benefit for a little cost—is characteristic of supporters' views.

Given this attempt to protect the market, it was only natural that eventually someone would come up with the idea of using economic incentives to discourage people from raising their wages and prices. Of the early attempts to do so, the most well known is a proposal by Henry Wallich and Sidney Weintraub (1971), and soon after the proposal's introduction, the acronym TIP (tax-based incomes policy) came to refer to their plan.

The Wallich/Weintraub TIP was a practical plan without much underlying theory, other than the eminently reasonable one that if raising wages costs corporations more, they are unlikely to raise wages as much as they were doing before. (To the non-economist such common sense reasoning might well make sense, but economists are wary of common sense, and prefer uncommon sense, or at least a demonstration of how a common sense policy can fit into their models.) Initially there was no development of what I call a generic TIP that integrated the plans into the general theoretical structure of macroeconomics, and most economists saw the plans as yet another gimmick—a type of controls by another name.

The few early attempts to develop the underlying theory of TIPs (Peter Isard (1973), R.W. Latham and D.A. Peel (1977), Yehuda Kotowitz and Richard Portes (1974)) were unsatisfactory and TIP remained a policy, quite unintegrated into macroeconomic models. The high inflation of the 1970s stimulated interest in TIPs, and in 1978 the Brookings Institution held a conference on TIPs. At that conference TIP advocates failed to convince other participants either that TIPs had any underlying theory or that they could be practically applied. This conference (discussed in Miller, Koford, and Schneider, Chapter 3), dealt a serious blow to the Wallich/Weintraub proposal and with it to most fellow travelers' interest in TIP. Robert Barro's comment (1979: 54) in considering the proposal for a tax-based incomes policy summarizes the view of many economists at the time: "I honestly have no idea what sort of private market failure or externality is supposed to rationalize this sort of government interference in the market process."

Nevertheless, for lack of alternatives, the idea survived and was partially incorporated into President Carter's real wage insurance proposal (a proposal that many TIP proponents opposed). Had Carter been re-elected, more work on designing a practical TIP would likely have been forthcoming.

With Carter's defeat in 1980, TIP as an immediate policy option disappeared and anti-inflation policy followed a somewhat different path. The economy went cold turkey; unemployment rose to almost 11 percent and the inflation was choked out of the U.S. economy. In the process, a much higher rate of unemployment was accepted as natural. While in the 1960s and 1970s, 7 percent unemployment was seen as a recession, in the 1980s, it was seen as natural.

In 1983, expansionary policy re-emerged, although it was no longer justified on Keynesian grounds. The cyclical expansion continued through 1985 without generating accelerating inflation. In some ways, the inflationary experience of the 1983–85 expansion was quite similar to that in earlier expansions. Consumer prices were up about 7.5 percent over the two years compared with 7 percent in the average post-war expansion. Thus, it seemed that the cold-turkey process eliminated much of the core inflation of the 1970s and returned the economy to the pre-1970s low inflationary regime. Contributory factors to the improved inflation picture include the high value of the dollar, which strengthened foreign competition pressures, the continued high (by historical standards) unemployment (7-7.5%), and the changed policy regime. Inflation fears persisted, however, and prevented the Federal Reserve System from further increasing the money supply. Within this new environment, little immediate policy interest in TIP existed.

Theoretical interest in TIP did not die, however. To understand the theoretical development of TIP, we need to consider another way in which an idea can develop. TIP was propounded as a policy, and then the underlying theory was considered. Another way for an idea to evolve is for it to emerge in theory and then be modified from theory into policy. It is that second approach that Abba Lerner and I followed independently. My interest evolved from my Ph.D. dissertation and an earlier unpublished paper I wrote in 1974 on what I called market-based incomes policy. Lerner's interest evolved from his attempt to expand the TIP concept into one that was more generic. In expanding the idea to its most general form, we both arrived at an incomes policy that relied on the creation of a new market – in rights to raise wages (Lerner) or value-added input prices (Colander). These were combined into what we called a market anti-inflation plan (MAP) (Lerner and Colander 1980). MAP created a new set of rights – to raise and lower prices – and then allowed individuals to trade those rights. In so doing MAP held the price level constant by definition but allowed individual prices to remain flexible. Firms raising their prices were encouraged to do so as long as they were willing to pay for the necessary MAP credit. A firm that raised prices was not in any way doing anything wrong: MAP merely eliminated the nonfunctional aspect of the price rise, leaving the functional (change in relative price) aspect.

Because MAP used pure market incentives and involved the government only in determining initial property rights (as it must do in any market), MAP avoided, or at least confused, many of the normal complaints about the workings of incomes policies. Specifically, MAP used a market to set price of raising price, and therefore the simple argument that MAP violated the market could not be used.

In contrast to administrative incomes policies (wage and price controls) that forced individuals to make an either/or choice, MAP allowed the individuals to choose their own price rise with the MAP price (the price of raising price) offering a disincentive, not a control. Thus MAP allowed partial price controls. MAP also provided a neat theoretical justification for the program – the macroeconomic externality. When individuals set their price, they did not take into account the effect their setting their price had on the general price level. Only if there was an additional market would individuals do so and would the externality be internalized.

Whereas TIP focused analysis on partial equilibrium practical questions, MAP focused the analysis on general equilibrium theoretical questions. It raised interesting new questions, such as, What does it mean to the aggregate economy if the MAP price is not zero? Will it imply a different equilibrium unemployment rate? If so, why? The late 1970s and early 1980s saw some preliminary answers to these questions and a convergence of the theoretical and practical aspects of the MAP and TIP (reviewed in Colander and Koford 1984), and it is those answers and that convergence that are conveyed in the chapters in this volume.

Lerner, I, and others had many useful discussions about both the theory and policy, and, as was Lerner's way, he spread the word on MAP. In England he introduced the MAP/TIP idea to Richard Layard, who began a working group there and continued the development of the idea. At the University of Delaware, a similar working group was started.

Simultaneously, Sidney Weintraub was modifying his original TIP and together with Larry Seidman was making it more politically acceptable. Arthur Okun became interested and also worked on designing a politically acceptable plan. This core group interchanged ideas and various proposals became intertwined.

The late 1970s and early 1980s were a difficult time for incentive anti-inflation plans. Three out of four of their most powerful, forceful, and well-known supporters died. Because their interest had given the idea merit to the press and academic economists, many felt that the death knell of TIP/MAP had sounded. But the seeds of the idea had taken root (some would say, had grown like weeds), and work continued on incentive anti-inflation plans, by a younger, less well-known, group.

At the same time, other fellow travelers, some quite well known, continued with their quiet support and encouragement. The role of that encouragement and subtle support should not be underestimated; without it these ideas would have been dropped. One personal story will give some idea of the importance of that quiet support. In 1974 I was working on a rather boring, but quite acceptable (quite acceptable often means boring) dissertation on optimal taxation theory. In my spare time I wrote a paper on an idea that I had been toying with and sent a copy to William Vickrey, who, along with Edmund Phelps, was my dissertation advisor. Vickrey wrote me a strong letter of encouragement, a letter that gave me the courage to toss my "acceptable but boring" dissertation out and write a "just acceptable"—but not boring—dissertation that explored the idea of a market in rights to raise prices. Vickrey played an important part in the subsequent development of the idea and is responsible, no doubt, for many of the ideas that I believe come from my own imagination.

Vickrey also said that he believed that my early paper would be easily publishable, but I soon discovered that he was wrong in this regard: The original was vehemently rejected by numerous journals and was never published. Had I been the only proponent of the idea, it would have died a quick death. Only when Abba Lerner came up with a similar market plan and we worked together was the market approach even considered.

Slowly a core group developed; its members worked on the proposal and the ideas represented in it. This volume embodies some of that work and is taken in large part from the proceedings of a conference on the ideas, held in Middlebury in the spring of 1984.

The book is divided into four sections: an introductory section, a theoretical section, an administration problem section, and a political problem section. The introductory section provides an initial look at inflation and incentive anti-inflation plans—a general name encompassing both TIP and MAP. Chapter 1, by James Galbraith, considers the recent history of inflation and provides a context within which incentive anti-inflation plans can be analyzed. In Chapter 2 William Vickrey provides an overview of the theoretical issues and the need for some type of structural change. In Chapter 3 Jeffrey Miller, Kenneth Koford, and Jerrold Schneider place the plans in the larger comparative institutional framework and relate them to a wider set of plans. These three chapters provide a good introduction to incentive anti-inflation plans and the previous literature.

The theoretical issues raised by MAP can be seen by reconsidering the institution of wage and price controls during World War II. Output expanded enormously. This is not what economic theory would have predicted. Controls should have caused shortages, unless the economy had not been operating at full employment. Chapter 4, by Walter Salant, puts the issue about controls in perspective in a paper that has been in his mind for over forty years, giving a good sense of the way in which the economic framework holds down, by its very structure, questions about incomes policies. As Salant shows, the key to defining a theoretical role for incomes policies is to give up the perfectly competitive framework and to shift to a monopolistic, or monopolistically competitive, framework where a firm is limiting output and workers are limiting entry into the labor market. Salant argues that a firm's margin is squeezed by controls and that it follows that after controls are lifted the price level will rise to where it would have been had the controls not been implemented. Although he doesn't draw it, the logical conclusion of his argument is this: Only a permanent system of controls will permanently affect the long-run equilibrium.

In Chapter 5 Koford and Miller develop a model of MAP. They argue that MAP changes the elasticity of demand facing the firm and thereby changes the equilibrium of the economy. The parallel between the Koford/Miller paper and the Salant paper provides good insight into the theoretical argument for income policies and price controls. Their purpose is to squeeze out monopoly from the system. Controls do it completely; they make the demand curve faced by the firm perfectly elastic, just as it would be for a perfectly competitive firm. Thus output expands and price falls. The problem with controls is that the control price may not be at the perfectly competitive price. If it is not, there will be continued shortages. Incentive anti-inflation plans avoid that problem by leaving the firm to choose whatever price it wants. Miller and Koford show how, in choosing that price, the plans (by increasing the marginal revenue of lowering price and decreasing the marginal revenue of raising price) make the perceived demand curve facing the firm more elastic.

The next two chapters approach the theoretical problems of tax-based incomes policies differently. They consider the dynamic flow equilibrium and the equilibrium relationship between vacancies and unemployment and how a TIP will affect that equilibrium. In papers that complement their other theoretical work (Layard 1982a, 1982b; Jackman, Layard, Pissarides 1983), Richard Layard, Richard Jackman, and Christopher Pissarides show how incentive anti-inflation plans can reduce the equilibrium level of unemployment. The Jackman and Layard chapter (Chapter 6) considers the issue for a wage TIP and relies on lowering the real wage as the method with which the plans achieve the lower equilibrium. In Chapter 7 Christopher Pissarides, using a different formulation, comes to the conclusion that a value-added TIP would have a greater effect on the elasticity of demand for labor and would have a stronger effect on reducing equilibrium output.

The three formal papers on the theory of TIP, while suggestive, are unsatisfying, even to their authors. The rigors of analytic exposition preclude specification of the model in a way that captures the dynamic general equilibrium workings of the plan. For example, Jackman and Layard agree that within their model a wage tax would achieve the same results as a tax-based incomes policy. Thus the reader is left with the questions, Is there something special about incentive anti-inflation plans, and what is the intuition behind the plans? The final paper of Part II (Chapter 8) considers these questions. It does not present a formal theoretical model but instead informally ties together the various theoretical approaches. In it I argue that conceptually one can move from the static models of the Koford/Miller and Salant papers to a dynamic general equilibrium model. The key to that movement is the concept of monopolization and viewing monopoly as the result of competition for monopoly. Excess supply equilibrium results (as is assumed in the Jackman/Layard and Pissarides models) from an asymmetry in the costs of monopolizing. Sellers monopolize more than buyers do, creating sellers' monopoly, but the costs of monopolization increase as the ratio of excess supply to excess demand increases, and eventually a non-accelerating inflation rate of unemployment (NAIRU), rather than a natural rate equilibrium, is arrived at. Tax- and market-based incomes policies work by increasing the cost of monopolization.

ADMINISTRATIVE FEASIBILITY

Even if one accepts the theoretical arguments for incomes policies, one might still oppose a TIP or MAP on the grounds that it cannot be administered. Part III considers these administrative issues. Since much has been previously written on the administrative problems of TIPs (Colander 1979a; Colander and Koford 1984; Slitor 1979) and many of the papers use these as starting points, I will briefly outline the administrative choices that need to be made with an incentive anti-inflation plan. The first decision is between a market plan such as MAP and a tax-based plan such as TIP. Second, choices must be made about the control variable (wages, prices, value-added prices), coverage, and implementation time. These various options are summarized in Tables I-1 and I-2.

In Chapter 9 Jackman and Layard present some of these options in more detail. They admit that numerous arbitrary decisions must be made but argue that these can be made without significant problems. At the conference from which these papers derive, there was substantial discussion of the relative merits of market and tax incentive anti-inflation plans. A market plan, such as the one analyzed in the Koford/Miller paper, sets the price level by law and allows trading in rights to raise price. TIP sets the price of the right to raise prices and thus cannot guarantee a specific rate of inflation. Because of the persuasiveness of the Triplett and Russell papers, many of the U.S. participants reevaluated the relative problems of tax and market plans. Market plans, which are theoretically superior because they set the rate of inflation and allow the incentive to fluctuate, were previously considered administratively more complicated and politically more acceptable. Given the strong opposition, however, to combining the incentive with the tax code, the clean separation that the market plans provide made them more desirable.

More desirable does not necessarily mean more administratively feasible, and, like the tax plans, the market plans have numerous administrative complications—some that parallel TIP and some that don't. In Chapter 10 Vickery discusses how some of the problems that will develop for a value-added market-based incomes policy can be resolved. He also introduces the term *gross markup*, which captures the idea of the value-added approach better than *value added*.

Chapters 9 and 10 were written by believers, and while believers were the majority at the conference, they are not the majority in the profession. Chapters 11 and 12 present something closer to a majority view, and they make their points forcefully. Drawing on their experience as members of President Carter's Council on Wage and Price Control, Jack Triplett and Robert Russell argue that the administrative decisions are anything but easy and that, if the Carter controls are any example, TIP won't work.

The TIP advocates' response is given by Larry Seidman in Chapter 13. He agrees with much of what Triplett and Russell have to say about the difficulty of administering TIPs, but still he argues the benefits outweigh the costs and that the design characteristics of TIP have proceeded beyond and avoided many of the problems Russell and Triplett mention.

Table I-1. Alternative TIP Proposals.

	"Price" Controlled	Fiscal Macro Effect	Tax System	Inclusiveness	Structure of Incentive	Guideline	Determination of Initial Base "Price"
Colander (1978)	Value added per unit input	Neutral	Value-added tax or separate exise tax	Firms > $500,000 net sales	Proportional or progressive	Decreased over 5-year period to 2–3 percent	Weighted average of past 3 years
Layard (1982)	Wage rate, dividends	Neutral	Social Security tax	All firms	Proportional	Zero inflation norm	Wage rate of equivalent quarter in previous year
Seidman (1981)	Wage rate and value added price	Neutral at guideline inflation	Corporate income tax	Largest 2,000 corporations	Hurdle, then proportional	5 percent wages, 4 percent prices, decreasing to 2–3 percent wages, 0 percent prices	Average of past 3 years
Wallich-Weintraub (1971)	Wage rate	Positive or Neutral	Corporate income tax	Large corporations	Hurdle, then proportional	—	Previous year's wage rate
Weintraub (1979)	Wage rate	Neutral at guideline inflation	Corporate income tax	Firms 500+ employees or wage bill > $5 million	Hurdle, then proportional	3 percent subsidy hurdle, 5 percent penalty hurdle	Previous year's wage rate

Table 1-2. Alternative MAP Proposals.

	"Price" Controlled	Market Operation	Inclusiveness	Guideline	Macroeconomic Supply Effect
Lerner (1978)	Wage rate	Unspecified	All firms	Immediate reduction to 2–3 percent	Increased labor supply
Lerner and Colander (1980)	Value-added rate	Run by Federal Reserve	Firms over $500,000 in net sales	Gradual reduction	Increased input supply

POLITICAL FEASIBILITY

John Kenneth Galbraith, at the end of his book on the theory of price control, wrote that it was not for lack of theoretical foundation or for lack of administratability that controls programs will not be implemented. It is for lack of political will. If incentive anti-inflation plans are to achieve their desired goals, somehow the plans must be instituted within a political environment. The final section considers these political problems.

Chapter 14, by Sheetal Chand, provides a transition from the administrative to the political problems. He considers the French and Belgian experiences with incentive anti-inflation plans and draws some lessons about the feasibility of TIP. He finds that the plans "require a substantial commitment to institutional change" and that lead times are long. However, he argues that a value-added TIP is feasible, at least for a country with a well-developed VAT system. In short, administratively the plans can be implemented; the problems are in many ways political.

In Chapter 15 Jerrold Schneider considers whether the present U.S. "quasi-monetarist" policy regime is politically sustainable and whether there is a realistic political bargain that could be adopted for a less costly means of fighting inflation. In it he examines the effect that books such as this one have on policy development. He argues that policy development cannot take place within government but must take place outside of government. He argues that given the right set of political conditions, the political coalition exists if the economic entrepreneurship is there.

James Galbraith, in Chapter 16, presents a different view. He argues that "formal anti-inflation policies offered to date have suffered an organic defect. They are politically costly to put into effect. Therefore nothing happens before inflation becomes a serious problem. But when inflation does become a serious problem, it is too serious for these policies to effectively contain."

In the final chapter of the book, I summarize the TIP defenders' response to the political argument. Yes, the plans are administratively and politically difficult to implement, but they can be implemented. It is simply wrong to use unemployment to hold down inflation. If not these, then some other plan is needed.

I
INCENTIVE
ANTI-INFLATION PLANS
General Issues

1 THE CONTINUING IMPORTANCE OF PRICE STABILIZATION

James K. Galbraith *

By 1985 inflation was no longer the leading economic problem in the United States. Since 1981 inflation had fallen, more quickly than most expected, to rates lower than before the Vietnam War. The defeat of inflation proved a vital ingredient in restoring national morale in 1983–84 and along with economic recovery contributed mightily to President Reagan's re-election landslide.

Yet the durability of this accomplishment remains in doubt. Deficits of unprecedented peacetime dimension are part of the reason. Surveys of inflation expectations still show widespread fears of a significant rise. Interest rate yield curves reflect these fears. Respected voices in government and in the financial community, including that of the chairman of the Federal Reserve Board, continue to warn that inflation is only dormant, not dead.

This chapter reviews the recent history of inflation in the United States in order to assess the present degrees of risk. It then surveys and places in their appropriate context some of the major proposals for price stabilization policy put forward in this book.

RECENT INFLATIONARY PATTERNS

The characteristic inflation process of recent times may be divided into three distinct phases. First are the gradual tightening of markets and the build-up in inflationary pressures, which appear to be natural concomitants of economic

*The views expressed are not necessarily those of the Joint Economic Committee or its Members. The author thanks Peter Neumann for exceptional research assistance.

15

growth. At the very least, this process strengthens a wide variety of different economic actors, to the point where many may feel partially empowered to displace an adverse terms-of-trade shift onto others. Second, there is the possibility that such a shift—a supply shock—may occur. Finally, the shock is transmitted though the economy, it is incorporated in contracts and in wage and price expectations, and there ensues a struggle over who ultimately will bear the real income loss.

The typical experience of postwar business cycle expansions has been that inflation rates rise slowly, beginning within a year or so after the trough quarter. They continue rising until policymakers perceive an inflation crisis and react with controls or other measures to end the expansion. Within these cycles, upward shocks to the inflation rate have tended to occur relatively late in the expansion phase. This may not be wholly coincidental: As a recovery matures, vulnerability to shocks increases. The first oil shock of 1973 occurred after real output in the United States had risen 16.7 percent above the 1970 trough, and the second oil shock of 1979 occurred after U.S. real output had risen 22.3 percent above the 1975 trough. (As of the first quarter of 1985, real U.S. GNP was 12.8 percent higher than it was in the fourth quarter of 1982.)

Supply shocks in and of themselves need not precipitate an inflation policy crisis. But if they occur after a sustained period of robust expansion, then the danger arises that economic agents hurt directly by the shock will seek to recoup their real income losses. The inflation impulse may then be transmitted from external shock to internal cost-push. Internal cost-push measures can reverberate through the economy for a long time and may come to an end only when all important parties accept as permanent at least some of the redistribution of real income implied by the original supply shock. On past occasions, that has required a massive change in agents' perceptions of the strength of their bargaining positions, something achieved only at high cost.

The expansion of 1975–80 provides a reasonably clear example of this process at work (Figure 1-1). Inflation had been cut in half by the preceding recession. It then began to increase very slowly, as growth resumed, from 1976 through 1978. In 1979 inflation surged, under the influence of the oil shock, rising food prices, and higher interest rates. In 1980 these sources of inflation spread through the economy as a whole, in a process of struggle over the allocation of real income losses. An effort to allocate the losses chiefly to the household sector, via the credit controls of March 1980, was only partly successful. In 1981, however, the Federal Reserve put an end to the argument. The move to extreme restriction in April 1981 created an environment in which no one could escape large losses. In the general concern over falling absolute levels of real income, the secondary dispute over relativities was temporarily lost sight of.

External shocks are inherently unpredictable. Perhaps the development of the Strategic Petroleum Reserve, coupled with stockpiling in other countries, con-

Figure 1-1. Changes in the Consumer Price Index, 1968-84 (*changes from December to December based on unadjusted indexes*).

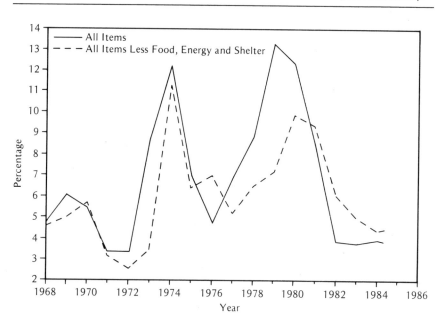

servation measures, and the declining solidarity of OPEC, will prevent another shock from that source. Perhaps not. Food may present a less reassuring picture; the policies of 1983-84 have eaten away at officially held surpluses of most grains. Other potential sources of commodity price pressure are simply not known.

A chief reason for continuing low inflation in the 1983-85 expansion was the high value of the dollar. This exerted competitive pressure on U.S. wages and kept import prices low. In a sense, we were exporting inflation during this time. Unfortunately, as Krugman (1983) has observed, inflation lent abroad through an artificially high exchange rate must be borrowed back, sooner or later, with appropriate interest. Any number of events, such as a change in U.S. policy or in central bank leadership, could precipitate an international portfolio shift and a sharp fall in the dollar. If so, many fear that inflation will come back with a vengeance. Durable victory over inflation cannot be taken for granted. Though inflation remains low, work on better, more efficient, less costly anti-inflation policies continues to justify the commitment of scholarly resources represented, among other things.

CRITERIA FOR PRICE STABILIZATION POLICY

It is important to distinguish between political and economic reasons to oppose inflation, because the nature of an anti-inflation policy varies according to which reason is accorded the greater importance. For most Europeans, Germans and Austrians in particular, the evil of inflation is axiomatic. Inflation destroys the constitutional order. It does so, as Keynes wrote, by a process of pernicious and arbitrary redistribution. His argument likens inflation to a revolutionary process (Keynes 1920: 235–36):

> The sight of this arbitrary rearrangement of riches strikes not only at the security, but at the confidence in the equity of the existing distribution of wealth. Those to whom the system brings windfalls, beyond their deserts and even beyond their expectations or desires, become "profiteers," who are the object of the hatred of the bourgeoisie, whom the inflationism has impoverished, not less than of the proletariat. As the inflation proceeds . . . all permanent relations between debtors and creditors, which form the ultimate foundation of capitalism, become so utterly disordered as to be almost meaningless, and the process of wealth-getting degenerates into a gamble and a lottery. . .
>
> Lenin was certainly right. There is no subtler, no surer means of overturning the existing basis of society than to debauch the currency. The process engages all the hidden forces of economic law on the side of destruction, and does it in a manner which not one man in a million is able to diagnose.

Modern economists are not so accustomed to thinking in symbolic and political terms, and so the postwar literature on inflation has deemphasized its political dangers and sought to define instead its economic costs.

Part of the purely economic costs of inflation is said to stem from effects on relative prices. One view is that the variability of relative prices—and hence of the costs of gathering information about prices and investment opportunities for the future—increases as inflation rates rise. A second is that inflation depresses business confidence, raises questions about the sustainability of effective demand, and so undermines investment and productivity growth. Unfortunately, while a persuasive case for such costs can be made in principle, they are not susceptible to being measured.

Economists also point to the effects of inflation on holders of money. One result is financial innovation: the creation of liquid financial instruments that are more or less fully indexed against inflation, to be held as substitutes for non-interest-bearing money. A second form of innovation attempts to increase the velocity of money that must be held for transactions purposes: more frequent trips to the bank, electronic transfers, and so on. These effects absorb real resources; however, it may be argued that such costs are small in relation to the size of the economy.

Another effect of inflation, particularly where indexed financial instruments may not be available, is excess holding of stocks of real materiel: inventories, commodities, works-in-progress, and the like. In extreme situations, such activities can seriously impede real production, as in Germany toward the end of World War II, when manufacturers held inventories rather than deliver on orders for real goods, since delivery would have merely added to cash balances that were rapidly becoming worthless (Galbraith 1952). Hoarding of real resources is an especially serious consequence of hyperinflation, particularly in economies with underdeveloped financial markets. On the other hand, one may question its relevance to recent experience in the United States.

It is a source of discomfort to some economists that the economic costs of inflation are so hard to measure and so largely defined in terms of market imperfections: uncertainty about the future, transactions costs, imperfect financial markets, and non-market-clearing behavior. It is difficult to model the real effects of inflation in the pure theoretical context where none of these things exists. It appears that the closer one's model comes to approximate the perfectly competitive, perfect-information, free-market economy of the neoclassical ideal, the less one can say with formal certitude about the costs of inflation.

The pursuit of pure theory, for many economists, seems to require a belief that the consequences of uncertainty, transactions costs, imperfect markets, and disequilibrium behavior are relatively small. As Frank Hahn (1980) pointed out, this is a problem for those economists whose instincts against inflation are the strongest. This paradox has led to one other ground for attack on inflation, which might be described as purely esthetic. We can have, the argument goes, any rate of inflation at any level of output and employment that we like. So why not zero? As John Rutledge testified to the Joint Economic Committee in 1981,

> Zero percent inflation is the only inflation that makes any sense. You may have wondered why God put a zero in the middle of all the numbers. That's because that's the optimal inflation rate. It's the only one; 6 is not much more than 5 or 11 is not much more than 10, but zero is right in the middle and that's the only credible inflation rate over the long term.

This argument has the virtues of clarity and simplicity. But it hardly motivates the loathing that the experience of inflation inspires in public life.

The citizenry exhibits a powerful preference for a near-zero rate of change in the general price level. Many are prepared to support politicians who deliver this result even at a very large cost in forgone real income. This suggests that for most people the political and constitutional reasons for opposing inflation may be the true ones. A political/constitutional interpretation of the costs of inflation helps explain the charged nature of the inflation policy debate and has implications for the design of anti-inflation policy.

In the first place, constitutional issues override economic concerns, and a threat to the constitutional order cannot be evaded. The appropriate question cannot be, as some would have it, How much inflation are we willing to put up with to achieve a given reduction in unemployment? Rather, it must be, How little inflation must we have, irrespective of all other considerations, so as to pose no significant threat to the constitutional order?[1]

This means that in the design of anti-inflation policy, all policies that keep inflation below the threshold level are appropriate; none that fail to do so are tolerable. The public is prepared to support extraordinarily costly means of reducing inflation to within tolerable bounds, so long as they are persuaded that no credible, effective, less costly alternative means of achieving the same objective exist.

The political/constitutional perspective suggests that we have perceived inflation in a way that is nearly the reciprocal of how we should have perceived it. We have sought to minimize the price change in a given unit of time. We should in addition seek to maximize those periods of time when prices do not change. These are not incompatible goals. But policy measures that would not be relevant to the former may become relevant when both objectives are considered in tandem.

Long periods of price stability, when inflation is below the threshold at which it is thought to be a problem, breed the self-assurance, confidence in government, and sense of resilience that healthy political institutions require. It is such periods that policy should seek to build, to reinforce, and to return to if they are interrupted. The plain may be subject to an occasional flood, and it is desirable to keep the floods small. Large or small, however, if floods are not too frequent, people continue to live on the plain: What matters for them is how long the plain can be expected to remain dry, not how much water passes over it when it floods.

That being so, anti-inflation policy will succeed—and be perceived as having succeeded—if it concentrates a given amount of price-level change into a short period of time and so permits a relatively rapid return to price stability following an external shock. This is true even though that stability may imply reductions in terms-of-trade or real incomes that are as large as or larger than those that might be achieved by allowing a longer period of inflationary adjustment.

The discussion so far suggests that four general questions should be asked of any proposed price stabilization policy. First, does it effectively deter inflationary behavior and reduce the total change in the price level below what would otherwise occur? This is the traditional question all analysts ask of all anti-inflation regimes. It addresses the issue of the economic costs of inflation itself. The apparent showing, in some models, that the Nixon price controls did not reduce inflation over the period 1971-74 as a whole has done more than any other single analysis to discredit price-wage controls with economists as an anti-inflation regime.

Second, does a proposed anti-inflation policy reduce the length of time during which a given change in the price level will occur and speed the return to stable prices? This question addresses the political and constitutional issues. To the policymaker, timing is everything, and time to recover in an atmosphere of price stability may be worth the cost of a larger change in the price level.

Third, what does implementation of the policy cost? Assuming that more than one credible alternative exists, it is imperative to choose the one that loses the least in production and employment and also infringes least on individual liberty, free collective bargaining, and other social values and that also requires the least in bureaucratic and administrative overhead to function. There are tradeoffs between the different parameters of cost: Some alternative policy may be designed that will dominate the three dimensions of economic cost, political cost, and administrative cost. Any such alternative would be highly desirable.

A subsidiary question is who gains and who loses. Some policies impose more costs on some groups than on others. A priori, it would seem that the ideal anti-inflation regime would not disturb the ex ante distribution of income and political power and so avoid entanglement in secondary disputes that might engender opposition to the regime itself.

Fourth, is the proposed anti-inflation regime feasible? This is a vital, difficult, and usually neglected question. But it does little good for abstract thinkers to propose grand changes in the constitutional order when such changes cannot be enacted.

A historical and scholarly record exists for four main alternative policies, which include two distinct types of principally monetary anti-inflation policies: guidelines and controls. I now briefly consider these in light of the criteria set forth above.

Conventional Monetary Policy

Conventional monetary policy works against inflation by exploiting the short-run Phillips curve tradeoff. That is, it creates unemployment, excess capacity, undesired inventories, and commodity gluts and so places a general downward supply-and-demand pressure on prices. Such regimes undeniably work; they lower inflation dramatically by comparison with what it would be under conditions of continued high production and employment. They are feasible but in a limited sense: It is possible to launch conventional monetary policy into action against inflation only *after* inflation has emerged as an important political problem. The preemptive or preventive value of such policies is nil. Such regimes are insensitive to the fine points of timing raised above; they do not seek to lessen political risks by crowding a given change in the price level into a shorter period of time, but only to reduce the total change in the price level from beginning to end of any given time frame. Finally, although it implies no formal impairment

GENERAL ISSUES

of political liberty and carries no administrative cost, the conventional monetary regime is immensely costly in economic terms—in lost output, lost employment, and lost opportunities for productivity gains.

Expectations-Altering Monetary Regimes

Since 1979 the new idea in monetary control of inflation has been an effort in both the United Kingdom and the United States to shift the Phillips curve inward (as well as move along it) by altering market perceptions of the maximum rate of inflation that the monetary authorities will tolerate. In an environment where it is known that rising rates of price inflation will be met with an overpowering response from the authorities, the argument goes, individual actors will be deterred from seeking price and wage settlements incommensurate with official stabilization objectives. In this way, an indirect political cost, the constraint on liberty inspired by fear of official reaction, is introduced in hope of reducing the direct economic cost of achieving a given anti-inflation objective.

There is something obviously desirable about the effort to substitute the indirect, internalized concept of deterrence for part of the direct material impoverishment on which monetary anti-inflation policies otherwise depend. However, the effectiveness of and economic cost-savings achieved by the particular means employed are both subject to doubt.

In the first instance, expectations-altering monetary policies seek to deter inflationary price and wage behavior by making an even greater impression on private parties of the ultimate costs of such behavior. That is, to establish credibility they impose vast preemptive costs on real output and employment over and above what would be required to reduce inflation to acceptable levels in a conventional monetary policy, and then seek to persuade all concerned that a return to inflationary wage-price setting will bring a return of the same repressive policies and associated costs. To this extent, when the announcement of a shift to a noninflationary policy is not automatically credible to begin with, expectations-altering policies are actually more costly immediately than conventional policies and can be justified only if the deterrence works—if the success in bringing down inflation is more durable under such regimes as production and employment recover. I have examined the evidence for this proposition in an earlier paper (1983) and have not found it especially hopeful.

Once the consequences of inflationary behavior have been defined through example in the public mind, expectations-altering monetary regimes seek to continue effective deterrence by establishing norms for social behavior in the aggregate. This is the function of the annual money supply targets, which imply a composite annual target for acceptable inflation and for real output growth.

This aspect of the new monetary policy most likely has had no effect whatsoever on public behavior. In the first place, the relationship between the various

Figure 1-2. Federal Reserve Targets and Performance, 1978-84.

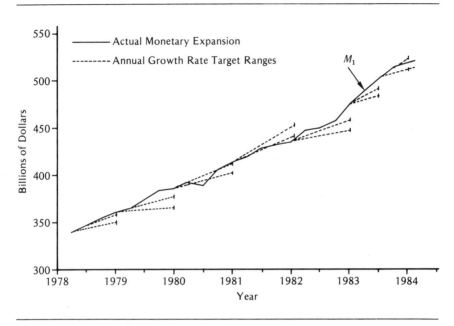

monetary targets and real economic variables is unstable, obscure, and poorly understood, a problem compounded by the good-bad composite nature of an implied nominal GNP target. Second, the targets are not credible, having been hit rarely in the seven years since they were introduced (Figure 1-2). Third, they provide no explicit guidance to individuals, unions, or companies on appropriate wage-price settlement behavior, an issue further confused by the authorities' ideologically motivated denial that monetary targeting/signaling policies could in principle be translated into guidelines. Finally, even if monetary signals were translated into wage-price targets, it does not follow that particular individuals have incentives to abide by them. To the contrary, any one can gain, though all may later lose, by acting in a way which is incommensurate with the official stabilization objectives.[2]

Thus expectations-altering monetary regimes may prove not more effective, and yet more costly, than their conventional predecessors. They do introduce an important new concept, that of the *costless signal* to market participants. But the attempt is obscured by jargon and unaccompanied by any mechanism that would enable even the susceptible businessperson or trade unionist to translate a willingness to cooperate into meaningful action.

Controls and Guidelines

Mandatory price or wage controls have been imposed in the United States on three occasions in history: during World War II, during the Korean War, and from August 1971 through January 1973.

No one seriously questions the effectiveness of price control in the first two cases, but the Nixon controls have been the cause for dispute. Some analysts claim that inflation suppressed during the control period came back entirely after controls were lifted, so that the total change in the price level from 1971 through 1974 was not different than it would have been absent the controls (Cagan 1979). This view is not universally accepted, however (Blinder and Newton 1981). In either event, as the objectives of the controls were arguably set by Nixon's reelection requirements in 1972, and as no one doubts that inflation from August 1971 through the election was lowered by the controls, it seems unreasonable to judge the Nixon controls by a broader historical standard.

Effective controls eliminate the direct output sacrifice of fighting inflation and permit the economy to generate vastly higher rates of production and employment than would otherwise be considered possible. (Between 1940 and 1945 real GNP increased 112.4 percent, but after 1941 controls kept average rates of price inflation down to 3.3 percent per year.) On the other hand, controls impose the highest possible political costs on individuals and imply the highest administrative overheads of any anti-inflation regime. They eliminate one entire dimension of market freedom. They imply either a system for rationing or a toleration for shortages. And if designed to last for more than a very brief time, they require thousands or tens of thousands of administrators to assure compliance.[3]

If critics of the Nixon controls are right and controls are not effective in reducing the total change in the price level from the beginning to the end of the relevant analytical time frame, then the only thing that controls accomplish is to reorder the timing of price changes. In the Nixon period they did so in a perverse way: A period of price stability achieved at great political cost was followed by a burst of rapid inflation. Of all imaginable time distributions of price level changes, from the standpoint of constitutional stability this was probably the worst. Thus if one grants a benefit of the doubt to the anti-control position on the general criterion of effectiveness, one must also rule against controls on the timing question, and inversely. (However, the World War II experience points to the opposite conclusion. In that case, controls reestablished price stability *after* a burst of inflation in 1941. And so, controls built confidence in the political authority for the duration of the war.) Finally, the feasibility of controls in peacetime for more than a brief period of time is open to question. Price controls in wartime worked with the assistance of production controls, rationing in the World War II case, and large numbers of volunteer enforcers over and above the very large official bureaucracy established for this purpose. In peacetime, prolonged controls require an element of flexibility and must withstand tests of fairness and due process, both of which imply even larger demands on the legal-juridical and administrative systems. The effective use of controls in the future may be confined to the use of a limited-duration, universal-coverage price or price-wage freeze, useful only as a transitional device.

A second dimension of feasibility in the case of policies for which no legal authority presently exists is whether such authority can be enacted. For the present generation of political leaders, peacetime price controls are a silver bullet that has already been fired. Authority to impose controls on a standalone basis will not again be granted to the executive branch, except possibly in a galvanizing emergency. (Conceivably, though, authority to impose controls on a stand-by basis might be granted, under a different administration, as part of a comprehensive reform of the wage-price determination process.)

Guidelines have all the properties of mandatory controls but to a lesser degree. As to their effectiveness, weaker claims are made by proponents, and, as to their costs, weaker criticisms are mounted by detractors. There is a fair consensus that the Kennedy-Johnson guidelines may have had some significant effect, though small, through the collaboration of labor in keeping wage claims within the growth rate of productivity. In the case of the Carter guidelines, experts quibble over whether an effect can be found; no one suggests that it was important.

Guidelines, unlike controls, do not permit economic expansion much, if at all, beyond what could otherwise be accomplished; thus they do not materially reduce the economic cost of fighting inflation. On the other hand, their political and administrative cost, while not negligible, is far smaller. As with controls, the administrative complexity of guidelines tends to grow as time passes, so that their usefulness in any given episode may be constrained to periods of short duration. At present, guidelines are as feasible politically as controls are: They are discredited but not necessarily permanently.

CONCLUSION

Given these problems, it is not surprising that interest in alternative anti-inflation plans remains alive. Through the design of incentive plans, economists have sought to achieve the effectiveness of monetary disinflation or controls without the extensive economic costs of the former and political costs of the latter. Whether they have succeeded in designing programs that will work in practice remains a matter of vigorous debate. No one questions, however, the unsatisfactory nature of the historical menu of choices or the immense potential payoff to creative work in this domain.

NOTES TO CHAPTER 1

1. Technically, the social welfare function becomes lexicographic in the inflation rate if the rate gets too high or stays high for too long.
2. A 1981 JEC study addressed similar questions in the context of the United Kingdom experience under Mrs. Thatcher, where it has been shown that "contrary to prediction, it is not necessarily irrational for wage earners to negotiate for wage settlements in excess of the money supply targets." (Hill 1981: 82.)
3. According to a Congressional Research Service, "The Nixon Administration needed almost 4000 staffers to administer its selective controls program in 1971–74. During the Korean conflict over 15,000 administered the controls program. In World War II, the controls program, in full operation, required a staff of 60,000, plus the efforts of 100,000 volunteers throughout the country who monitored compliance at the local level."

2 THE NEED FOR A DIRECT ANTI-INFLATION PROGRAM

William Vickrey

THE TRADEOFF BETWEEN INFLATION AND UNEMPLOYMENT

As the U.S. economy is currently organized, there is a built-in medium-long-run tradeoff between the level of unemployment and the rate of inflation. This relationship is sometimes represented by a Phillips curve. In any short run, situations substantially above or below any such curve would be observed and would be to some extent cyclical in nature. Indeed, the curve itself is often conceived as gradually tending to shift outward, the rate of shift being related to recently experienced rates of inflation, especially if these are not thought of as corresponding to nonrecurring impacts such as wars or oil crises.

The point on this curve at which inflation is zero indicates what is sometimes referred to as the natural rate of unemployment, a term that misleadingly connotes that there would be something normal and acceptable about such a rate of unemployment. Currently, it seems, the "natural" rate of unemployment is often thought of as being in the neighborhood of 6 or 7 percent. To those who are concerned with the efficiency of the economy and the quality of life it provides, however, such a level of unemployment is entirely unacceptable as a long-run goal. Not only is the loss of production that it represents a serious matter in itself, but the way in which the unemployment is concentrated on particular individuals and groups poses serious social problems in terms of morale, crime, the destruction of family life, and general malaise.

Such a level of unemployment could be considered tolerable if it were spread evenly in the form of shorter hours, longer vacations, and earlier retirement. But even this would not solve the inflation problem, for unemployment in these forms does not furnish the downward pressure on wages and prices necessary to keep in check the underlying tendency to inflation. Even at best this would be an inefficient frustration of preferences for higher incomes resulting from higher employment levels.

Actually, if the Phillips curve could be thought of as stable, a preferable solution would be to select a point on the curve representing an optimal level of unemployment and accept whatever rate of inflation corresponds. An optimal level of employment could be defined as one that reflects a suitable compromise between (1) the loss of production from the idle resources and (2) the sacrifice of efficiency resulting from the lack of flexibility and reserve capacity to meet unexpected developments and the other constraints involved in operating with an "empty pipe line."

If the corresponding rate of inflation could be maintained in an accurately predictable fashion, such an inflationary environment could be adapted to by suitable adjustments in rates of interest and in other long-term contracts. The main loss from the inflation then would be limited to the mechanical difficulties involved in keeping prices up-to-date and the psychological task of learning to think of money as having a changing value over time. It is the unpredictability of inflation, rather than its level, that is the essence of the evil properly attributable to inflation. Indeed, at one time I believed that a modest level of inflation, by keeping the corresponding value of the real money stock low, would make it easier to control the rate of inflation within narrow limits and therefore would provide a better economic environment than an attempt to hold to a zero rate of inflation on the average. The larger real money stock associated with a zero average inflation rate would, it seemed possible, make it difficult to manage a relatively large real money stock so as to keep the actual inflation rate within a range of, say, -1 to +1 percent—more difficult, for example, than it would be to keep the inflation rate within the range of, say 4 to 6 percent by dealing with a correspondingly smaller real money stock. However, it must be admitted that there is something unique about zero that makes it easier to keep this as a target than to keep 5 percent as a target, and this psychological focusing may be more important than whatever difference there may be in the mechanical factors between the two situations.

A crucial difficulty with this approach, however, is that there appears to be a tendency for the experience of inflation to generate expectations of further and increased inflation, so that inflation itself accelerates the outward shift of the Phillips curve. The level of inflation associated with an optimal level of employment would thus tend to increase until the system eventually breaks down. Maintaining an assured constant rate of inflation as a long-run policy seems thus to be extremely difficult if not practically infeasible with traditional tools, though it might be possible with a market anti-inflation policy (MAP). At least in the short run, however, the damage done even by incorrectly anticipated inflation is far less serious than the damage done by unemployment. Incorrectly anticipated inflation (or deflation) results in arbitrary and often inequitable transfers between debtors and creditors and between traders in markets where prices have not kept pace with inflation, in either direction. (In the 1930s it was complained of on behalf of farmers that industrial prices and especially utility prices had not fallen as much as had the overall price level.) There may thus be some inefficiency or inequity in the way that the aggregate product of the economy is distributed among the participants, but if employment is kept at the same level, the aggregate amount to be distributed will be substantially the same. Some lose but others gain by roughly similar amounts in the aggregate. Unemployment, however, results in a roughly corresponding reduction in the total amount of product to be distributed. Many suffer substantially, and few, if any, gain. Essentially, unanticipated inflation is akin to embezzlement, while unemployment is comparable to vandalism.

The popular conception, however, is quite different. The overwhelming majority of individuals feels that people have been injured, on balance, by inflation. The illusion is that if only inflation had not occurred, incomes would have climbed almost as much but prices would not have increased. This illusion is reinforced by politicians and financiers who constantly refer to the burdens of inflation and who characterize inflation as "the cruelest tax." The political reality is thus that for every person who directly experiences losses from unemployment several will regard inflation as the greater threat to themselves. In a system of majority rule that provides little opportunity to register the intensity of preferences at the ballot box, practical politics pushes strongly in the direction of giving first priority to the abatement of inflation over the reduction of unemployment. Attention paid to the lesser problem tends to preclude adequate attention being given to the greater problem.

In a sense, inflation does operate as a tax, but this effect is almost trivial in the modern context. When nearly all transactions were effected by means of coin or non-interest-bearing notes or scrip, inflation amounted to a tax on the holding of such instruments and could enable the sovereign to obtain control over significant amounts of resources. Under modern conditions, when most transactions are by check and checking accounts generally earn interest at a rate that reflects the rate of inflation, this tax on holdings of currency is relatively trivial. To the extent that there is a burden on the holding of cash balances, when interest on deposits fails to keep pace with inflation, the beneficiaries are the banks and not the government. Even so, competition may compel the banks to return some of this tax in kind, albeit inefficiently, through enhanced services or lower service charges.

The incidence of such a tax on currency holdings may be somewhat regressive, since lower-income individuals are likely to use cash for a relatively larger amount of their buying. On the other hand, where life is eked out on a hand-to-mouth basis, average holdings of currency may be quite small even relative to income. In any event, a tax of say 10 percent per year on the average holdings of currency can hardly be properly described as "the cruelest tax."

THE MISLEADING NATURE OF THE NOMINAL DEFICIT

Concentration on inflation as the prime evil coupled with a widespread conviction that government deficits increase the rate of inflation leads to a pervasive deficit-phobia shared in varying degrees by many on both sides of the political arena. This deficit-phobia tends to preclude any adequate action in the direction of a full-employment policy aimed at an optimum level of employment (as contrasted with acceptance of a "natural" rate of unemployment). This fear, however, is exaggerated, if not seriously misplaced.

As long as the federal budgeting process operates on essentially a cash-flow basis and makes no attempt to distinguish in any systematic way between outlays on current account and those on capital account, the resulting deficit figure is highly arbitrary and misleading. For example, if a government borrows to build an office structure on its own account, this shows up as an increase in the deficit, while if it merely enters into a long-term lease with a private firm who will build the structure on its own and lease it to the government, there is no deficit created, though the effect on the economy is hardly different.

This failure to distinguish between capital and current outlays imparts a pervasive bias in decisions as to how government business shall be transacted. An agency will contribute less to the cash-flow deficit if it rents or leases rather than purchases outright or if the post office operates in rented rather than owned quarters. In many cases the arrangements thus induced will be significantly less efficient than those that would have been chosen without the bias induced by deficit phobia. Indeed, a relatively painless way of substantially reducing this nominal deficit, or even eliminating it altogether, would be to sell off the Pentagon and other government buildings to private investors, subject to a long-term lease and repurchase agreement. To attempt to do this openly on a large scale would probably provoke widespread cries of "Foul" but might be a salutary method of bringing the issue to the fore.

There is no way to make sense out of the government budget without distinguishing outlays on capital account and those on current account, including appropriate current account charges for interest and depreciation on past capital outlays. If a balance sheet is drawn up that shows assets and liabilities in the same way that General Motors does, a totally different picture of the government deficit and its impact on the economy emerges.

Indeed, Robert Eisner and Paul Pieper have done just this (1984). They show that at the end of 1946 as we emerged from the war the net worth of the U.S. government was -$56 billion, reached a low of -$92 billion at the end of 1949, ran close to a balance from 1956 to 1962, and showed a healthy surplus of

$279.4 billion in 1980. While one may quarrel with the details of this calculation, it is clear that from a balance sheet point of view the picture is quite different from the impression one gets from the nominal budget figures usually presented. Even the extraordinarily large nominal deficits since 1980 and projected for the next few years would appear much less threatening if adjusted to include only the real interest on the debt and exclude net government capital formation. In terms of the regular federal budget, far from mortgaging the future to pay for present extravagance, future citizens would seem to have been presented with assets worth considerably more than the associated debt burden.

DEFICIT PHOBIA

A budget deficit should, properly viewed, not necessarily be a cause for alarm. Unfortunately, the rampant deficit-phobia prevalent to varying degrees among government officials and congressmen of both parties, as well as throughout the financial community, can engender reactions that convert predictions that large deficits would be eventually disastrous into self-fulfilling prophecies. A failure to take adequate steps in the direction of "balancing the budget" may be viewed by the chairman of the Federal Reserve Board as calling for him to take action to ward off the increased inflationary pressure that he foresees. Even before this action is actually taken, financial markets may react by increasing interest rates in anticipation of such action. This in turn curtails investment, cancelling out whatever stimulus to the economy might have been produced by the budgetary deficit and stymying the potential improvement in the level of unemployment. If monetary contraction is in fact undertaken, monetarists will point to the coincidence of monetary contraction and reduced nominal income flows as a vindication of their theory.

In the orthodox Keynesian model, as long as adequate real resources remain available, it should be possible for the monetary authority to prevent the government borrowing involved in a budget deficit from "crowding out" private investment by implementing an appropriately expansionary monetary policy. In the current state of deficit-phobia, however, a substantial increase in the government deficit may be taken by the financial community as a harbinger of impending increased inflation, increases in nominal interest rates in the long run, and anticipatory increases in long-term interest rates in the short run. In the face of such a market psychology, the Fed may indeed feel that any attempt to keep short-term rates down by expansionary monetary measures would merely exacerbate an eventual reaction.

Indeed, there are indications that the Fed operates under the assumption that it lacks the capability of lowering current long-term interest rates in the face of large government deficits and the psychology of the market. For long-term interest rates to go down would require that the market anticipate that short-term rates would stay down in the future. While in principle the Fed possesses the power through its rediscount operations to continue keeping short-term interest rates low, given its recent postures it would be unable to generate a confident expectation in the market that it would in fact do so in the face of continued deficits. Thus even though a lowering of long-term interest rates might stimulate long-term investment that does not depend for its attractiveness on an expansion of demand, the financial community does not feel that this is achievable. Without lower long-term rates, lower short-term rates are relatively ineffective in stimulating investment, since investments that are financed by short-term rates, such as expansion of inventory, are unlikely to prove attractive in the absence of an increase in demand.

In this way, while the real availability of resources would make it unnecessary for government borrowing to curtail private investment, deficit-phobia may prevent making the financial arrangements that would be necessary to allow these idle resources to be put to work. Thus deficit-phobia with its associated fear of a resurgence of inflation may diminish much of the expansionary effect of deficit financing. Even if it were true that much of what we have to fear from a deficit is fear itself, the existence of that fear is a fact that must be dealt with. Only by installing a confidence-inspiring anti-inflation program can the potential beneficial effects of deficit financing in periods of low utilization of resources be fully realized.

SECULAR INCREASES IN INFLATIONARY TENDENCIES

In the simple Keynesian model, inflation is the result of "too much money chasing too few goods" in a context of full employment of resources, such that expansion of supply to meet expanded aggregate demand is not possible. Nonuniformity in the degree to which various resources are idle and the sluggishness of adjustments in relative prices to reflect such variations in scarcity would lead to some inflationary tendency even at points somewhat short of full employment. But substantial inflation under conditions of severe unemployment was supposed not to be possible, except perhaps where inflation had become so intense as to cause unemployment to result from sheer confusion and uncertainty. Unemployment was supposed to sound a bell calling for expansionary policy, while inflation was supposed to blow a whistle calling for restraint. But of recent years the bell and the whistle have had a habit of going off simultaneously, with unemployment greater than could be accounted for by mere confusion.

Inflation, of course, is nothing new. But in the past it has occurred either in times of prosperity and reasonably full employment or as a consequence of and an aggravating factor in the breakdown of an economic system. In most politically stable economies, substantial unemployment has usually been accompanied by steady or falling prices. Now something seems to have been added to the picture.

At the most immediate level, price inflation is the result of individual prices being raised. This raising of prices takes place under varying circumstances according to the nature of the respective markets. For present purposes prices may be classified according to how they are set. Some are set in a manner closely approximating the competitive model in organized markets such as the commodity exchanges, auctions, and the like. Some are set through bargaining and haggling between buyer and seller where the influence of the two parties is roughly symmetrical and results average out to be not far from the result in the competitive model. Some prices are set primarily by the buyer, as when a canner posts a price that it will pay for tomatoes delivered to the plant.

Increasingly, however, prices are set by sellers. This is the natural result of increasingly differentiated products of a more and more technical nature, where the suppliers are few relative to purchasers, have a greater interest in the price, and have superior knowledge of the characteristics of the product and of prices and characteristics of competing products. Even where the products are closely similar in physical characteristics, substantial differentiation can occur in terms of conditions of delivery, location and transportation costs, reliability of supply, and ancillary services. Differentiation of products is often associated with economies of scale in the production of any one variety. Such economies of scale can be important in a relative sense even in small-scale industry, as with the production of specialty buttons, books, or encyclopedias.

As is frequently the case, the economies of scale involve substantial sunk costs, which constitutes a substantial barrier to the entry of new firms, at least in the short run. This thus provides an opportunity for each seller to raise its price above what would be comparable to those of its competitors without immediately losing a large part of its trade. As all competitors in such a market act similarly, price can increase substantially above costs before there is a temptation for a given competitor to lower its price in an attempt to capture a sufficiently larger share of the market to result in higher profits. Even this possibility is strongly inhibited by the realization that any such move would incur a significant danger of provoking competitive price cuts or even a price war.

If such seller-set pricing predominates at all stages of the production and distribution cycle, a price increase at one stage of production becomes an increase in the costs of the next stage, and a continuous process of price increases can develop even in the presence of substantial unemployment and other idle resources. Formerly, the cycle tended to be interrupted at the labor market stage, where buyer-set prices tended to prevail. In recent years, however, the seller side of the labor market has tended increasingly to influence the setting of wages, so that the break in the inflationary cycle has tended to close. Among the factors working in this direction have been increased coverage and replacement ratios of unemployment insurance; more common appeals to cost-of-living rises as a justification for generous wage settlements; and greater investment by employers in the training and organization of a sophisticated labor force that must be held and even hoarded over periods of slack production if this investment is not to be lost. Minimum wage laws, social pressures against the payment of substandard wages, and social approval of policies of paying higher wages even in the face of a not too clearly perceived likelihood that this might lead to price increases may also have played a role. Politically, also, producers, especially of agricultural products, appear to have been better organized than consumers when it comes to legislative action affecting the price of such items as milk.

Note that this inflationary cycle of oligopolistic pricing can operate independently of restrictions on the money supply. The resulting increase in the aggregate of money transactions can send interest rates up and cause contraction of investment, employment, and real disposable income, but it does not directly interrupt the cycle of price increases. Indeed, increases in interest rates can exacerbate the cycle by raising costs and providing a justification for further price increases. The inflationary process stops only if unemployment gets so severe that it does break the cycle at the labor market.

As a result of this inflationary cycle the Phillips curve has moved outward to a point where a "natural" rate of unemployment has become entirely unsatisfactory and where the maintenance of a truly satisfactory level of employment is likely over any medium long run to entail an unacceptable and even accelerating rate of inflation. There is thus an urgent need for some form of direct countervailing pressure on prices that will move the Phillips curve inward sufficiently to provide a satisfactory level of employment and price stability. Incentive antiinflation policies do precisely that and thus must be considered far more carefully than they have been previously.

3 PLANS FOR FIGHTING INFLATION WITH MICROECONOMIC INCENTIVES

Jeffrey B. Miller, Kenneth J. Koford, and Jerrold E. Schneider

The last fifteen years have been unsettling for macroeconomists. In the 1960s economists felt that they had learned a great deal about the macroeconomy. The 1970s saw this self-confidence unravel as both inflation and unemployment soared above the level of the 1960s. The decade of the 1970s was also a period of dramatic change in macroeconomic theory as the earlier Keynesian theories came under attack and new theories like rational expectations came to the fore.

These two events are not unrelated. As Hicks (1969: 255) has stated in discussing advances in monetary theory:

> Monetary theory is less abstract than most economic theory; it cannot avoid a relation to reality.... [A] large part of the best work on "money" is topical. It has been prompted by particular episodes, by particular experiences of the writer's own time.... So monetary experiences arise out of monetary disturbances.

The same could be said for macroeconomics in general.

Among economists doing research in the area of macroeconomics, there is a group that believes that the economy's macroeconomic performance can only be improved by changing some of the economy's basic institutional arrangements. While the recommendations are varied, they have a common theme. Each proposal attempts to achieve higher employment levels and lower inflation rates through changes in incentives under which agents at the microeconomic level make decisions about prices and wages. This book covers one area of this research: Incentive anti-inflation plans, which are novel forms of incomes policies. While these new proposals differ from previous incomes policies, it is useful to analyze these new proposals in part by comparing and contrasting them with incomes policies that have been tried in the past.

Historically incomes policies have been tried in many different countries. These policies have not been overwhelmingly successful, but as Flanagan, Soskice, and Ulman (1983: 21) state:

> It is interesting that the policymakers of Europe should have returned so persistently to an instrument whose record has been as spotty and unreliable as the record of incomes policy has been. That record raises the question whether incomes policies are inherently ineffective, even self-defeating, given the nature of the underlying inflationary process, or whether the design and administration of past policies have been inadequate to cope with the institutional forces that they are designed to resist.

The issue that we address in this chapter is whether the design of these new proposals will be able to overcome the inadequacies observed in past incomes policies.

We begin by analyzing the policy most closely associated with incomes policy in the United States: wage and price controls. We then describe the impact of wage/price guidelines and the problems that have arisen when this policy has been tried. We then describe new proposals and compare them to wage and price controls. Finally we briefly discuss other policies that might work in a similar fashion—Meade's arbitration scheme (1982) and Weitzman's share economy (1983, 1984).

Incentive anti-inflation plans are directed at microeconomic incentives but are designed to achieve macroeconomic effects. Thus to analyze them requires an integration of macro- and microeconomics. This integration is an important area of ongoing research. At present no consensus exists as to how it should best be done. Rather than enter into this debate we consider the various proposals using a uniform microeconomic framework of firm behavior. Because it is a microeconomic model, the model says nothing directly about macroeconomic performance. The framework is useful, however, in clarifying the differences among the various proposals, and from it some indirect macroeconomic inferences can be drawn.

To stress that these proposals would become crucial features of the economies to which they were applied, following Weitzman, we use the terms "wage and price control economy," "TIP economy," etc. This terminology emphasizes that each of these "economies" has a different structure and behavior.

THE WAGE AND PRICE CONTROL ECONOMY

For most people in the United States, incomes policy is essentially wage and price controls. Their view of controls is often based on the experience of the early 1970s when Nixon first imposed a wage and price freeze and then through a series of stages – or "phases" – relaxed the controls.

Numerous problems arose during this period. First, because of the rigidity of prices, unacceptable inefficiencies, shortages, and inequities eventually arose. For example, during the controls period shortages of logs, fertilizer, and molasses occurred when higher world prices caused domestic suppliers to send their output abroad. Domestic buyers could not offer higher prices if they wanted the goods because the controls program prevented prices from rising. These shifts affected other firms. For instance, sawmills shut down because of the curtailed supply of lumber (Gordon 1981b: 265). Controllers tried to make exceptions in cases like this. However, as time passed, the exceptions proliferated. In the Nixon program, at about this point the controls were slowly lifted, but it seems apparent that before long such a program will reach a point where so many exceptions exist and so many people believe they are treated unfairly that the program collapses from political opposition. For these reasons, it is apparent that a wage and price control program can have only a short lifespan.

This leads to a second problem. If the program is only temporary, then it will eventually end. When this happens, there can be a "bounce back" in which inflation surges again after the program is terminated. This apparently occurred after Nixon's Phase II, though it did not occur after the Korean War controls ended. As discussed below, some increase in prices is likely after controls are removed, but it will be more dramatic if aggregate demand pressures are allowed to build as they did during the Nixon controls.

Another important issue that arose during this period was whether such a program is administratively feasible. During the Nixon controls all prices and wages were frozen for three months while the administrative machinery was put into place. Then guidelines were issued and decisions were made as to the extent of program coverage and permissible wage and price changes. The complexity of these rules increased as pressures built in different areas of the economy and as the use of the precontrols period as a base became more strained.

This experience suggests that for the program to be administratively feasible it probably will have to be focused on a relatively few firms (although in the case of the Nixon controls this was politically difficult for reasons of the appearance of equity (Pohlman 1976: 205)). If this is done, the rest of the economy would be only indirectly affected by the program, and competition would have to hold down prices and wages there. If the scope of an incomes policy program is narrowed in this way, the complexity and the potential distortions of incomes policy can be reduced along with administrative costs, but the program then relies on competitive elements for its success.

The 1971 wage/price controls were also perceived by many people as a temporary shield behind which excess aggregate demand was generated to reelect Nixon in 1972. Under controls it should be possible to achieve higher employment without setting off new price increases. But there is a limit. If aggregate demand pressure increases, then shortages are likely to appear, and political opposition will build as the perception of fairness is harder to maintain. This is true of any incomes policy, although how the "breakdown" occurs will depend on the specific policy.

Much of the immediate success and later unhappiness with controls (Pohlman 1976: 204–05) can be explained by a microeconomic model of the firm with downward-sloping demand.[1] In this model the firm produces at an output level where marginal cost is equal to marginal revenue. Figure 3-1 shows this as (Q_o, P_o). The imposition of controls prevents the firm from raising its price. This changes the demand curve so that it now looks like AEB. With this new kinked demand curve, as long as the overall level of demand for its product has not changed, the firm has no motivation to move from its original production level, since profits will still be maximized at (Q_o, P_o).

But behavior will differ when there is either a change in demand or a change in cost. If demand increases, the demand curve will move out to $AE'B'$. At this level of demand, production by the firm will actually be higher than it was without controls, since the demand curve looks horizontal to the firm along this section. Thus during the early part of the Nixon controls program as aggregate demand rose there seemed to be a large increase in output. Only later did shortages begin to appear.

Shortages arise as demand continues to increase. If demand moves out to $AE''B''$, then the firm will no longer produce enough to meet demand at the price P_o. The firm will now produce at Q_o'' where the marginal cost curve crosses the horizontal section of the demand curve. The shortage is (Q_o'', Q_1'').

Under controls, if aggregate demand is raised, any firm experiencing increased demand would like to raise its price, giving it an incentive to go to the wage/ price control administrators and argue that the increase in demand in their sector is an unusual circumstance and deserves special consideration. Furthermore, as time passes more firms are likely to experience significant increases in demand, and the pressure on the control system will build.

Shortages can also arise from increases in cost. Costs can rise because of increases in wages, increases in prices in uncontrolled sectors, or price increases on imported inputs. An increase in marginal costs will cause the marginal cost curve to shift upward. If the increase is sufficiently large, then the intersection of the horizontal section of the demand curve and the marginal cost curve will occur at a point like Q_o'', and there will be a shortage.

This analysis suggests that markets can absorb some increase in costs without creating shortages, but large increases in costs, such as those experienced when imported oil prices rose in the 1970s, will produce serious shortages.

The model can also explain why agents who anticipate the implementation of a controls program will raise prices. If firms expect demand for their product to rise soon after the implementation of the controls program, they will raise prices

Figure 3-1. Effect of Price Controls on a Monopolistic Firm.

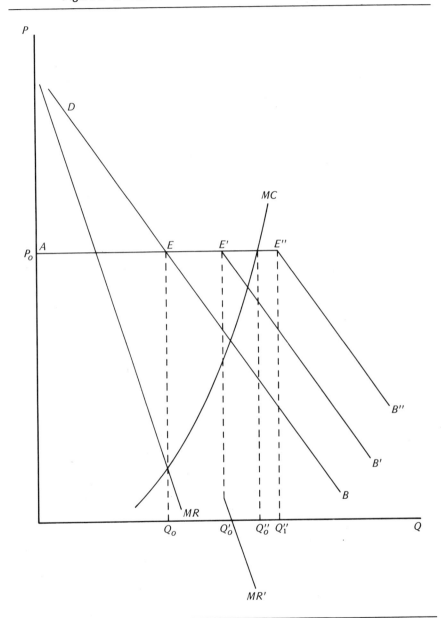

now while they can and suffer a short-term reduction in profits in order to increase profits during the controls period.

From this analysis it can be seen that controls can produce some benefits. As time passes pressures begin to build, however, when shortages begin to appear in more and more sectors. If at this stage controls are abandoned, firms will raise prices. This occurs because the demand curve now snaps back to its original shape and firms that were previously operating at output levels along the horizontal segment of the kinked curve will see that they can increase profits by raising their prices. Thus we get a "bounce back" as prices rise. Furthermore, if the end of the controls program is anticipated by labor, there may be greater insistence on higher wages, increasing cost pressures on firms, and a larger bounce back.

The difficulties associated with maintaining a viable controls program for more than a short period of time have led to a search for a more flexible program. One such program that has been tried is wage and price guidelines.

THE WAGE AND PRICE GUIDELINES ECONOMY

There have been two recent experiences with guidelines in the United States. The first was during the 1960s and the second was during the Carter administration in the late 1970s. During the 1960s government policy was directed at increasing aggregate demand in an attempt to reduce unemployment, and the guidelines were directed at keeping inflation low. In 1978 when Carter announced his program, the country was pulling out of the recession of 1974–75. Inflation had been in the 6 to 8 percent range, and an anti-inflation program was deemed necessary.

In many ways a guidelines program is very similar to a controls program except that the enforcement mechanism is different. Rather than legislating that price adjustments must be held within certain boundaries as in the case of controls, guidelines tend to be more "voluntary" and enforcement is accomplished through persuasion. Often this persuasion takes place in private. At other times it takes the form of a public pronouncement of noncompliance.

Because the enforcement mechanisms are less clearly defined than with controls, there must be broad and sustained support from both business and labor if there is to be compliance. Such support will come if the policy is demonstratively effective, efficient, and perceived to be fair. The perception of some degree of noncompliance by some will swiftly unravel compliance by others.[2]

Since guidelines and wage/price controls are very similar, their interpretation in terms of the microeconomic model of downward sloping demand is very much the same. If the guidelines are interpreted to mean that prices cannot rise at all, then the graph of a firm under a guidelines program is identical to the graph in Figure 3–1 for a firm under a controls program.[3]

If the program is more flexible than this and prices are allowed to rise some-what under the guidelines, then the demand curve could adjust to shortages, eliminating non-marginal solutions.[4] With higher prices firms will supply more before a shortage arises. Still, as relative demands and costs shift, before too long shortages can be expected to arise in some areas of the economy unless specific exceptions are granted.

The problem with guideline programs, however, appears to be enforcement, not shortages. Without enforcement the guidelines do not constrain inflationary pressures: The horizontal section of the demand curve does not exist. Both in the late 1960s and at the end of the Carter administration inflation rose. This has led to a search for a program that is both more flexible than wage/price con-trols and prevents inflation better than guidelines.

THE TAX-BASED INCOMES POLICIES (TIP) ECONOMY

TIP is the first of a number of programs that allow relative price flexibility but prevent the overall price level from rising. This approach grants that no central administration can determine when a particular price change is appropriate and when it is not. Price adjustments must be made in a decentralized way. Thus the proposals permit economic agents to continue to make price and wage decisions, but the proposals change the incentives under which agents operate to create an environment in which decisions will not lead to inflation.

TIP was made famous by Wallich and Weintraub (1971). Their idea was to adjust corporate profits taxes if the increase in the firm's wage bill exceeded a government guideline. They argued that by giving management an additional incentive to keep wages down, inflationary pressures could be better controlled. Corporate taxes were chosen because adjusting them was seen as less economi-cally distorting. Controlling wage adjustments was the objective because wage inflation was viewed as the principal problem.

This proposal has been criticized for both its use of the corporate profits tax and its focus on wages. Use of the corporate profits tax has been attacked be-cause the tax is not paid by all corporations and the significance of the tax to different firms does not reflect their economic importance.[5] The focus on wage inflation has been criticized by those who believe that wage inflation is not the only cause of inflation, and the proposal has received strong political opposition from labor groups that are particularly sensitive to its wage focus.

This has spawned several related TIP proposals designed to overcome the economic and political problems of the original proposal. For example, there have been suggestions that guidelines be established for variables other than wages, such as price changes. Some proposals recommend both price and wage guidelines with the level of taxation depending on some combination of the changes that have occurred in both. Still another possibility is taxing increases in "value added." As we will see below, that would make TIP very close to the market anti-inflation policy of Lerner and Colander (Colander and Koford 1984; Lerner and Colander 1980).

TIP can also be changed along other dimensions. Okun (1977) argued for subsidies rather than penalties. Moving one step further, a mix of tax penalties and rewards is possible. Also one could adjust tax rates progressively depending on the variance from the guidelines rather than using a single tax rate above the guidelines.

Given the number of possibilities it is important to establish some criteria for distinguishing among them. Three criteria that should certainly be considered are (1) effectiveness in reducing inflation and unemployment, (2) administrative feasibility, and (3) political feasibility. We shall first examine criteria 2 and 3; later we will analyze 1 in terms of our economic model.

The administrative and political feasibility of these proposals are often intricately intertwined. It has been suggested, for instance, that using a reward TIP, where payments would be given for compliance, would not be politically feasible unless all economic agents were eligible for the grants. Such a program might be administratively infeasible, since to monitor it would be extremely costly, and the reward payments might be very expensive for the government. Increased tax penalties would not need to be applied so broadly, and therefore would be administratively easier to implement.

Much of the recent work on the administrative and political feasibility of these proposals is an outgrowth of a 1978 Brookings Conference which evaluated the early TIP proposals. As might be expected, given the novelty of these ideas at the time, a number of problems were identified. Since that time proponents of these proposals have attempted to address the criticisms raised at the conference.

Perhaps the most serious political criticism of the early plans was that they were unbalanced by the focus on wages (for example, Rees 1978). Since 1978 more work has been done on how prices or value added can be included in the incentive schemes and how measurement problems related to these variables can be handled. For example, Lerner and Colander argue that placing the incentive on value added reduces the problems of measurement and is politically fair (Lerner in Okun and Perry 1978; Lerner and Colander 1980; Colander 1981; Koford 1983). In their MAP proposal the sum of wages and profits is controlled, but wages and profits are not controlled individually.

Many of the other criticisms at the Brookings Conference were directed at how the various plans might be implemented. These problems can vary considerably across plans. Indeed the choice of plan may well be based on these issues. For instance, Joseph Pechman, one of the more skeptical conferees, was for these reasons particularly critical of proposals that involve a subsidy, but he agreed (in Okun and Perry 1978) that "a penalty on profits based on wage changes is feasible" under certain conditions.

One of Pechman's principal reservations regarding the use of a TIP that controls wages is the timing problem. He argues that it would be very difficult for the firm to anticipate ahead of time what its situation will be at the end of the period and, therefore, what tax should be paid at the end of the period. Paying a subsidy rather than collecting a penalty would be much more difficult under these conditions. To demonstrate this he posits the following situation: Suppose a union agrees to a small increase in wages in order to comply with the program. Later negotiations between other unions and that firm lead, however, to changes in the overall wage bill that are so large that the firm is no longer in compliance, and benefits that the members of the first union anticipated no longer accrue to them. This concern, like others Pechman expresses, depends on a TIP scheme that specifically rewards workers directly for their willingness to comply with the program. A penalty TIP would not suffer from this problem.

The administrative burden of a TIP program applied to millions of U.S. firms was also addressed at the conference. This is a problem that is particularly severe for a reward TIP but not necessarily for a penalty TIP. Proponents of the penalty TIP also recognize this problem and suggest that the program be applied only to the largest 2,000 corporations (Seidman 1981). Whether this would be politically feasible remains to be seen. As pointed out above, the Nixon administration was unable for political reasons to keep its controls program from being extended into competitive areas of the economy.

Another administrative problem is the identification of an appropriate unit when implementing the program. What do you do about the diversified firm? Actually, the more diversified the firm the better the program should work. The objective of a tax-based incentive program is to keep the overall price level from rising. Distortions are caused when the program inhibits the movement of relative prices. A diversified firm has more latitude in its individual price decisions, since it is operating in several markets. Allowing the diversified firm, which is sensitive to the tradeoffs of pricing decisions among its different products, to make the decisions about price adjustments should actually improve the effectiveness of the incentive scheme. A firm that recognizes limitations on how much it can raise its overall price list will be forced to select carefully when deciding which prices to raise. Indeed the most serious problems are likely to arise in such firms as automobile manufacturers, where only a few goods are produced and firms have little flexibility.

A related problem is what to do when the unit being taxed undergoes some fundamental change (such as a new firm, merger, or spinoff) so that it is difficult to use past history as a guideline for what should be done next year. Pechman is particularly concerned about the parallels between these problems and those that have arisen under the excess profits tax, where litigation has been common. The most difficult case would be where new firms are created; but if the program is addressed to only the largest firms, this is not really an issue. With mergers or spin-offs there is a past history that can be used to make a judgment.

Richard Slitor, a tax economist with long experience in the U.S. Department of the Treasury, argues (1979) that this ability to identify a past history actually distinguishes TIP from an excess profits tax.

As can be seen from this discussion, the Brookings Conference called attention to some important issues concerning the viability of a tax-based scheme. These issues have formed the basis of a research agenda that is still being worked through.

The effects of tax-based incomes policies have also been explored in a series of papers by Layard, Jackman, and Pissarides. These papers investigate the impact of tax-based policies in models where there is search unemployment and where wage determination is specifically modeled. Layard (1982a) argues that another force besides monetary policy should be brought to bear on the inflation/unemployment problem and that incomes policy is the obvious candidate. While monetary policy can be expected to determine the rate of inflation, he sees incomes policy as a means of lowering the natural rate of unemployment.

More recently Jackman, Layard, and Pissarides (1983) explored a number of different wage setting arrangements and policies. They find that at least in theory a tax on wages is equivalent to a tax on wage increases. In each case unemployment is reduced. These papers provide theoretical support for the notion that a TIP program would reduce unemployment, giving the monetary authority more freedom to control inflation.

A related but less sophisticated way of looking at the impact of a TIP is in terms of our microeconomic model of the firm. Rather than try to model the theoretical implications of all the different forms of TIPs we focus on the wage TIP. This is the form studied by Jackman, Layard, and Pissarides and is the most common form discussed in the literature. It is also possible to design a TIP based on value added (Colander 1981). Value-added schemes have more commonly been associated with a market anti-inflation policy (MAP). Since a value-added TIP is very similar to a MAP that uses value added, we will put off analyzing value added until the next section where MAP is discussed.

Since we are focusing on the choice of a wage rate, our analysis is framed in terms of the labor market. Suppose the firm sees the supply of labor as upward sloping. This follows from the argument that the firm is the largest agent in the market and therefore will establish the price (Arrow 1959; Seidman in Okun and Perry 1978).[6]

Just how a TIP program will affect the supply of labor to a firm depends on labor's perception of how firms will react to the program and how this will affect the workers' actions. For example, if a firm faces a union, the supply of labor will depend on the union's reaction to the new bargaining situation. A union that recognizes that it is now more costly for the firm to raise wages may be less insistent on large increases since this could affect the viability of the firm. A firm in a nonunion environment may also find that labor costs are reduced if workers' perceptions of the availability of high-paying jobs change under TIP.

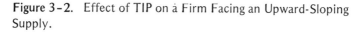

Figure 3-2. Effect of TIP on à Firm Facing an Upward-Sloping Supply.

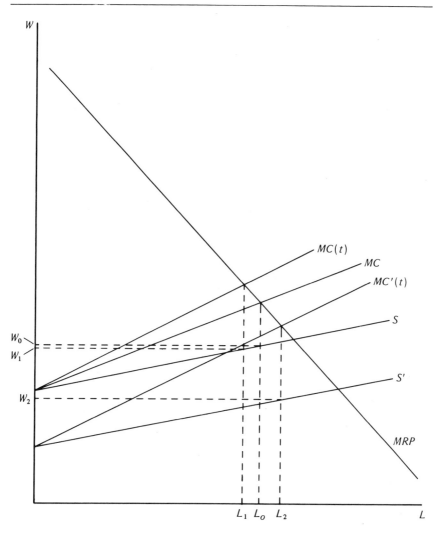

In describing the impact of TIP in a nonunion environment, we must distinguish between the immediate impact on the firm and what occurs after market adjustments have been made. The immediate impact of a "balanced budget" TIP (where money collected by the tax is used to finance an employment subsidy) is to tilt the marginal cost curve upward as shown in Figure 3-2. Initially the firm will hire less labor, L_1, and pay a lower wage, W_1. If this firm is a representative firm, and there is no entry of other firms into the market, the unemployment rate will rise, and workers who are seeking employment will find that wage offers in general are lower. But both the increase in unemployment and the lower wage can be expected to change workers' perceptions of what is a reasonable wage offer. This will shift the supply curve of labor outward (Jackman, Layard, and Pissarides 1983). Firms can now hire more workers at wage rate W_1, and unemployment will fall. While this will cause the supply curve to shift back toward the original supply curve, S, as perceptions change again, as long as wage offers in the economy as a whole remain below their initial level, the new supply curve will be to the right of the original curve.

Figure 3-2 shows that one possible outcome of a TIP is that wage rates fall and employment rises to (W_2, L_2). If the firm is also a price maker in the output market, the firm will increase output and charge a lower price. Increases in demand for the firm's product will shift the MRP curve outward. This would move the firm to higher employment levels and lower marginal cost levels than would have been the case in the absence of TIP. Thus TIP can lead to higher output and lower price levels.

If TIP tilts the $MC'(t)$ curve more or the shift in the supply curve is less than shown in the diagram, then the results are not as positive. The intersection of the $MC'(t)$ curve and the MRP curves is to the northeast of where it would have been without TIP. This will lead to lower wages and less employment than would have occurred without TIP. Since output is lower, prices would be higher. A more complete and sophisticated treatment of this case has been analyzed in papers by Jackman and Layard (Chapter 6), Pissarides (1985b), and Oswald (1984b).

A TIP program, like wage and price controls, can generate higher output and lower prices than would have occurred otherwise. As long as tax rates on wage changes are not prohibitively high,[7] firms will adjust prices and wages as pressures build, and, unlike the result of controls, shortages will not arise, for expansion of demand will not generate situations where the firm will refuse to supply sufficient quantities at the prices established in the market. Increases in demand will instead result in increases in price and output. The increases in output will be greater and the increases in prices will be smaller than they would have been in the absence of TIP.

The TIP economy, therefore, would look quite different than the wage and price control economy. While there are incentives to keep down wage and price increases, they are not as strong as in a controlled economy. If pressures build, increases in wage and price levels will occur. On the other hand there is less rigidity in relative price movements, and sectoral shortages will not arise.

How effective the TIP program will be in controlling inflationary pressures will depend in part on labor's perception of the new economic environment. If labor does not adjust its behavior (that is, the supply curve does not move), then (in the absence of employment subsidies) TIP will only add to the firm's costs, causing higher prices and lower output. If, however, labor claims are moderated, then TIP can improve both inflation and unemployment. In particular, if workers have rational expectations, labor will moderate its claims and TIP will improve the overall economic climate.

THE MAP ECONOMY

An incentive policy that is similar to TIP is Lerner and Colander's (1980) MAP (market anti-inflation plan). This plan would create a market in licences permitting firms to raise prices. The idea is that firms that intend to lower prices can sell their government-assigned MAP credits to those firms that wish to raise prices. The overall price level will then (under certain configurations) remain unchanged, and the cost of raising a price will be determined in the marketplace.

The price that firms pay for raising their output prices is very similar to the tax that firms would have to pay if TIP were applied to price changes. One difference is that under MAP there are no transfers to the government, since all payments are made to other firms. Thus MAP is like a TIP scheme where there are both rewards and penalties and a balanced-budget constraint. Another difference and possible advantage of MAP over a tax-based proposal is that the MAP credit price adjusts as inflationary pressures change, while the tax rate in a TIP must be determined administratively and may not adjust well to fluctuating pressures for price increases in the economy.

Like TIP, MAP can be applied to different variables under the control of the firm. For example, MAP could be applied to wage changes or price changes. However, MAP has usually been thought of as being applied to "value added," as in Lerner and Colander's original proposal.

MAP also has serious measurement problems. In order for trades to take place in the MAP market, a firm must establish whether or not credits have been earned, and a buying firm must establish what its needs are. Thus the administrative problems involving TIP described above also relate to MAP. Lerner and Colander chose value added as the variable to be controlled partly because they believed value added would be easier to measure. Value added, which in this instance is gross sales minus inputs purchased from other firms, is calculated as part of normal accounting practice and therefore would not be difficult for firms to determine. While the measurement problems associated with value added per se are clearly less severe than those associated with other measures, the diversity and dynamics of an ever-changing economy will still create significant measurement problems. In particular, under MAP a method must be found to measure changes in the input *quantities* of capital and labor. While Lerner and Colander propose some solutions, technical problems still exist, and a fully worked-out solution awaits further research.

The other reason that Lerner and Colander chose value added was their belief that it presented a more balanced picture of where the sources of inflation may arise. Unlike trying to control only prices, which might squeeze profits, or only wages, which might reduce workers' real incomes, value added attempts to control the sum of the two. They argue that since it does not single out either group it is a more politically viable proposal.

To examine how MAP would function, we shall analyze a MAP on price increases. Our rationale is that it is easy to get an intuition for this form of MAP, and it is very similar in its economic implications to the more familiar MAP on value added. It is important to keep in mind, however, that MAP can be applied to other variables much as TIP can.

The effect of a price MAP applied to a firm with a downward sloping demand curve is illustrated in Figure 3-3. Since MAP raises the cost to the firm of increasing its price, the firm will receive smaller net revenues when it attempts to raise its price. Similarly, the firm is being subsidized when it lowers its price. If the D' curve is interpreted as the net demand curve after the MAP credits have been bought or sold, the D' curve will be flatter than the original demand curve. Since at that level no MAP credit transactions need to be made, the new curve will pass through the original price and quantity on the D curve.

With the new D' and MR' curves the firm will now produce more output and charge a lower price than it did before. The greater the inflationary pressure the higher the MAP price and the more the curve rotates. Unlike a wage and price control economy, in a MAP economy if the inflationary pressure does not build to the point where the demand curve becomes horizontal, there should not be sectoral shortages.[8] It does not matter whether this pressure comes in the form of wage inflation pushing up costs or demand pressure shifting up the demand curves of individual firms. As long as the demand curve does not become horizontal, shortages should not arise.

There are some differences between a MAP economy and a TIP economy. In the TIP economy if demand pressures increase, firms will begin to raise their prices and pay the penalties. With MAP the cost of the MAP license increases and the benefit of price cuts rise as the inflationary pressures rise, keeping the price level constant. MAP therefore operates as a kind of "shock absorber" that keeps the price level from rising. This contrasts with a TIP economy where prices will eventually rise. TIP and MAP will perform in a similar fashion if taxes are increased along with the rise in inflationary pressures. If this were done in a way to keep the price level constant and the budget balanced condition satisfied, then TIP and MAP would have essentially equivalent economic effects. In practice, however, it would be difficult to make such changes in tax rates administratively. In the United States it is also unlikely that Congress would be willing to relinquish its control over tax rates (see Vickrey, Chapter 10, this volume).

In summary, a MAP economy can be expected to function differently than either a wage and price control economy or a TIP economy although it has more

Figure 3-3. Effect of MAP on a Monopolistic Firm.

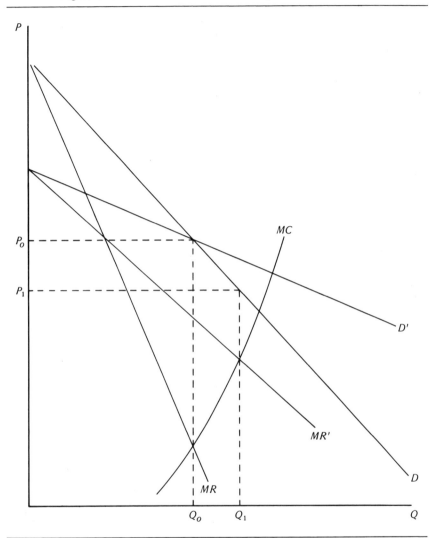

in common with a TIP economy. Theoretically at least, MAP offers a way to control the overall price level while permitting relative prices to adjust. In practice, for MAP to perform well the market in MAP credits must function properly. As yet there has been little research on this question. In part the difficulties that might arise here are related to the measurement problems described above, for if trades are to take place, MAP credit units must be well defined.

We now turn to other approaches that avoid some measurement problems.

THE ARBITRATION ECONOMY

This policy, designed to improve the inflation-unemployment tradeoff, is based on some arbitration procedure. Labor and management come together to resolve their differences without government intervention. If they fail, the government imposes binding arbitration. The incentive to keep settlements within announced government guidelines is the knowledge that if the process goes to arbitration, the arbitrator will follow these guidelines in determining what the settlement will be. There are many possible variations of these proposals. Some have been tried in Australia. Meade (1982) recommends a distinctive approach that is really a policy designed to provide incentives to encourage more employment rather than an anti-inflation policy per se. He proposes that the arbitrator be told to choose the wage rate that will maximize the level of employment in that particular firm or industry. The government would become involved only when agreement could not be reached. The hope is that this would be such a small subset of the whole that its members can be looked at in detail without large administrative costs. If both the firm and the workers agree that higher wages are appropriate, then wages can be raised by simple agreement without arbitration.

Incentives to stay close to the government guideline are twofold. First, if the two parties want to retain control over the situation, they will try to settle their differences without an arbitrator. Second, they will be pushed toward settling near the guidelines because the two parties know that if there are disagreements, the position closer to the guideline will be selected by the arbitrator.

To see what Meade (1982: 44-57) has in mind we again turn to our theoretical model. Since Meade focuses on the labor market, our analysis looks at this market. Figure 3-4 shows a downward sloping MRP curve that reflects a downward sloping demand faced by the firm in its output market. In Meade's model the firm is also a monopsonist in the labor market; so there is also an upward sloping supply of labor curve and a MC cost curve that lies above it. In the absence of a union the firm will employ L_O labor and pay a wage W_O.

If there is a union, it will try to bargain for a wage higher than W_O. Since the wage rate is constant regardless of the number of people hired, the labor supply curve will appear horizontal to the firm. If the wage agreed to is W_1, then the marginal cost of hiring an additional laborer will be W_1, and the firm will hire L_1 workers. Note that at W_1 the firm is willing to hire more workers than it did before, even though the wage is higher. If the wage is pushed higher than W_1, employment might fall below L_O.[9]

Meade's proposal encourages firms to set wages at W'. At W' firms will hire L' workers, where L' represents the maximum employment possible in this firm given the supply of labor and the demand for the firm's output. If the union and the firm fail to agree, the arbitrator would seek to find W'. Since both the firm and the union know that an arbitrator will likely attempt to choose W', there is

Figure 3-4. Effect of Binding Arbitration on a Monopolistic Firm with an Upward-Sloping Supply Curve.

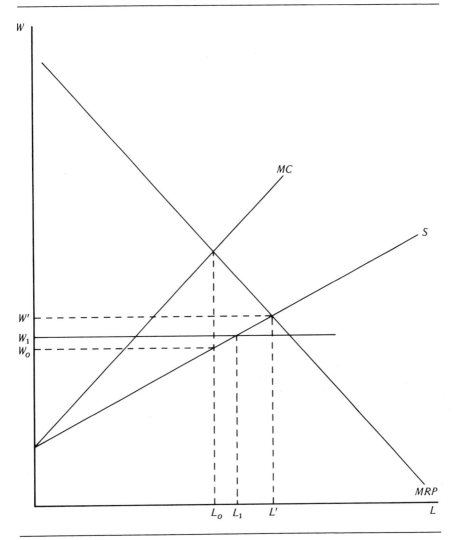

an incentive for them to settle and avoid taking a chance on what the arbitrator will actually conclude.

While this little model does not show the inflationary effect of Meade's proposal, the increased employment would take pressure off the monetary and fiscal authorities. With employment high the rationale for an expansionary policy would be reduced. On the other hand its effects on wage inflation are less clear.

Guidelines could be established and arbitrators could be instructed to keep wage settlements within the guidelines. But there could be conflict between this growth rate of wage goal and the goal of setting wages to maximize the firm's level of employment.

THE SHARE ECONOMY

Two new proposals aim at reducing unemployment by changing from wage payments to giving employees some share of the firm's income. First, Daniel Mitchell (1981) proposed that workers be paid on a profit-sharing basis. Mitchell sees the inflexibility of wages during the business cycle as causing unemployment to rise when business conditions are depressed. Under profit-sharing, wages would fall as profits are squeezed during a downturn. Since wages move procyclically under this arrangement, there would be fewer layoffs and unemployment would not rise as much as it does in the current "wage" economy.

Second, Martin Weitzman (1983, 1984) proposes what he calls a "share economy." A share system is any system where individual workers' compensation varies inversely with the number of workers. Since wages fall as more workers are hired, the owners have a greater incentive to hire more workers than under a wage system. Indeed Weitzman argues that the firm will always have an incentive to hire more workers until there are no more workers to be found. In the aggregate, firms hire more workers until no unemployed workers remain. The elimination of unemployment in this way means the problem of inflation can then be addressed more directly by monetary and fiscal policy.

CONCLUSION

This survey of recent developments in incomes policies has emphasized the variety of policy options. The fact that some of these proposals are very recent suggests that we have just begun to explore the possibilities. As weaknesses in existing proposals are found, we can expect new proposals to evolve.

Some guideposts for further research have also been laid out. The authors of these proposals all see problems in the existing set of economic institutions. Their recommendations would alter the decisionmaking environment of economic agents by changing the incentives that firms face when choosing output levels and wages and prices. Thus these proposals represent a basic restructuring of the economic system.

Disenchantment with past attempts to implement such policies may mean new developments will be slow in coming, for it has become more difficult to draw attention to new ideas in this area. This is unfortunate because the new proposals have been developed in response to the problems that were identified from this experience. The result is that the kind of economy that would evolve under these new proposals would look very different from what occurred under past schemes.

This is not to argue that any of these new proposals answer all the questions raised by this experience. Before we can judge them, more research is needed. None has reached the point where the problems have been fully investigated. But the importance of continued work in this direction is highlighted when compared to the costs of the alternative approach: recession or stagnation.

NOTES TO CHAPTER 3

1. This is the most convenient model to use because it is the simplest model we have where the individual firm sets its price. Also, Arrow (1959: 45–50) has pointed out that if the firm is a price setter, then at least for a temporary period, the firm must have a downward-sloping demand curve.
2. Broad public support is necessary if *any* controls program is to succeed. The problems of monitoring and enforcement are just too great. In the case of voluntary guidelines this aspect of incomes policy program is just highlighted. See Triplett (1983; Chapter 12, this volume).
3. Guidelines are often stated in terms of the rate of growth of wages and prices. These permissible rates are usually based on anticipated improvements in productivity. In the context of the static model described here this can be interpreted as no change in price.
4. Note that this is the same as a controls program that allowed for some price adjustment.
5. It should be noted that at the time Weintraub and Wallich presented their proposal, tax collections from the corporate profits tax were much greater than they are today.
6. Seidman also develops an analysis of TIP where the firm is a monopsonist. His models evaluate TIP when unions are present or where more long-term factors are considered.
7. If tax rates were sufficiently high, wages would never increase and TIP would be no different than wage controls. TIP would then exhibit the same inflexibility as controls.
8. The term *sectoral shortage* is used here to refer to shortages that occur under controls when demand or costs increase in a given sector. General shortages could appear in a MAP economy at full employment if demand continued to rise. Shortages could also appear in some sectors if labor is not homogeneous and there was full employment of certain types of labor.
9. This latter case where the wage is so high that employment is restricted appears to be the more likely case in Britain and other parts of Western Europe.

THE THEORY OF INCENTIVE INCENTIVE ANTI-INFLATION PLANS

4 EFFECTS OF PRICE CONTROL ON OUTPUT AND THE PRICE LEVEL

Walter S. Salant

For many years most economists have believed that once inflation got underway it could not be stopped by restrictive monetary and fiscal policy alone without some sacrifice of output. This belief has given rise to the view that such aggregate demand policies could accomplish the same anti-inflationary result with less restriction if they were reinforced by some form of control over prices or wages or both, whether direct or in the milder form of incentives for those who set prices and wages to exercise restraint.

This development reminded me of thoughts I had about controls during World War II, when I was officially concerned with stabilization policies in general and direct price and wage controls in particular. They concern the effects on the price level and on output of imposing controls and of removing them. This conference has provided me with the opportunity to put some of these forty-year-old thoughts on paper for the first time.

SOME WORLD WAR II BACKGROUND

It may seem that my ideas about the effects of imposing price controls and of removing them should have developed at the same time, since they are the reverse of one another, but as a matter of historical fact they did not. The thoughts about the imposition of price controls occurred to me when the Office of Price Administration was putting on some of those selective controls or altering selectively the price ceilings that resulted in the spring of 1942 from the initial freeze imposed (called the General Maximum Price Regulation). The question then was the effect on the output of an individual product of imposing a ceiling on its price. The thoughts about the removal of controls suggested themselves around 1945, when what was at issue was the effect of a wholesale removal of price controls on the general price level and whether the increase in the price level that it was widely assumed would ensue could be prevented if the decontrol were accompanied by a restrictive fiscal and monetary policy. Because the imposition or adjustment of ceilings was selective, that appeared as a problem in microeconomics, while the latter question of wholesale removal of ceilings was one of macroeconomics.

There was another difference, also, which affects the conclusions one draws about the effects on prices and output. When controls were imposed, there was substantial unemployment in the United States—later estimated to have been approximately 10 percent in 1941—while in 1945 the labor market was very tight, with the unemployment rate estimated at around 2 percent.

Finally, I should point out two aspects of views that were conventional in the 1940s, one of microeconomics and one of macroeconomics. The microeconomic point is that, although the works of Edward H. Chamberlin and Joan Robinson on monopolistic or imperfect competition had been published in 1933, the conventional expectation about the effect on a firm's output of imposing a ceiling on the price it could charge was based, however unknowingly, on the assumption of perfect competition. The macroeconomic point is that inflation was generally assumed to be not only initiated by excess demand but enabled to continue only if excess demand continued, so that it could be counted on to end if excess demand were eliminated. Cost-push and supply-shocks had little status, except as an accompaniment of excess demand.[1] Indeed, inflation came to be *defined* by some as excess demand, which led to the confusion that it was inflationary to hold prices down if the means of doing so increased excess demand or prevented its elimination or reduction. Questions, doubts, or denials of these views constitute the core of this paper and underlie the case for incomes policies.

PRICE AND OUTPUT EFFECTS OF IMPOSING PRICE CEILINGS ON SELECTED PRODUCTS WHEN COMPETITION IS IMPERFECT

When price controls were first contemplated, a common objection was that they would reduce output of the products whose prices were controlled. This objection is what accepted microeconomic theory tells us would happen under perfect competition. Theory tells us that under those conditions uncontrolled market prices would be equal to marginal costs, and the imposition of ceilings lower than those prices would force prices below marginal costs, causing firms to reduce their output.

Under monopoly and imperfect or monopolistic competition, however, the situation is different. The price-elasticity of demand for a firm's output is then finite and its marginal revenue is therefore less than the price. If, as conventional theory tells us, the rational firm chooses to produce the output at which marginal revenue is equal to marginal cost, price exceeds that marginal cost. Under those conditions the effect of imposing a price ceiling below the existing market price is to make the demand for the product infinitely elastic at all outputs that could have been sold before at high prices and thereby to raise the marginal revenue, which before control was below the ceiling price, to the level of the ceiling price. At these outputs the seller, when considering whether to expand his output, does not have to take into account that selling the additional output would require him to reduce the price of the output that he is already selling, as he would have to do if the price were uncontrolled, because with the price under control he cannot legally sell the existing (smaller) output at the higher demand-price. The price ceiling makes the demand curve infinitely elastic for all outputs that could have been sold before at higher prices, raising the marginal revenue associated with those outputs. Imposition of a price ceiling cuts monopolistic profits, but, so long as the ceiling is higher than the initial marginal revenue and marginal cost at the output prevailing with the uncontrolled price, the rise in marginal revenue induces an increase in output. The seller will have an incentive to reduce output only if the ceiling price is lower than the marginal revenue at the output that prevailed when the price was not controlled, which presumably is where the marginal revenue and the marginal cost were equal. With rising marginal costs output will be reduced only if the ceiling is set below the original marginal revenue.[2]

The conclusion that output would be increased if the price ceiling is set above marginal costs applies most clearly in the case of monopoly, as distinguished from monopolistic or imperfect competition, where both the interaction among the firms already producing similar products and the possible exit of such firms or entry of new ones must be taken into account. I shall proceed here with reasoning that excludes those two influences and that therefore can confidently be applied only to cases of monopoly. I suspect, however, that an analysis that included the effect of exit and entry would find that the net changes in output would be broadly similar, although of smaller magnitude.

The conclusion that imposition of a ceiling would increase output assumes that demand for the product is less than infinitely elastic at the uncontrolled price and that the price ceiling would be above the marginal revenue of the output associated with the uncontrolled price, so that the ceiling would raise the marginal revenue at that and smaller outputs. Of course, if the ceiling were less than the marginal revenue at the uncontrolled price, it would also be less than the marginal cost at the initial output, and its imposition would induce the firm to cut rather than expand its output if marginal cost is rising with output or falling more slowly than the uncontrolled marginal revenue.

The conclusion that imposition of ceilings will increase output does not really depend, as the above explanation may make it appear, on the assumption that firms actually set prices and output by estimating the elasticity of demand and the associated marginal revenue, as described in textbooks. The textbook description seems very abstract and unrealistic, requiring information that sellers do not have, but it may seem less unrealistic when expressed in less technical language.

Why does a firm not produce more than it does when the price is not controlled? Because, to sell the additional output, it would have to cut the price at which it sells the output it is already producing. This would make the addition to its sales receipts fall short of the receipts from sale of the additional output by the amount of reduction in the sales value of the existing output caused by the cut in prices at which it has been selling. But if a price ceiling is imposed at a level below the price the firm has been charging, it suffers that cut in sales even if it does not expand output. The enforced lowering of price creates excess demand for its product; the firm can sell more at the ceiling price than it was selling at the uncontrolled price, and the revenue from sale of the additional output will not be offset by any cut in the price of the initial output attributable to the expansion, since the excess demand makes such a cut unnecessary. The only offset to the increase in revenue from sale of the additional output will be the increase, if any, in total cost of production attributable to that additional output. It will be profitable, in other words, to expand output up to the point where marginal cost is equal to the ceiling price.

In short, all that the firm needs to know or estimate in deciding how to respond to the imposition of a price ceiling is how much more the market will take at the ceiling price than it is selling at the uncontrolled price and how much its total costs would be increased by producing and selling that additional output. These are two questions that a firm presumably tries to answer, if only approximately, when prices are not controlled.

The conclusion holds in any case where the ceiling price is lower than the uncontrolled price but higher than the marginal cost at the output associated with that uncontrolled price. The ceiling price can be in that range whenever the uncontrolled price is set by adding a fixed percentage to what firms believe to be the relevant costs, whether marginal, average prime, or average total costs.

Although imposition of a price ceiling in the range specified above provides an incentive for increasing the output of a product sold in imperfect competition, an increase in actual output can occur only if the additional labor and/or capital required is available in the firms affected or can be attracted from other firms or (in the case of labor) from the unemployed or those not in the labor force. To the extent that these necessary additional inputs are taken from other forms of production there would be offsetting decreases in other outputs. Under conditions of high employment, therefore, the conclusion based on partial analysis would have only limited macroeconomic applicability. But to the extent that a firm could increase output by using inputs that would otherwise have been unused, all or most of the increase in its output would be an addition to aggregate output. This would certainly have been the case in the United States during the very early 1940s.

There are also other reasons why the above conclusions about the effects of price controls on the output and prices of individual firms may not apply to the effects of universal or even very widespread price controls on aggregate output and on the general price level.

One of these other reasons is that the conclusions of partial equilibrium analysis about the effects of price changes on quantities demanded, quantities supplied, output, and other real variables refer to the effects of changes in *relative* prices, although that fact is rarely made explicit. If, in two situations, a difference in the money prices of one product or factor of production is accompanied by an equi-proportionate difference in all other money prices, including those of inputs, there is no reason to expect their outputs to be different in the two situations. The imposition of ceilings on a limited sector of the economy will affect the price of a controlled product relative to other prices by less than it affects its money price because ceilings are being imposed on some other prices, but it will have some effect on its relative price because some prices remain uncontrolled. This fact permits applying the microeconomic conclusion of partial equilibrium to aggregate output.

Another justification is that individual firms, when their products are subjected to price control, perceive these products to be among few that are being subjected to such control. As Lucas and Sargent pointed out in their effort to reconcile the equilibrium envisaged in rational-expectations theory with the existence of business cycles, this is true not only when this perception is correct but when the area of controls is larger than controlled firms perceive so that the constraint on their *relative* prices is less than they think.[3] So long as this perception is correct, the control does affect real variables. When it is incorrect, these writers hold that the misperception will be corrected and that the effect on real variables, therefore, will be transitory. But there will be an effect as long as that misperception persists.

I have already mentioned that the possibility of expanding total employment limits the possibility of expanding total output. Indirectly, the degree of unemployment also affects the extent to which the reduction of prices in one sector, even a large sector of the economy, also affects what happens to the aggregate price level. Any incentive for the controlled sector to expand its output under conditions of low unemployment will tend to push up wages and the prices of other inputs used by other sectors of the economy and thereby to push up prices charged in that sector. Certainly if the control is very widespread, firms are less likely to be able to expand output at costs as low as those on which they had planned because the effort to do so, if engaged in by many firms at the same time, would raise the relevant wages and perhaps prices of other inputs.

It may also be noted that insofar as the directly affected firms obtain additional labor and other inputs from other firms, the output of those other firms would be reduced, and if they were not subject to price control the imposition of such control on the first group of firms would not reduce the price level or restrain its increase because there would be a partially, wholly, or perhaps even more than wholly offsetting increase in the prices charged by the firms whose output would be reduced. Indeed, this offsetting increase would, or at least could, occur even if the firms subjected to control did not succeed in bidding labor away from other firms; their mere efforts to do so may force other firms to raise wages in order to retain their labor.

If the imposition of price ceilings induces an expansion of output by the controlled firms it will presumably raise their marginal costs and thereby reduce the margin between costs and prices by more than the actual or virtual price reduction. Such a rise of costs is not necessarily evidence that output has increased; costs could also rise for other reasons. For example, any widespread effort to expand output elsewhere in the economy would bid up the prices of inputs. In any event, the imposition of price ceilings implies that an inflationary environment exists, so that either excess demand or a wage/price spiral already exists independently of the imposition of controls. In these circumstances, margins are almost certain to be squeezed.

EFFECTS OF DECONTROL ON THE PRICE LEVEL

This abstract reasoning about the effect that imposing price controls has on margins and on the price level has obvious implications for the effects of removing those controls. As World War II ended, the administration and many people outside it feared that the removal of controls would give rise to a spiraling increase in the price level. But against this conclusion it was argued by some that demand restraints not only would permit price ceilings to be removed without much rise in the general price level—which, alone, I take to be undeniable—but could do so without causing a reduction of output and employment. It seemed clear to me then, and seems to flow from what I have argued so far, that restriction of aggregate demand great enough to prevent the price level from rising when controls were removed would force a cut in output and employment. If so, both would fall well before demand would be reduced enough to keep the general price level stable when controls were removed.

The reason is that after several years of excess demand effectively repressed by ceilings on prices, margins between prices and costs are compressed. It is safe to assume that the first effect of decontrol of prices will be an effort by sellers to restore the margins that had prevailed before control was imposed, unless the conditions that determined precontrol margins have changed. The consequence will be a rise of prices and a fall in output of firms in imperfect competition. This will be true whether the influence that changed margins during the control period was the effect of controls on elasticity of demand or some other influence.

Although a one-time rise in the level of prices, as well as margins, is to be expected when prices are decontrolled, this does not necessarily mean that the level of prices would be as high as it would have been if there had been no control, as is the presumption with margins. Why? Because if the nominal supply-price of labor is influenced by the level of consumer prices or of profits, control of a substantial proportion of prices would have limited the rise in money wages.[4] Over any prolonged period of inflationary pressure and control, this dampening effect on money wage rates would outweigh any stimulating one-time effect on output and on the demand for labor caused by the effect of controls in increasing the elasticity of demand for the controlled products.

I conclude that whenever margins between prices and costs have been compressed by comprehensive controls their removal will be accompanied by a one-time (although perhaps drawn out) rise in the price level at unchanged aggregate output unless monetary or fiscal policy suppresses the rise in the price level, and that before restriction of demand became great enough to suppress the rise in the price level, output and employment would fall. Thus, when decontrol occurred, there would be a zone of demand restriction in which the price level would rise and output would fall at the same time.

This view differs, or at least supplements, the view that a postcontrol rise in the price level is attributable to the spending of liquid assets that consumers and business firms have accumulated during the period of controls. That was Galbraith's (1952: 52) explanation of the rise of prices after the removal of World War II controls: "With the release from controls, the expenditure of these [accumulated liquid] savings is obviously capable of bringing on the inflationary upsurge in prices that the controls had previously restrained. . . . such a price increase occurred after the controls were lifted in 1946."

Attribution of the rise only to the accumulation of liquid assets, even if that is supplemented by attributing it also to the accumulation of unsatisfied wants, is not the whole explanation. Some rise will always occur when a control that has squeezed margins is abolished, even without excess demand. A purely excess-demand explanation misses what has in more recent years given rise to stagflation—the occurrence of cost-push at the same time as deficient demand—and could cause a price rise from the restoration of normal margins. Avoiding excess demand or even having excess supply is not enough to prevent a one-time rise of prices, even though it may be enough to prevent continuing inflation. It may not even do that, however. It is true that the restoration of squeezed margins is a one-time phenomenon, but it appears that a one-time push can cause a prolonged, even if not an indefinitely continuing, rise in the price level. Whether it will do so depends on what causes the initial rise in the price level and on the economy's response to that initial stimulus. For example, if an increase in the demand for shares in aggregate real income causes their sum to rise above the sum of national income and the current-account deficit and if the excess is not squeezed out by the consequent rise in prices, the rise can go on indefinitely. It is the possibility that one-time causes can have continuing effects that makes the one-time direct effects of control and decontrol more important than their relatively small magnitude would suggest. But whatever the size of the total effects of decontrol in any specific situation, my main point is that if market imperfections are restored when the economy is decontrolled, it is impossible to "liquidate the disequilibrium at stable prices" (Galbraith 1952: 55ff).

ECONOMETRIC TESTS OF EFFECT
OF CONTROL AND DECONTROL

At least a dozen writers have made estimates of the effects of price controls, mainly those of the Nixon administration. Some of them have attempted also to estimate the effects of controls imposed during other periods—the Korean War controls imposed at the beginning of 1951, the World War II controls, the minimum prices and wages imposed under the National Industrial Recovery Act during the first Roosevelt administration, and the controls exercised during World War I. To test the ideas I have advanced in the preceding section of this chapter, it is necèssary to estimate the effects of controls on the margins between prices and costs. Most of the existing estimates, however, are concerned with effects on the price level; only a few estimate effects on margins between prices and costs. Rather than present and discuss those estimates in detail I shall here merely summarize them and give examples of some of the difficulties in empirical testing of the effects of controls.

The standard finding about effects on prices is that the imposition of ceilings lowers prices or the rate of their increase and that their removal is accompanied by a more rapid rise of prices than was occurring before the controls were imposed or than it is thought would have occurred had they not been imposed. It is not always clear which, but the essential idea is that the rise makes up for time "lost" during the control period, and that it continues long enough to bring the price level approximately to where the estimates indicate it would have been had controls not been imposed. All the writers seem to take for granted that both of these effects would occur, and the questions they try to answer are how much the controls restrained the increases that would otherwise have occurred and how near the price level reached after controls have been removed for some time (usually for less than a year) is to the price level that they estimate would have prevailed had there been no controls.

Nearly all the empirical findings support the expectation that the World War II controls and the Nixon administration controls held the price indices down and that these indices rebounded when the controls were removed. The estimates of the rebound range between half the distance to the levels that would have been reached in the absence of controls to the entire distance, in the latter case leaving unsettled the question whether the controls had any long-run effect on the price level.

These findings, both of the repressive effects of controls on prices and the rebounding effect of their removal, are consistent with the point I have advanced that the effects on the price level of imposing controls and of removing them works partly through their effect on the elasticity of demand for monopolized or imperfectly competitive products, but I note that none of the explanations invokes that point.

The empirical tests of the effects of controls, like empirical tests of the effects of anything, consist of a comparison of what actually happened with what one would expect to have happened in the absence of the controls or other conditions whose effects are being appraised. These expectations of what would otherwise have happened are necessarily based on some theory. The obstacles to measuring the effects in the specific case of controls are examined in a thorough paper by Walter Oi (1976) and also in one by Michael Darby (1976a). There are obstacles connected with choice of theoretical expectations about what would "otherwise" have happened.

One difficulty is that the estimate of what would have happened if controls had not been imposed or had not been removed must be based on what happened during a sample period when the event or condition whose effects are being evaluated did not occur or exist and applying this to another period. Robert Gordon (1982a) warned his readers of this difficulty when he found that the removal of the Nixon controls was accompanied by a rise in the price level greater than the downward displacement accompanying their imposition. But, he pointed out, the method of estimating that gave this result is unable to incorporate information on the variables that were unimportant during the sample period but were important afterwards, notably the foreign exchange rate.

Another example is to be found in Hagens and Russell (1985), which presents an exception to the conventional conclusion that the effect of controls on prices ends with the controls themselves. They find that Nixon controls had large initial effects and that a catch-up of the price and wage levels occurred, but not after the controls were formally lifted in 1975, as was concluded by Alan Blinder and William Newton (1981). On the contrary, they find that it occurred when controls were relaxed, which was before their formal termination. They think that the 1974 price increases, which the Blinder-Newton paper attributes to a postcontrol catch-up, may have been the lagged effect of the explosion of energy prices in 1973–74. The Hagens-Russell paper also finds that the multiple increase of energy prices in 1979–80, when the Carter administration's Price and Pay Standards Program was in effect, was not passed through to the general price and wage level in "the usual manner" (p. 205) and that price and wage inflation were both lower for several years after the termination of controls than their model of the price/wage structure would have led them to expect. They recognize, however, that causes other than the control program may account for these differences; they note that a similar moderation of wage demands occurred in countries that did not introduce incomes policies during this period, although that counter-consideration could itself reflect the transmission to those countries of other effects of the U.S. program.

Finally, I want to give an example from the field of incomes policy of an empirical result that may be consistent with several theories that not only differ but conflict. Consider a finding that the relation between the price level and the money supply on some definition is the same when an incomes policy was in effect and after it ceased to be in effect as it was before. Such a result would be consistent with the theory that controls that leave a substantial proportion of the price level uncontrolled might not affect the general price level at all, even while they are in effect. That conclusion seems to follow from monetarist reasoning if the controls do not affect either the supply of money or real output. They may affect the allocation of spending between the controlled and uncontrolled sectors, but they will not affect its aggregate amount, and, in the absence of an effect on output, they will not affect the general price level.

Similarly, even if the policy applies to all prices and if it is conceded that the controls have kept down the price level while they are in effect, theoretical arguments can be given as to why, after the controls have been in effect for some time, their removal will cause the price level to rise to approximately where it would have been had there been no controls. A necessary assumption is that, as in the preceding case, the supply of money is determined exogenously and determines aggregate demand, so that the suppression of the free-market price gives rise to excess demand, which, when free to act on prices, drives them up to where they would otherwise have been.

The same empirical result could be consistent with the unconventional hypothesis, advanced by Thomas Mayer (1984), that an incomes policy, even though intended to restrain increases in the price level, might (Mayer does not say would) actually promote such increases. Mayer argues that because controls may be expected to, or may actually, restrain a rise in the price level, there is "a good chance that the imposition of wage and price controls will lead to a more expansionary monetary policy." Therefore, if their removal is accompanied by a rise in the price index more or less to the level indicated by the rate of growth in the money supply, as is said to have happened under the Nixon controls, one may conclude that the controls raised the growth rate of money, and that the "Nixon price controls led to a higher, rather than a lower, price level" (Mayer 1984: 50). This hypothesis assumes that the incomes policy is temporary. It also assumes, in contrast to the preceding case, that the incomes policy does affect the supply of money but does so by influencing the monetary authority to be more expansionary than it would have been in the absence of the incomes policy; the money supply is what might be called policy-endogenous.[5]

Finally, one can argue that the finding of a constant relation between the money supply and the price level is consistent with precisely the opposite hypothesis: that even limited controls may keep the postcontrol price level below what it would otherwise have been. If the controls are in effect for a substantial period of time, they may not only keep down the controlled prices, which keeps down the costs of producing other products for which the controlled products are direct or indirect inputs, but also limit the rise of wages by repressing the rise in the cost of living or in profits or both. These uncontrolled products thus have lower money costs and therefore lower prices when controls are removed than they would have had if there had been no controls, leaving the price level lower than it would otherwise have been.

It is clear that the issue here is closely related to the question of causality in close correlations between the supply of money and nominal GNP. If the money supply adjusts to the price level without sacrifice of real output, the last-mentioned argument implies that controls make it lower than it would be without controls. Mayer, in contrast, argues that it would be higher. Thus, both tend to undermine the monetary test of the effectiveness of controls, which assumes, among other things, that the money supply would have been what is implied by a model estimated from data for a period with no controls.

The implication of these points is that we have no reliable empirical test of either the magnitude or the duration of the effect of controls, except, I should add, in the case of a small and open economy whose price level is dominated by external influences.

SOME GENERAL OBSERVATIONS

I have said little about the micro theory of tax-based incomes policy, as distinguished from other policies to limit or influence price and wage increases, and I shall not take a position on the broad issue of making incomes policy a part of permanent macro policy. But I cannot refrain from making a few general observations about some of the arguments for and against such a policy.

First, let me say that an incidental benefit of any effective supplement to anti-inflationary demand measures is that it might spare us discussions of whether unemployment or inflation is the "worse" evil. This question, when posed in that way, has always struck me as nonsensical. For one thing, when so posed it does not specify how much unemployment is being compared with what rate of inflation. Obviously, it makes a difference whether one is comparing an unemployment rate of 4 percent with an annual inflation rate of 20 percent or more or is comparing an unemployment rate of 20 percent with an inflation rate of 2 percent, unless you rate the evil of one of these alternatives at zero. And it is not enough to specify those quantities. One must also specify how long the alternative unemployment and inflation rates are expected to last. A rate of unemployment lasting six months that prevents an inflation that would continue for, say, four years is obviously different from an alternative of the same unemployment rate lasting four years that saves the economy the same rate of inflation but one lasting only six months.

My second observation concerns a conflict between two views often held by the same person. On the one hand, it is said that stagflation of the degree that we have had in the past two decades is extremely harmful economically, socially, and politically, almost to the point of catastrophe. On the other hand, the difficulties of administering a tax-based incomes policies, fully described by Dildine and Sunley (1978), are so great that some people think such policies should not be tried. And some hold both views at once. Those who do so rarely either offer promising ways of avoiding the choice between stagflation and administrative difficulties or resolve the dilemma by making the choice. When a country, on being attacked by another country, declares war against its attacker, it knows that it is undertaking vast administrative problems. But nobody argues that countries should forbear from defending themselves because of those administrative difficulties. Similarly, if the difficulties of incomes policies are so great as to preclude adopting them, must the evils of stagflation not have been exaggerated? But if those evils have not been exaggerated, is the burden of administering incomes policies not worth assuming? It seems that at least one of the two evils is often exaggerated.

Another argument made against incomes policy is that "it politicizes the income distribution" (Mayer 1984: 51). One may concede that it does so and still not agree that this argues against trying it. Nothing politicizes the income distribution more than taxation, so the same logic should argue against taxing.

My last observation about the logic of the discussion has to do with the widely held conclusion that the effects of price and wage controls are temporary. This conclusion should be recognized as having two elements, one relating to the life expectancy of the controls themselves and the other to that of their effects on the levels of prices and money wages. This distinction is made necessary by the fact that the economic effects of controls may outlast their operating effectiveness. Of course, this conclusion is of no particular interest if the controls themselves were intended to be temporary; it is of interest only if it asserts that they break down or that they do not have their intended economic effects or that these effects are shorter lived than was intended.

The validity of the conclusion that the effects of controls are temporary depends largely on a correct measurement of those effects. Such measurement is difficult, perhaps impossible, for reasons discussed in the preceding section of this paper. These difficulties are so great that I have no empirically supportable judgment about either the magnitude or the duration of economic effects.

As to the conclusion that controls themselves are temporary because they are bound to break down, there is no question that they often do so, and perhaps do so in the majority of cases, so there is something in the argument. But I suspect that it is exaggerated. Some forms of incomes policies have lasted for a long time in some countries. To conclude that controls intended to be permanent would, in fact, be temporary, one would have to show that it is inherent in them or their consequences that their effects, or the perception of their effects, are so bad that they are terminated sooner than was intended.

I close with one further observation. The late Willy Fellner (1981: 578) said that "from the post-Korean period until the mid-1960s . . . the markets must have realized that the monetary authorities became increasingly willing to accommodate steepening rates of inflation that were considered necessary to achieve short-term employment policy goals." If vulnerability to inflation is largely the result of a combination of confidence that demand will be kept strong to meet employment goals and past experience of inflation, one must conclude that the problem with "fine tuning" is—to put it sharply although imprecisely—not that it won't work but that it will, for its initial success breeds confidence in the future maintenance of high employment that removes inhibitions against excessive pay demands. Or, to be more precise, the danger is that initial successes of fine tuning will lead, via inflation, to its subsequent abandonment. I see no escape from the proposition that without some form of incomes policy we have to choose between much less fine tuning, which is to say greater slack than we once hoped for, or a repetition of recent inflationary experience. But that, unfortunately, is not itself a reason to believe there would be no problems with incomes policy.

NOTES TO CHAPTER 4

1. This fact is what gave a pioneering character to the working out of mark-up models by Polak (1945) and Leontief (1946).
2. This idea proved to be an example of unnecessary originality for, soon after thinking of it during World War II, I found that it had been stated by Robinson (1933: 159–63). Only while writing this paper did I find that it is also in Hansen (1951: 104–14) and Darby (1976a: 237ff). Also, several months after revising this paper and submitting it for publication, I found, to my embarrassment, that Martin Bronfenbrenner had already stated the proposition that under imperfect competition, price control can increase output while lowering price (1947). Moreover, he pointed out that besides having been stated by Robinson in 1933, as I have noted, this proposition had been advanced at least as early as the first edition of Pigou's *Economics of Welfare* (1920: Chapter 21, Section 11 and Appendix 3, Section 23).
3. I am indebted to my colleague Martin N. Baily for reminding me of this aspect of the Lucas-Sargent article (1978: 60). Regarding the question discussed in the preceding paragraph, it may be of some interest that R.F. Kahn, referring in 1974 to his famous article, "The Relation of Home Investment to Unemployment" (1931), said, "What I explained in my article is that the price level is determined by the conditions of demand and supply in much the same way as the price of an individual commodity." See his letter to Don Patinkin (Patinkin and Leith 1977: 147). I do not know if Kahn ever gave a justification for applying the micro conclusion to aggregate demand and supply. Keynes appears on the point of dealing with this problem when he says, in *The General Theory* (1936: 294), "In a single industry its particular price-level depends partly on the role of remuneration of the factors of production which enter into its marginal cost, and partly on the scale of output. There is no reason to modify this conclusion when we pass to industry as a whole." But what follows does not come to grips

with the problem of whether conclusions about the effect of changes in relative prices on a firm's or industry's output may legitimately be applied to the effect of changes in money prices on aggregate output.

4. This argument is advanced forcefully by Galbraith (pp. 63–65) in his 1952 book where he explains why he thinks "open and suppressed inflation do not represent the same magnitude of danger." He says:

> In modern labor and product markets, . . . a price increase [resulting from general excess demand] leads inevitably to wage demands. These, if granted, lead, on the one hand to expanded wage income and to still further pressure on given supplies in the product markets and, on the other hand, via cost increases to still further price increases. . . . If prices and wages are controlled effectively, then the interaction of wages and prices cannot so act as an accelerant of the inflationary movement. . . . Herein lies the difference between open and suppressed inflation. The first has a powerful dynamic of its own; the rate and extent of the movement need bear no relation to the initiating excess of demand. The effects of suppressed inflation are limited to the initiating excess of demand. In lay terms open inflation can run away; suppressed inflation cannot."

5. Regarding the substance of Mayer's point, I think that the outcome he hypothesizes is a possible one but that there is some confusion in the argument, and the confusion may add to the plausibility of the conclusion. If controls hold the price level down they may permit monetary policy to be what Mayer calls "more expansionary," in the sense that the *real* money supply would be allowed to be larger than would have been permitted had the price level been allowed to rise or rise more rapidly. But that does not necessarily mean that the nominal money supply would be any larger. The argument assumes that without the controls the price level would have been higher. This argument seems to ignore its own initial assumption that controls do have some effect on holding down the price level, and therefore, as economists concerned with World War II price controls then argued, they help to hold down money incomes and aggregate demand. If so and if the level of nominal income influences the money supply in the same direction, controls presumably keep down the money supply. Thus, one is led to conclude that the nominal money supply and the price level, even after controls are removed, would be lower than if there had been no controls; a conclusion precisely the opposite of Mayer's.

5 INCENTIVE ANTI-INFLATION POLICIES IN A MODEL OF MARKET DISEQUILIBRIUM

Kenneth J. Koford
Jeffrey B. Miller*

The enormous costs of reducing inflation by monetary contraction and recession have triggered a search for better ways to reduce inflation. Wage and price controls clearly can reduce inflation in the short run but generally lead to shortages, inefficiency, and a breakdown of the control system in the long run. Thus, there has been a search for "incentive" anti-inflation policies that can reduce inflation without the associated shortages and inefficiency of traditional wage/price controls. The most successful proposals appear to increase the long-term level of output (or reduce the natural rate of unemployment) while maintaining price stability. For example, Meade (1982), Layard (1982a), Pissarides (1985a, b), and particularly Jackman, Layard, and Pissarides (1985) examine wage incentive plans under various assumptions as to how the labor market works: quit and search equilibria, labor union monopoly, and competitive sector/monopoly sector models. They find that in general a wage tax that reduces workers' equilibrium wages also reduces unemployment. (We shall return to this analysis in our conclusion.)

Whether a price or value-added incentive scheme would increase output and reduce unemployment is not yet clear. For a perfectly competitive industry, Baumol (1979) and Okun (1981) found that a price TIP would reduce output. We examine the effects of a value-added incentive, Abba Lerner's and David Colander's (1980) market anti-inflation plan (MAP), for a multisector economy in which firms face downward-sloping demands and industries are in short-run disequilibrium. Koford (1983) examined MAP in a multisector economy with

*We would like to thank Rudiger Dornbusch, Laurence Seidman, and other participants at the conference for helpful comments.

firms in short-run equilibrium, and Koford (1984b) examined MAP in a single-industry economy with labor-market search and monopolistically competitive firms.

The disequilibrium model we use was developed in Benassy (1982). It extends work pioneered by Clower (1965, 1967) and Barro and Grossman (1976). However, Benassy has a more fully developed microeconomic foundation for his disequilibrium results.

Why use Benassy's "disequilibrium" framework? (Why not a "new classical" equilibrium model, or a stochastic-search equilibrium model?) An economy might fail to adjust quickly—or optimally—to shocks for many reasons. Research may ultimately identify fundamental "contracting costs" that prevent the complete set of Arrow-Debreu markets from existing. For now, we think it reasonable to model the adjustment problems specific to the most important sectors, consistent with the adjustment problems found in current microeconomic work. They involve failure of prices to adjust immediately to clear markets. The price of capital may fail to equilibrate, the wage rate or goods price may fail to equilibrate, and disequilibrium in one market may create disequilibrium in other markets. Benassy's model captures the second and third problems and so provides a good description of disequilibrium in markets for current output. (To our knowledge, no model captures all three disequilibria, although Grandmont (1983) and Malinvaud (1977) provide good models of financial and investment disequilibria.) We now describe the three disequilibria in more detail.

1. Financial sector adjustment failures find "sticky" interest rates or a failure to equilibrate the supply and demand for loans. In Stiglitz (1985), price determines quality and so cannot be easily adjusted. Rationing on credit markets creates, in the extreme, a Clowerian world in which agents require money to obtain goods and goods to obtain money. Such models have been dominant in the analysis of adjustment failure (for example, Diamond 1984; Smith 1983; and Benassy 1982). (With perfect credit markets, failure of the labor market to clear merely causes workers to adjust their optimal intertemporal consumption path (Barro 1984).)

2. Labor and goods market disequilibria may occur when auction markets are absent. An agent on one side of the market sets the price and often enjoys temporary or permanent monopoly power. The price set typically does not equate supply and demand. Often the participants on the price-taking side of the market search for a good opportunity, so that markets never fully clear (Pratt, Wise, and Zeckhauser 1979; Salop 1979). When the market fails to clear, the price-setter usually has little information as to the magnitude of the shortage or surplus and cannot quickly adjust to the market-clearing price. Benassy (1982: chs. 3 and 4) develops this model in some detail.

3. Intermarket disequilibrium occurs when disequilibrium in one market spills over into another market, affecting its equilibrium and potentially creating disequilibrium there as well. Such spillovers can easily occur, since complete

contingent prices in markets do not exist and price-setting agents are not aware of changes in all related markets. Benassy (1982: ch. 4) models this intermarket disequilibrium, developing an important part of Clower's original (1967) insight.

Given the variety of disequilibrium models, it is reasonable to determine the effects of a value-added MAP (or TIP) in several of them, since none yet captures all crucial facets of the macroeconomy. This paper continues that effort by examining how MAP would operate in a Benassy-type economy.

Lerner's and Colander's MAP gives firms the right to a certain level of net sales (gross sales minus the cost of purchased inputs): the net sales of the firm prior to the adoption of MAP. Firms may obtain the right to additional net sales in two ways. First, firms are free to buy or sell these rights at whatever price they choose. This implies an economywide competitive market in these rights, "MAP credits," at a competitive price. Second, firms gain additional credits when they employ additional inputs—capital, labor, land, R&D. They lose credits when they employ less of these credits. MAP allocates credits for these inputs at their competitive price. In addition MAP should allocate credits for intangible inputs—goodwill, or entrepreneurship, although that is quite difficult to measure in practice.

We first develop a model of an economy with many industries, firms with some control over price, and sticky wages. In this model we show the effect of the incentive anti-inflation plans, MAP and an equivalent TIP,[1] for an economy with labor-market disequilibrium, a goods-market disequilibrium that is due to firms' price-setting behavior, and some intermarket disequilibrium. Then we consider some dynamics and the impact on the natural rate of unemployment. In the conclusion we review other current work on incentive anti-inflation plans.

THE BENASSY MODEL

Benassy (1982) concentrates on the general equilibrium consequences of quantity supplied not equaling quantity demanded. Each market has a price-setter who knows that the price chosen may or may not clear the market that period. If the market fails to clear, the short side of the market prevails and some of those on the long side of the market go without a transaction.

Price-setters recognize this possibility and adjust their profit-maximizing decisions, as do price-takers. In that sense, the model incorporates rational expectations. The possibility that a firm cannot buy or sell all it plans to reduces the firm's "effective demand" (Clower 1965, 1967) below what its "notional demand" at market-clearing prices would be.

Each price-setting firm has a degree of monopoly power: It faces a downward-sloping demand curve. A well-designed MAP or TIP incentive rewards firms for lower prices and penalizes them for higher prices, thus reducing firms' effective monopoly power. Figure 5–1 shows a firm facing a conventional downward-

Figure 5-1. Effect of MAP or TIP on Monopolistic Equilibrium.

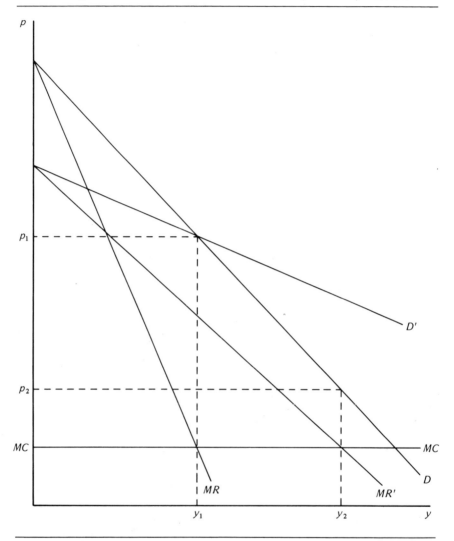

sloping demand curve, D. The incentive rotates the average revenue the firm received from D to D', causing the firm to increase output and reduce price, for any given demand conditions. (In terms of our later analysis, this is credit rule C.)

The Benassy model is not a complete model of a price-setter's economy. In particular, it assumes for most results that wages are sticky, without providing a choice-theoretic explanation for that stickiness.[2] The model nevertheless shows that disequilibrium could be very common, since Benassy's assumptions seem reasonable for most major industries. We now examine the effect of the MAP incentive when wages are fixed and the firm is a price-setter in the output market (Benassy 1982: 150-52).

In this case each firm faces a perceived demand curve, where expected demand at price p is $\theta g(p)$. θ is a multiplicative parameter that varies across firms and $g'(p) < 0$. The elasticity of the perceived demand curves is $\epsilon(p) > 1$, so that the firm's profit-maximizing price is always finite. Demand is then (Benassy 1982: 158)

$$\theta g(p) \;=\; \theta p^{-\epsilon}$$

Absent MAP the firm's profit-maximization problem is

$$\text{maximize} \qquad py \,-\, wL \qquad \text{s.t.}$$
$$y \leq q \;=\; F(L) \tag{5.1}$$
$$y \leq \theta g(p)$$
$$L \leq L_o$$

That is, the firm maximizes price times output (py) minus labor costs. The firm faces three constraints. The first constrains output sold, y, to be less than or equal to output produced, q. (Traditional models assume equality here.) Produced output is a positive function of labor input, $q = F(L), F'(L) > 0$. Effective demand, or output sold, is less-than or equal to notional demand $\theta g(p)$. Finally, there is a labor input constraint: L cannot exceed L_o. A solution may be found for two cases: (1) when the constraint $L < L_o$ is not binding and (2) when the constraint $L = L_o$ is binding. When the capacity constraint does bind, we have $y = F(L_o) = y_o$. On the other hand, when the constraint does *not* bind, we substitute the problem

$$\max \quad pF(L) \,-\, wL \tag{5.2}$$

The first-order condition is

$$\frac{dp}{dL} F(L) + pF'(L) \;=\; w \tag{5.3}$$

Now, $\epsilon(p) = \dfrac{-p}{g(p)} \dfrac{dg(p)}{dp}$. But since $F(L) = \theta g(p)$, this elasticity can also be expressed as

$$\epsilon(p) \;=\; -p \, \frac{F'(L)}{F(L)} \frac{1}{\dfrac{dp}{dL}}$$

so from equation (5.3)

$$p\left(1 + \frac{dp}{dL}\frac{1}{p}\left[\frac{F(L)}{F'(L)}\right]\right) = \frac{w}{F'(L)} \qquad (5.4)$$

or by substitution

$$p\left(1 - \frac{1}{\epsilon(p)}\right) = \frac{w}{F'(L)} = \frac{w}{F'(F^{-1}(y))} \qquad (5.5)$$

since $L = F^{-1}(y)$. Next, we solve equation (5.5) for y, yielding

$$y = F\left[F'^{-1}\left(\frac{\epsilon(p)}{\epsilon(p) - 1}\frac{w}{p}\right)\right]. \qquad (5.6)$$

Substituting in the constant-elasticity demand formula, equation (5.6) becomes

$$y = F\left[F'^{-1}\left(\frac{\epsilon}{\epsilon - 1}\frac{w}{p}\right)\right]. \qquad (5.6')$$

Equation (5.6') must be interpreted carefully since the firm is a price-setter, and the price is not exogenous. What (5.6') describes is the relationship between y and p given that the firm faces a particular w, ϵ and θ. If θ rises, the demand curve shifts upward and both p and y will increase. If w increases, marginal costs rise, p goes up and y falls. If ϵ were greater, the output-price combination would be one where output was higher and price lower.

Equation (5.6) allows us to find the microeconomic effects of different incentive anti-inflation policies. Thus, the goal of the Layard wage-tax approach is to reduce w/p in equation (5.6) and so increase the firm's output for any given level of demand. The goal of MAP and the equivalent TIP, as we see it, is to increase firms' effective price elasticity of demand, increasing output and lowering price.

When the economy is at full employment, the effects of MAP differ greatly from its effects with slack employment. (For example, increased nominal demand then cannot cause increased output and is not allowed to increase the price level.) Full employment occurs when all firms reach $L = L_o$; we must investigate both the disequilibrium-unemployment and the full-employment behavior of the system. Each firm has a "supply function"

$$S(p) = y = \min\left[\left(F'^{-1}\left(\frac{\epsilon}{\epsilon - 1}\frac{w}{p}\right)\right), F(L_o)\right] \qquad (5.7)$$

that restricts supply to the minimum of its profit-maximizing output when labor is in surplus (from equation (5.6')) and its maximum output when $L = L_o$.

THE MAP INCENTIVE IN A
MULTIPLE-MARKET MODEL

MAP creates an economywide market in rights to increase prices, and so its effects can be seen only in an aggregate model. Our model consists of two sectors, each containing n_i firms. Within each sector the firms face identical constant elasticity of demand functions, $\theta_i p_i^{-\epsilon_i}$. If these demands are satisfied, then total output in each sector is

$$
\begin{aligned}
y_1 &= n_1 \, \theta_1 \, p_1^{-\epsilon_1} \\
y_2 &= n_2 \, \theta_2 \, p_2^{-\epsilon_2}
\end{aligned}
\tag{5.8}
$$

Aggregate supply is then

$$N = p_1 y_1 + p_2 y_2 \tag{5.9}$$

Aggregate demand in nominal terms is found by summing consumption demand and government demand

$$N = C + g \quad . \tag{5.10}$$

Following Benassy (1982: 160-61) we specify consumption demand as

$$C = \alpha(1 - \tau)N + \beta \overline{m}$$

where α is the marginal propensity to consume out of nominal income, τ is the government's tax rate, β is the marginal propensity to consume out of nominal balances, and $\overline{m}$ is the money supply. If government demand is a fixed proportion, γ, of national income, then equation (5.9) can be reduced to

$$N = \frac{\beta \overline{m}}{1 - \alpha(1 - \tau) - \gamma} \quad . \tag{5.11}$$

The crucial point of equation (5.11) is that the government determines nominal demand, N, by choice of money supply, $\overline{m}$. (We do not investigate fiscal policies, although (5.11) allows one to investigate combinations of fiscal and monetary policies and MAP.)

Aggregate demand is divided between the two industries according to a constant-proportion sharing rule determined by the original levels of nominal demand:

$$\frac{p_1 y_1}{p_2 y_2} = k = \frac{\overline{p}_1 \overline{y}_1}{\overline{p}_2 \overline{y}_2} \quad . \tag{5.12}$$

By equations (5.11) and (5.12), nominal demand in each sector is fixed (that is, $\epsilon = 1$). It should be noted that firms perceive their individual demand to be more elastic, since ϵ_1 and $\epsilon_2 > 1$, due to the higher cross-elasticities within each sector.

The profit function for each firm j in sector i under MAP is

$$\pi_{ij} = p_{ij}y_{ij} - wL_{ij} - \phi CR_{ij} \quad \text{s.t.}$$

$$y_{ij} \leq q_{ij} = F_{ij}(L_{ij})$$

$$y_{ij} \leq \theta_{ij}p_{ij}^{-\epsilon_{ij}} \qquad\qquad (5.13)$$

$$L_{ij} \leq L_{o_{ij}} \ .$$

(Since all firms in sector i are identical, we drop the j subscript when it is redundant.) The major difference from equation (5.1) is the cost of purchasing MAP credits, ϕCR_{ij}. ϕ is the market price of MAP credits, which the firm considers to be exogenous. CR_{ij} is the number of MAP credits the ijth firm must purchase. CR_{ij} may be negative, in which case the firm would receive income from sales of MAP credits.

We shall examine three specific MAP credit rules, and then at the end of the section we compare our results to what might occur under a wage/price controls regime. (We omit the ij subscripts in describing these rules.).

Credit rule A,

$$CR(A) = py - \bar{p}\bar{y}$$

gives the firm the right to its original sales revenue, $\bar{p}\bar{y}$, regardless of changes in price and output. If, however, sales exceed previous levels, the firm will be required to purchase additional credits. It is not a desirable rule and has not been proposed by anyone, but it is a very simple rule that gives some insight into the nature of a MAP credit rule.

Credit rule B,

$$CR(B) = py - \bar{w}L - (\bar{p}\bar{y} - \bar{w}\bar{L})$$

grants the firm a right to additional revenues without buying additional credits equal to the firm's increase in labor inputs valued at the original wage $\bar{w}$. $CR(B)$ is close to Lerner and Colander's definition of MAP, as it allows for an increase in the only explicit input, labor, at the original wage. However no credit is given for capital or entrepreneurial inputs, as Lerner and Colander do, as these other inputs are only implicit in the function, $F(L)$.

Credit rule C,

$$CR(C) = py - \bar{p}y$$

gives the firm the right to increased or reduced revenue as it increases or decreases output, at the level of the original price $\bar{p}$.

$CR(C)$ is closest to the original intentions of Lerner and Colander (1980), although it is stated as an output price rule, not an input price rule. Lerner and Colander argue that there is a margin between the firm's price and its labor cost per unit of output that is due to entrepreneurship. So the firm should be credited with a return for this entrepreneurial capital.

A rule very similar to $CR(C)$ gives firms MAP credits for increases in these intangible inputs as well as increases in tangible inputs. Define $\bar{a} = \bar{\pi}/\bar{L}$ as the original profit per unit of labor input. Then provide credit to the firm for $\bar{a}$ in proportion to changes in the measured input L:

$$CR(C') = py - \bar{p}\bar{y} - (L - \bar{L})(\bar{a} + \bar{w}) .$$

With constant returns to scale and fixed input coefficients, $CR(C')$ reduces to $CR(C)$. For $\bar{a} + \bar{w} = \bar{p}\bar{y}/\bar{L}$ = original profits plus original costs per unit of labor. The constant returns to scale/fixed input coefficients assumption implies that $y/L = \bar{y}/\bar{L}$. Then

$$CR(C') = py - \bar{p}\bar{y} + \bar{L}(\bar{p}\bar{y}/\bar{L}) - L(\bar{p}\bar{y}/\bar{L})$$

$$= py - \bar{p}\bar{y} + \bar{p}\bar{y} - \bar{p}L(\bar{y}/\bar{L}) .$$

Substituting y/L for $y/\bar{L}$,

$$CR(C') = py - \bar{p}y .$$

While our model does not utilize a fixed input coefficient technology, this suggests that $CR(C)$ is an approximation of $CR(C')$.

The model is closed by noting that the market for MAP credits must clear, however they are defined:

$$\sum_{j=1}^{n_1} CR_{1j} + \sum_{j=1}^{n_2} CR_{2j} = 0 . \tag{5.14}$$

The model thus consists of an aggregate nominal demand-supply equation (5.9), a government determination of aggregate demand (5.11), individual demands (5.8), which are controlled by a demand-sharing relationship (5.12), and individual supplies in the two markets (solutions to (5.13)).

Now we consider the effect on aggregate supply of the three MAP credit rules when the labor constraint is not binding.

In credit rule A, each firm's supply function is[3]

$$S_i(p_i, w, \phi) = F_i\left[F_i'^{-1}\left(\frac{w}{p_i} \frac{\epsilon_i}{\epsilon_i - 1} \cdot \frac{1}{1 - \phi}\right)\right] \tag{5.15A}$$

$$S_p > 0, \ S_w < 0, \ S_\phi < 0, \ \text{for } 0 < \phi < 1 .$$

So an increase in the price of MAP credits reduces individual firm's supply. From equation (5.14)

$$\sum_{j=1}^{n_1} (p_1 y_{1j} - \bar{p}_1 \bar{y}_{1j}) + \sum_{j=1}^{n_2} (p_2 y_{2j} - \bar{p}_2 \bar{y}_{2j}) = 0$$

so

$$p_1 y_1 + p_2 y_2 = \bar{p}_1 \bar{y}_1 + \bar{p}_2 \bar{y}_2$$

As y_1 and y_2 are reduced by an increase in ϕ, p_1 and p_2 must rise. So credit rule A would reduce output and increase prices. It does not keep the price-level constant.

Credit rule A also creates a knife-edge equilibrium: nominal demand, $N = p_1 y_1 + p_2 y_2$, must equal aggregate allowed credits, $\bar{p}_1 \bar{y}_1 + \bar{p}_2 \bar{y}_2$, for the economy to be consistent. If demand exceeds allowed credits, the MAP price presumably rises to 1 and shortages result. If demand is less than allowed credits, either MAP has no effect—if firms can sell less than their allowed credits—or the MAP price falls to -1—if firms are required to hold the credit rule with equality.

In credit rule B, each firm's supply function is

$$S_i(p_i, w, \phi) = F_i \left[F_i'^{-1} \left(\frac{w - \phi \bar{w}}{p_i} \frac{\epsilon_i}{\epsilon_i - 1} \frac{1}{1 - \phi} \right) \right]$$

$$S_p > 0, S_w < 0, \text{ while} \qquad S_\phi > 0 \text{ if } \bar{w} > w$$

$$S_\phi = 0 \text{ if } \bar{w} = w \qquad (5.15B)$$

$$S_\phi < 0 \text{ if } \bar{w} < w$$

When $\bar{w} = w$, case B is equivalent to a MAP rule on profits. Nothing changes as a result of the constraint except that profits will be reduced for output levels where profits are positive and increased for output levels where profits are negative. Figure 5-2 shows this case. π is the original profit function; π' is .8 of π. The maximum profit output, y^*, does not change.

Aggregate relationships may be obtained by substituting $CR(B)$ into equation (5.14) and summing across firms

$$(p_1 y_1 - L_1 \bar{w}) - (\bar{p}_1 \bar{y}_1 - \bar{L}_1 \bar{w}) + (p_2 y_2 - L_2 \bar{w}) - (\bar{p}_2 \bar{y}_2 - \bar{L}_2 \bar{w}) = 0$$

where $L_i = \sum_j L_{ij}$. Separating out the constant terms,

$$p_1 y_1 + p_2 y_2 - (L_1 + L_2)\bar{w} = \bar{p}_1 \bar{y}_1 + \bar{p}_2 \bar{y}_2 - (\bar{L}_1 + \bar{L}_2)\bar{w} . \qquad (5.16)$$

The left-hand terms of (5.16) are $N - (L_1 + L_2)\bar{w}$, which are held constant by the aggregate $CR(B)$ constraint. Therefore, defining aggregate employed labor as $L = L_1 + L_2$, and the constant right-hand side of (5.16) as C, $L = (N - C)/\bar{w}$.

Figure 5-2. Effect of MAP on Profit-Maximizing Output.

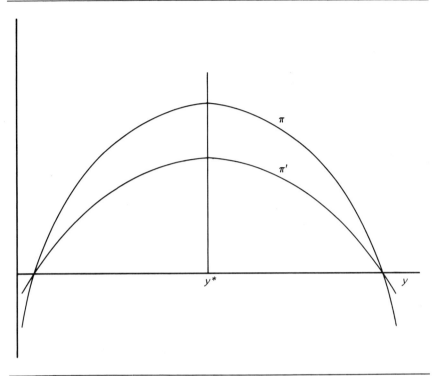

Figure 5-3 shows this positive linear relationship between L and N: Increased nominal demand increases labor input (and output) until one market or the other reaches its labor constraint, L_{o_1} or L_{o_2}. If labor could move freely between the two sectors, an aggregate labor constraint, L_o, would hold, as shown in Figure 5-3. If nominal demand rose beyond this point—that is, if $(N - C)/\overline{w} > L_o$—there would be repressed inflation and shortages. For then neither aggregate output nor aggregate prices could rise in response to the increase in nominal demand. If labor cannot adjust freely between the two sectors, given our assumption that increased nominal demand is shared by the two sectors, one sector, say sector 1, is likely to reach its labor constraint L_{o_1} first, as shown in Figure 5-3. By our assumptions, demand cannot shift from that sector, so shortages will develop in that sector. Increases in N will still increase L, but at a slower pace, until sector 2 reaches its labor constraint. However, $\phi = 1$ at L_{o_1}, so a monetary policy rule never to allow nominal demand to rise enough for $\phi = 1$, would prevent shortages. We believe, but have not shown for $CR(B)$, that at $N = C$, equilibrium $\phi = 0$, and that it then rises monotonically until at L_o, $\phi = 1$. We might note that equation (5.16) holds regardless of whether $w > \overline{w}, w = \overline{w}, w < \overline{w}$.

Figure 5-3.   Relationship between Nominal Demand and Labor.

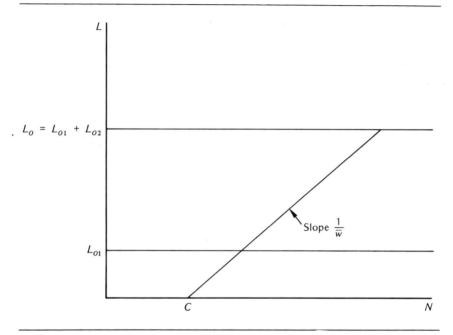

Our general result for credit rule B is that for any given N

if $w < \bar{w}$, the y_i are larger and so the p_i are smaller

if $w > \bar{w}$, the y_i are smaller and so the p_i are larger

than without MAP. Thus, to increase output (for a given nominal demand), it seems sensible to look for a policy that *assures* an incentive to increase output.

In credit rule C, the supply function is

$$S_i(p_i, w_i, \phi) = F_i \left[F_i'^{-1} \left(\frac{w}{p_i} \frac{\epsilon_i}{(\epsilon_i - 1)(1 - \phi) + \phi \epsilon_i \bar{p}_i / p_i)} \right) \right]$$

$$S_{p_i} > 0, \; S_w < 0, \; S_\phi > 0 \text{ if } \bar{p}_i > p_i(1 - 1/\epsilon_i)$$
$$S_\phi = 0 \text{ if } \bar{p}_i = p_i(1 - 1/\epsilon_i) \tag{5.15C}$$
$$S_\phi < 0 \text{ if } \bar{p}_i < p_i(1 - 1/\epsilon_i)$$

The condition $p_i(1 - 1/\epsilon_i)$ comes from the firm's marginal revenue, while the $CR(B)$ condition, w, came from the firm's marginal cost. For most firms if $\bar{p}_i$ is close to p_i, then $\bar{p}_i > p_i(1 - 1/\epsilon_i)$. In fact, in the aggregate $\Sigma p_i y_i = \Sigma \bar{p}_i y_i$, so it is highly probable that aggregate output Y will increase (though output may fall for particular firms that face unusual shifts in demand).

We should also note that by equation (5.14)

$$p_1 y_1 - \bar{p}_1 y_1 + p_2 y_2 - \bar{p}_2 y_2 = 0 \text{ or}$$

$$p_1 y_1 + p_2 y_2 = \bar{p}_1 y_1 + \bar{p}_2 y_2 \ . \tag{5.17}$$

In this notation, and assuming that $\bar{p}_1$ and $\bar{p}_2$ were the earlier prices, the Paasche price index is

$$Pa = \frac{p_1 y_1 + p_2 y_2}{\bar{p}_1 y_1 + \bar{p}_2 y_2} \ .$$

But equation (5.17) assures that $Pa = 1$, for any allowed changes in prices and quantities. Thus MAP assures a constant Paasche price level.

We can use (5.17) to derive a quite general effect of credit rule C on aggregate output. An increase in nominal demand increases $p_1 y_1 + p_2 y_2$ in (5.17) and so increases $\bar{p}_1 y_1 + \bar{p}_2 y_2$ as well. But that implies an increase in the Laspeyres quantity index

$$Y_L = \frac{\bar{p}_1 y_1^1 + \bar{p}_2 y_2^1}{\bar{p}_1 y_1^o + \bar{p}_2 y_2^o}$$

regardless of any changes in the individual y_i. Thus, without using any of the structure of the Benassy model, we can see that credit rule C forces increases in nominal demand into an increase in (Laspeyres) aggregate output.

By looking at a specific production relationship, we can also reduce the model to two equations in p_1 and p_2 and investigate what happens under a variety of circumstances. The first equation in p_1 and p_2 is found by combining the MAP constraint (5.17), the distribution of demand equation (5.12), and equation (5.9):

$$p_1 = \frac{\bar{p}_1 p_2 k}{p_2 (1 + k) - \bar{p}_2} \qquad \frac{dp_1}{dp_2} < 0 \ .$$

The other relationship is found by equating demand and supply for output in each industry. These equations are then solved for ϕ in terms of the industry price. By setting the ϕ's equal to each other we obtain a second equation in p_1 and p_2. We can rewrite equation (5.15C) as:

$$\phi = \frac{1}{\bar{p}_i E_i - p_i} \left[p_i - \frac{w E_i}{F_i'(F_i^{-1}(y))} \right]$$

where $E_i = \epsilon_i / (1 - \epsilon_i)$.

Table 5-1. Relationship between Elasticities, Prices, Output, and the Market Price of MAP Credits.

			p_1	p_2	ϕ	Y_1
$K = 1$	$\epsilon_1 = \epsilon_2$	$N = \bar{N}$	$3.90	$3.90	0	10
$K = 1$	$\epsilon_1 = \epsilon_2$	$N = (1.1)\bar{N}$	3.90	3.90	$.01	11
$K = .1$	$\epsilon_1 = \epsilon_2$	$N = (1.1)\bar{N}$	3.90	3.90	.01	11
$K = 1$	$\epsilon_1 = 1.1$ $\epsilon_2 = 1.4$	$N = (1.1)\bar{N}$	3.79	4.01	.016	11.3
$K = .1$	$\epsilon_1 = 1.1$ $\epsilon_2 = 1.4$	$N = (1.1)\bar{N}$	3.52	3.94	.03	12.2

$C_1 = 10, \bar{Y}_1 = 10, \bar{p}_1 = \$3.90, \bar{p}_2 = \$3.90, \epsilon_1 = 1.1$ and $w = \bar{w}$ throughout the calculations. The bar over variables indicates the initial level.

While an increase in nominal demand, N, keeps the aggregate price level constant and increases aggregate output, it would be nice to see how sensitive ϕ is to changes in N, and how the relative prices and quantities adjust.

To solve for actual values, a specification of the production function is necessary. We chose

$$F_i' (F_i^{-1} (y)) = C_i/y_i$$

and analyzed the problem using numerical techniques. The results appear in Table 5-1. We find that when $\epsilon_1 = \epsilon_2$, p_1 and p_2 do not change as nominal demand increases. ϕ, the MAP credit price, does rise, encouraging firms in both industries to produce more. In this case, therefore, we get an unambiguous increase in output while prices remain constant.

When $\epsilon_1 < \epsilon_2$, ϕ again rises when N increases to reflect the greater pressure on the system. In this case, p_1 falls and p_2 rises. With increases in both ϕ and p_2, y_2 clearly rises. y_1 also rises but for a different reason. The increase in N means that the nominal value of output in sector 1 must also rise. $p_1 y_1$ is, therefore, greater than before. With p_1 falling, y_1 must be greater. Thus both y_1 and y_2 will rise.

These results can also be seen graphically. Figure 5-4 shows the Benassy supply and demand curves. (p^o, y^o) is the original equilibrium for the industry. Without MAP the new equilibrium which will result from an increase in aggregate demand to $D'(p)$ is (p^1, y^1). With MAP ϕ increases and $S(p)$ shifts upward to $S_0(p)$ reflecting firms' willingness to increase production at any value of p. (This is contingent, of course, on $\bar{p} > p(1 - 1/\epsilon)$.) Figure 5-4 is drawn for the case $\epsilon_1 = \epsilon_2$. Here price stays at p^o and output rises to y^*. If $\epsilon_1 < \epsilon_2$, the shift to $S_0(p)$ for industry one will be greater than shown in the figure and p_1 will

Figure 5-4. Benassy Supply and Demand Curves.

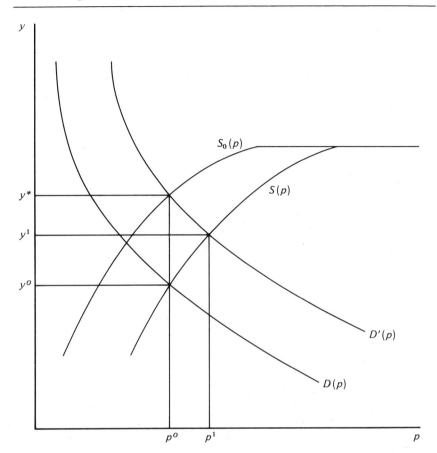

fall. The shift to $S_0(p)$ will be less for industry two, and p_2 will rise. In both cases output will be greater and price lower than without **MAP**.

This improvement in price output behavior does *not* come from a reduction in real wages. In the case where $\epsilon_1 = \epsilon_2$, real wages remain the same; neither price nor the wage rate change. The improvement comes from a reduction in monopoly power as depicted in Figure 5-1.

These results can now be compared with what would happen in a wage/price control regime. If controls are placed on the economy at the original prices, $\bar{p}_i$, this would change the demand curves so that they are now kinked. This is shown in Figure 5-5. There is now a horizontal section at $\bar{p}_i$. Initially this does not change either price or output levels. If demand increases, at first output will rise

Figure 5–5. Shortage Caused by Price Controls.

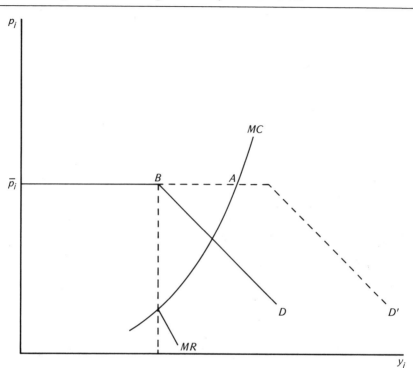

more rapidly under controls, but if demand shifts enough, there will be a point where producers will refuse to produce all that is demanded at this level. In Figure 5-5 the demand shift to D' illustrates how a shortage AB could arise.

In contrast to the wage/price control case, with a **MAP** like $CR(C)$ the demand curve will now appear to be flatter, but demand will be met as long as $\phi < 1$. If ϕ reaches 1, then in equation (5.13) the firm will be maximizing $\bar{p}y - wL$, which is equivalent to the problem faced in the controls case. By monitoring ϕ, and releasing pressure on the system when it rises too much, government policy makers can prevent price control type shortages from arising.

SOME DYNAMICS

In this section we consider the microeconomics of wages and prices over time when the **MAP** credit price affects the firm's decision. We look at two cases. We first follow Benassy's (1982: 161) very simple wage rule: Workers bargain for a constant real wage, W, that is fixed in nominal terms according to the previous period's price level:

$$w_i(t) = W p_i(t - 1) \ . \qquad (5.18)$$

Thus workers are following a simple adaptive expectations rule (or, assuming that they have poor information or high bargaining costs, a rational expectations rule with information or bargaining costs).

The second case uses a wage adjustment model developed by Okun (1981). Okun discusses labor search when workers and firms are tied together because of certain start-up costs, which he calls *tolls*. Furthermore, firms are restricted in terms of wage adjustment because of implicit contracts that exist between workers and firms. These notions lead to a wage adjustment equation where the rate of wage adjustment depends on some concept of a normal rate of increase and the tightness of the labor market. After analyzing each model, we then compare the two models.

Benassy Wage Adjustment

We begin by investigating how the economy would react to wage adjustments consistent with equation (5.18). To simplify, we assume that all firms have identical costs, wages, and demand elasticities, so that a single representative firm may be considered. We first solve (5.15C) for price to obtain the firm's behavior under MAP credit rule C.

$$p_i(t) = \frac{\epsilon_i}{\epsilon_i - 1} \frac{[w_i/F_i'(L_i) - \phi\bar{p}]}{1 - \phi} \ .$$

For simplicity, normalize all prices, so that $p_i(t - 1) = 1$; then, under Benassy's simple wage-adjustment process, $w_i(t) = W$. Substituting,

$$p_i(t) = \frac{\epsilon_i}{\epsilon_i - 1} \frac{[W/F_i'(L_i) - \phi\bar{p}]}{1 - \phi} \ .$$

If

$$\left.\begin{array}{l} p_i(t) > 1 \\ p_i(t) < 1 \\ p_i(t) = 1 \end{array}\right\} \quad \text{its price has} \quad \left\{\begin{array}{l} \text{risen} \\ \text{fallen} \\ \text{remained constant} \ . \end{array}\right.$$

The inflation rate

$$i(t) = \frac{p_i(t) - p_i(t - 1)}{p_i(t - 1)}$$

$$= p_i(t) - 1 \ .$$

We can calculate the effect of MAP on inflation by taking

$$\frac{dp_i(p)}{d\phi} = \frac{\epsilon_i}{\epsilon_i - 1} \frac{[W/F_i'(L_i) - \bar{p}]}{(1 - \phi)^2} \ .$$

So if

$$W > \bar{p}F_i'(L_i), \text{ then } \frac{dp_i(t)}{d\phi} > 0 \ .$$

Since all firms are identical, $u(t) = L_{io} - L_i(t)$, can be thought of as the unemployment attributable to any one firm. Then the unemployment/inflation relationship is

$$1 + i(t) = \frac{\epsilon_i}{\epsilon_i - 1} \frac{[W/F_i'(L_{io} - u(t)) - \bar{p}\phi]}{1 - \phi} \ .$$

Is full employment possible, without inflation? Full employment occurs when $u(t) = 0$. Inflation ceases when $i(t) = 0$.

$$1 = \frac{\epsilon_i}{\epsilon_i - 1} \frac{[W/F_i'(L_{io}) - \phi\bar{p}]}{1 - \phi} \ .$$

Let $E_i = \epsilon_i/(1 - \epsilon_i)$, then

$$\phi = \frac{E_i W/F_i(L_{io}) - 1}{E_i \bar{p} - 1} \ .$$

For $\phi < 1$, $W < \bar{p}F'(L_{io})$: or, the demanded real wage must be less than the product of $\bar{p}$ and the marginal product of labor at full employment. In principle, it is always possible to obtain a sufficiently high $\bar{p}_i$ to assure the inequality. If that inequality is not satisfied, alternative policies to assure consistency might be needed either to reduce the demanded real wage, or to increase firms' marginal product of labor. But for a basically consistent economy, MAP can assure simultaneous full employment and zero inflation.

It should be noted that the possibility of an inconsistency is not due to any problem in controlling inflation. The MAP credit constraint guarantees for the economy as a whole that the price level will be constant. Wages also will stop rising with a one period lag once prices stop rising, so inflationary pressure is controlled as long as the target real wage is not so high as to make the MAP system break down. Trying to reach full employment, however, further increases the pressure on MAP. So it is less likely that ϕ will remain less than one at full-employment than at lower output levels. Still, it is possible to reach higher output levels without inflation under MAP than without MAP.

Okun Wage Adjustment

Because wages adjust quickly to adjustments in price, the rate of wage change slows rapidly with MAP in the Benassy formulation. This is not true in the Okun model. Okun's wage equation (1981: 244) is:

$$\dot{w} = r + S(X)$$

$\dot{w}$ is the rate of change of wages and r represents a "norm . . . for wage increases." $S(X)$ is a function which describes the relationship between "tightness of the economy," X, and its impact on the rate of wage adjustment. At some level of output $S(X) = 0$. If output is higher than this, wages adjust more rapidly than the norm; if output is less, then wage adjustment is slower.

Tightness might be considered less unemployment. This yields a Phillips curve with wage inflation increasing as unemployment falls. Shifts in the curve occur as perceptions of r, the norm wage change adjust.

What might affect the norm, r? Perhaps price inflation influences r adaptively. This leads to an equation like (Okun 1981: 250):

$$r = (1 - \alpha)r_{-1} + \alpha\dot{p}_{-1}$$

where $\dot{p}$ is the rate of price inflation.

If wages are set in this manner, the implications for MAP are seen most simply by observing what would happen with the economy at a tautness level where $S(X) = 0$. With the MAP constraint, $\dot{p} = 0$ so $\dot{w} = (1 - \alpha)r$. The increase in wages would cause ϕ to rise, but prices would be constant. Next period, $\dot{w} = (1 - \alpha)r_{-1}$ and ϕ will rise again, since wages are still increasing. Unless α were very large ϕ would eventually reach 1, and shortages would appear.

This suggests that if MAP is imposed on an economy where wage inflation is already ongoing, a severe credit constraint could cause the eventual breakdown of the MAP system. A better strategy would be to issue additional MAP credits during a transition period to zero price inflation. For example, if the existing inflation rate were 6 percent, firms would not be required to purchase additional credits until their needs exceeded 104 percent of their previous allocation. Under $CR(C)$, this could look like: $CR(C) = py - (1.04)\overline{p}y$. As the wage norm came down, the pressure ϕ would also come down, and the cap could be lowered until inflation was eliminated.

The Okun equation also suggests that there might be a limit to how far the economy could be expanded before the MAP system breaks down. If the economy expands beyond the point where $S(X) = 0$, the constantly increasing wages will put even more pressure on ϕ. Thus the system seems to be limited in that pushing beyond this point is self-destructive.

An advantage the MAP system has over the present use of recession as an anti-inflation tool is that inflation could be brought down without having to increase unemployment beyond the $S(X) = 0$ level.

A Comparison of the Two Models

While MAP can control inflation in both the Benassy model and Okun model, the two models differ as to whether the unemployment rate can be permanently affected. In the Benassy model, under MAP unemployment and inflation can be brought down together, and if the target real wage workers seek is not too high, full employment without inflation can be achieved. In contrast, if money wages adjust as Okun suggests, moving below $S(X) = 0$ and trying to remain there will eventually put intolerable pressure on the MAP system.

The differences in these two models are best explained in terms of how they treat real wages. In Benassy full employment is possible as long as the exogenous real wage does not happen to be too high. In Okun constantly increasing demand for higher real wages creates the pressure on MAP.

In the real world real wage demands are not static as in Benassy's model, but if productivity is rising these demands may not create the kinds of problems suggested by our discussion of Okun's model. The "truth" probably lies somewhere in the middle: Some improvement in unemployment is possible but not on the scale suggested by our discussion of the Benassy model. One possibility is a compromise between the Benassy and Okun models.

Suppose that workers expect a real wage that depends on the rate of unemployment. Then the nominal wage demanded is

$$w(t) = [W + S(X)] p(t - 1)$$

where $S(X)$ is the function between tightness and the desired real wage. It is still possible to affect output via the MAP credit price, but as output rises, the higher real wage puts pressure on the system more rapidly than in the Benassy case.

SUMMARY AND RESULTS

Our goal in this chapter was to investigate the operation of Lerner and Colander's MAP in a specific model of a disequilibrium economy. We had to specify the precise form of the MAP credit rule to make it consistent with the variables available in the Benassy disequilibrium framework. We examined the results of three such rules.

The specific form of the credit rule is crucial to MAP's incentive effects. Thus, the simplistic credit rule A, that gives credit for net revenue with no adjustment for outputs or inputs, causes firms to raise their price and reduce both outputs and inputs.

A second rule, credit rule B, gave credits at an allowed price for increased measurable inputs, here labor. For MAP to have a positive effect on output the firm's allowed wage had to exceed its actual wage. This rule would probably have small effects on output, since the allowed and actual wage are likely to be close.

The third rule, credit rule C, gave credits for increased output at an allowed price. If that price is greater than the firm's marginal revenue, which is very likely, MAP increases the firm's optimal output, at any level of demand. Credit rule C also keeps the economy's Paasche price index constant, so that increased aggregate demand cannot cause a higher price level. Instead, the (Paasche) level of output is increased.

In simulations, we found that the MAP credit price rises gradually as aggregate demand is increased. A modest increase in aggregate demand (say 10 percent) increases the MAP credit price only moderately. Thus, a policy of moderately increased aggregate demand—in this model—increases output at a constant price level without pushing up the MAP credit price very far. And credit rule C implies a stable market in MAP credits: Modest errors in demand management would cause modest changes in the MAP credit price.

Credit rule C thus appears to dominate rule B. But we wonder whether an even greater incentive for increased output could be obtained? If so, how much incentive would be desirable?

We see two ways in which this work should be extended. First, neither credit rule B nor rule C captures exactly what Lerner and Colander had in mind. A rule like C' should be considered in more detail along with the dynamics of MAP, to find the best transition to zero inflation.

IS MAP A USEFUL POLICY TOOL?

This chapter has shown that some versions of MAP will create an incentive for firms to expand output, while the MAP constraint keeps the price level constant. The policy works automatically; firms use the market-determined MAP price to make their own decisions regarding price and output. All the government does is determine the money supply and assure that there is no cheating on the MAP credit constraint. Thus, MAP creates a new, limited form of property right, owned by private firms and freely tradable. The property rights rule, that firms' prices should be consistent with a stable price level, seems the appropriate one, since a stable price level is a highly desirable "public good" to the public and to most economists.

Our results presume that the labor market does not clear rapidly, so that a divergence between labor supply and demand often occurs. We have not proved that, but we believe that this assumption is more plausible than the alternative "new classical" assumption that markets always are at equilibrium—that there is no unemployment. We would like to see the conclusions drawn from other sorts of nonauction models, however; particularly stochastic search models, models of entrepreneurial innovation, and models in which prices and wages are optimally sticky but not fixed. Since the aggregate economy is quite complex, each of these models appears to contain valid insights, even though as currently conceived the models are not mutually consistent.

When MAP increases output, it in effect creates a subsidy to increase output (and a tax to decrease output). It is not clear that this specific MAP subsidy/tax is the best possible, even though it appears to be beneficial on net. If we had a more precise idea of the actual externalities that cause what appear to us as excessive unemployment and inflation, we would be better able to design a tax/subsidy scheme to internalize it.

Nevertheless, in the disequilibrium framework that we examined, a reasonably designed MAP, such as credit rule C, is clearly superior to no incentive policy at all. Similar results have been found in other models. For example, Koford (1983) found that MAP kept the Paasche price level constant and increased short-run output in price-searcher industries, in a short-run multimarket model that included inputs purchased from other firms. There credit rule C acted as a Ramsey pricing rule, optimally reducing monopoly across industries toward marginal cost pricing. Koford (1984b) examined MAP in a long-run equilibrium model of labor search (adopted from Pissarides 1985a, 1985b). There MAP reduced the long-run rate of unemployment, but not in a clearly optimal way: The incentive was not tied to the workers' search externality, although it was related to the firms' price/cost margin and so to the firms' wage-setting externality. More precise modeling of the credit rule might find a rule that builds in the Lerner-Colander version of an anti-monopolizing incentive to labor search (Koford 1984a). However, MAP's effects on innovation are ambiguous. These papers find that MAP increases some kinds of innovation and reduces other kinds, depending on the specific form of the incentive. We don't have a standard for optimal innovation to compare this with, however, and so cannot be sure if MAP does good or ill in this respect.

The analysis of TIPs with budget balance, mostly of wage TIPs (Jackman, Layard, and Pissarides 1985) but also including a value-added TIP in Pissarides (Chapter 7), finds that they reduce equilibrium unemployment in a variety of labor market models. These papers develop models of labor search and bargaining that give a relatively satisfactory microeconomic foundation to long-run wage behavior. That is encouraging. But these TIPs act on different labor-market externalities than those modeled in this chapter, where a wage-only incentive, credit rule B, has almost no effect.

MAP appears to us to have some desirable features. However, it needs to pass further examination, both theoretical and practical (as noted in Chapter 3 of this volume). And more work on the nature of macroeconomic externalities might lead to a better form of incentive than currently exists. Given the lack of reasonable alternatives at present, we do feel positive enough about MAP (and related TIPs) to believe that their adoption should be seriously considered.

NOTES TO CHAPTER 5

1. In principle, a value-added TIP can be devised that is identical to MAP. It would contain a single uniform tax rate on prices above a fixed criterion price, and the same uniform subsidy for prices below that criterion. If the tax/subsidy rate equals the (market-determined) MAP credit price, and the revenues collected from the tax just equal the subsidy payments, the TIP is identical to MAP. (In a dynamic context, the analogy breaks down, since TIP fixes the tax/subsidy rate but MAP allows it to fluctuate.)
2. So far, a good analytic explanation for wage stickiness or rigidity has not been developed. See Stiglitz (1985) for a critical review of current efforts.
3. In theory ϕ could take negative values, so that an increase in ϕ would increase supply in this case. That could occur if firms were required to supply the amount of net sales they were allowed. However, we expect that firms would be allowed without penalty to supply less than their allowed net sales. Then the MAP credit price would never fall below 0 or exceed 1.
4. The MAP credit price is the value of the Lagrangian multiplier in a Ramsey pricing scheme: the marginal value of relaxing the price constraint.

6 THE ECONOMIC EFFECTS OF TAX-BASED INCOMES POLICY

Richard Jackman
*Richard Layard**

Tax-based incomes policy is worth having only if it is both economically effective and administratively feasible. In this chapter we discuss the first of these: how a TIP might have positive economic effects.

What is the purpose of a TIP? The advocates of TIP vary in their answers. Some see it as a temporary measure to reduce inflation, without the unemployment costs that would otherwise be involved. In the eyes of such people the NAIRU is not itself too high; one just wants to avoid going above it when one disinflates. We do not agree with this approach—at least for Great Britain. We see the basic problem as being that the NAIRU is too high. Thus the aim of TIP is not to reduce inflation but to reduce the NAIRU. Once the economy is at the NAIRU, inflation will be constant, determined inertially by its own level at the time when the economy reached the NAIRU. But the crucial objective is to ensure that the NAIRU is lower than the depressingly high levels that seem to be required these days in many European countries at least.

If the aim is to reduce the NAIRU, then an effective policy will have to reduce the real cost of labor to employers.[1] It is no good saying that we do not want TIP to reduce the real wage (relative to productivity). We do. However with luck we can do this without reducing the living standards of workers, for two reasons. First, the higher level of employment will raise the tax base and cut transfer payments to the unemployed. Hence it will be possible to reduce tax rates, quite possibly by enough to maintain real take-home pay.[2] Second, the

*We are grateful to George E. Johnson and Christopher Pissarides, with whom many of the ideas in this chapter were developed. The chapter draws heavily on Jackman, Layard, and Pissarides (1985) and Johnson and Layard (1984). For earlier statements of the general points in this chapter see Layard 1982a and 1982b and Jackman and Layard 1982b.

higher level of economic activity will raise the level of investment, at least during the transition to the NAIRU. There will thus be a higher capital stock, and thus higher real wages.

The route to higher welfare is thus through gross real wages that are lower relative to productivity, but this is not an attack on labor—not even on those workers who are employed, let alone those who are unemployed. We will return later to consider devices that might make our approach more acceptable to labor. But for the moment we shall proceed with our analysis of how TIP could increase employment by reducing the cost of labor.

The basic point is that TIP should be thought of as a tax on the real wage rather than on the money wage. The tax that we propose is simpler than the original suggestion of Wallich and Weintraub (1971). They suggested that the rate of corporation tax could be varied in relation to the excess of wage growth over a norm. This suggestion is certainly inappropriate for a country like Britain where, due to various exemptions, roughly half the firms pay no corporation tax. But in any case it seems less distorting to operate the tax in such a way that incentives to cooperate are independent of profitability. The Wallich/Weintraub argument for relating the tax to profits was that it was then less likely to be passed on. But this is to misconstrue the problem, since the aim of the tax is not to affect the long-run rate of inflation but to affect the level of unemployment.

Thus we suggest a norm (n) for the growth in average hourly earnings. The firm then pays a tax (positive or negative) equal to $t(w - w_{-1}(1 + n))N$ where t is the tax rate, w is hourly earnings (nominal), w_{-1} is lagged hourly earnings (nominal), and N is employment. We want the scheme to be fiscally neutral, so we accompany it by a small subsidy scheme by which firms get a per capita subsidy per worker (s) such that ex post in a world of homogenous workers $s = t(w - w_{-1}(1 + n))$. (We call this the government balanced budget condition.)

The key question is the choice of norm (n). Provided the norm is ex post equal to the rate of price inflation, the scheme amounts to a tax on real wage growth, offset by a small real per capita subsidy. The net real tax per worker is thus

$$T = t(W - W_{-1}) - S$$

where W is real wages and S is the real per worker subsidy. Since it is politically, as well as economically, sensible to set the norm at a level which turns out equal to the rate of price inflation, we assume this is done.[3] We then find that a self-financing scheme with a tax on real wage *growth* at rate t operates exactly like a tax at rate δt on the *level* of real wages (where δ is the relevant discount rate). In each case the scheme has the effect of reducing the level of the real wage. Against this has to be set the cost-increasing effect of the tax payment itself, but this is of course exactly offset by the cost-reducing effect of the subsidy. So labor cost falls by the same amount as the fall in real wages. And this is what increases the level of employment.

To demonstrate this, we use a variety of models of wage-setting behavior: In some, firms set wages, and in others wages are set by unions. But in all of them the basic mechanism is the same: Wage-setters have an incentive to set lower real wages in the presence of the tax.

HOW TIP AFFECTS THE NAIRU

How would TIP affect employment? To examine this we have to use models in which wages are set, not by supply and demand but by agents who have genuine latitude in the wages they can arrive at.[4] In some markets wages are set by employers, in others by unions, and in others by bargaining between the two. For our purpose it is enough to look at the two polar cases, since we find that they give similar results.

Wage-Setting Models

In all these models the basic idea is this: Wage-setters choose their optimal real wage (W) in a way that is affected by the wages ($\overline{W}$) that they expect to prevail elsewhere in the economy, by the level of unemployment (U) and by the TIP rates of tax and real subsidy (t and S). Thus

$$W = f(\overline{W}, U, t, S) \ . \tag{6.1}$$

But in general equilibrium wage-setters must all be setting the same wage:

$$W = \overline{W} \ . \tag{6.2}$$

So the function of unemployment is to make wage-setters choose the same wage as they expect others to set. If unemployment is too low, they will choose a higher wage, and wages will spiral upward with each group chasing the wages others have set.

We thus have (with $W = \overline{W}$) an equilibrium wage equation with a common wage determined by

$$W = f(W, U, t, S) \ . \tag{6.3}$$

The actual wage and unemployment levels are determined jointly by this wage equation and the labor demand relation:

$$U = g(W) \ . \tag{6.4}$$

This is illustrated in Figure 6-1. The role of TIP is to shift down the wage equation and thus increase employment.

Figure 6-1. Determination of the NAIRU

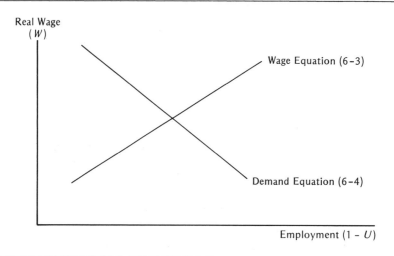

Models Where Firms Set Wages: A Quits Model

So let us begin by looking at a world where firms set wages. In doing this firms are concerned about the effect of their wage levels on their ability to retain or to hire workers or on the morale and productive efficiency of their workers.

Consider first the case where the main concern is quitting.[5] For simplicity we shall assume that the marginal product per worker is constant (γ) and that free entry ensures zero profits.[6] If a worker quits, this imposes a resource cost $\gamma\phi$ on the firm. The firm's quit rate depends on its wage W relative to the income which a worker not employed in the firm could expect elsewhere, which for simplicity is $\overline{W}(1 - U)$, where $\overline{W}$ is the prevailing wage and U is the unemployment rate. Thus the quit rate is shown by the function

$$Q = Q\left(\frac{W}{\overline{W}(1 - U)}\right) \qquad (Q' < 0, \ Q'' > 0) \ .$$

To get a feel for the mechanism by which TIP works let us start with a simple tax on the *level* of the wage bill (tWN) where N is employment. This is accompanied by a per capita subsidy in which the firm receives SN. The scheme is self-financing.

The firm maximises its profit per worker, which is

$$\frac{\pi}{N} = \gamma - (1 + t)W + S - \gamma\phi Q\left(\frac{W}{\overline{W}(1 - U)}\right) \ .$$

The firm chooses W to do this, so that, after setting $W = \overline{W}$, we have a wage equation

$$- (1 + t) - \frac{\gamma\phi Q'\left(\frac{1}{1-U}\right)}{W(1-U)} = 0 \ . \tag{6.3'}$$

The demand relation comes from the zero profit condition:

$$\gamma - (1 + t)W + S - \gamma\phi Q \left(\frac{1}{1-U}\right) = 0 \ . \tag{6.4'}$$

Eliminating $W(1 + t)$ from these two equations we find that

$$Q \frac{1}{1-U} - Q'\left(\frac{1}{1-U}\right) \frac{1}{1-U} = \frac{\gamma + S}{\gamma\phi} \ .$$

Hence

$$\frac{\partial U}{\partial S} < 0 \ .$$

As the level of subsidy (and tax) is raised, the level of unemployment falls. In terms of the diagram, the demand curve $(6.3')$ has not shifted, since by definition tW equals S; but the wage equation $(6.4')$ has shifted down. The lower wages (at given employment) make it profitable for firms to expand employment until the level of quitting has risen enough to push profits back to zero.

It is interesting that in this model the tax is fully passed back into real wages, since $W(1 - t)$ appears as a single variable. Thus the tax as such leaves labor cost unaffected, while the subsidy reduces it. This is a general feature of all our models. It may be a somewhat extreme result, but the basic argument is clear. If wages are taxed, there will be an incentive to reduce wages, and, if there is no net change in labor taxes, this means a fall in labor costs.

We can now use these insights to analyze TIP. The profits of the firm are

$$PV = \sum_j N_j \left[\gamma - (1 + t)W_j + tW_{j-1} + S - \gamma\phi Q \left(\frac{W_j}{\overline{W_j}} X_j\right) \right] (1 - \delta)^j$$

where δ is the real discount rate and $X = 1/(1 - U)$. The optimal choice of wage in the steady state requires that

$$- (1 + t) - \gamma\phi \frac{Q'X}{\overline{W}} + t(1 - \delta) = 0 \ .$$

Second order conditions imply $- Q'' < 0$. In equilibrium, all wages are the same (W) so that $Q = Q(X)$ and

$$(1 + \delta t)W + \gamma\phi Q'(X) = 0 \ . \tag{6.3''}$$

Also, since competition ensures zero profits,

$$\gamma - (1 + t)W + tW_{-1} + S - \gamma\phi Q = 0 \qquad (6.4'')$$

where W_{-1} is the value in the previous year. We now use the government balanced budget condition that ex post the net tax proceeds are zero ($T = 0$). In addition we assume for simplicity that there is no economic growth ($W = W_{-1}$)— this could easily be relaxed. In consequence equation (6.4'') becomes

$$W = \gamma(1 - \phi Q(X)) \ . \qquad (6.4''')$$

Thus, substituting for W in (6.3'')

$$(1 + \delta t)(1 - \phi Q) + Q'(X)X = 0 \ .$$

This determines the natural rate of unemployment, since $X = 1/(1 - U)$.
   From this we find that

$$\frac{\partial X}{\partial t} = \frac{-\delta(1 - \phi Q)}{\phi(Q''X - \delta t Q')} < 0 \ .$$

Thus the wage inflation tax reduces unemployment. At the same time it reduces real wages, as can be seen from equation (6.4''').
   If the discount rate is zero, the tax has no effect. For if a firm raises its wages by £1 this year, it pays an extra £N in tax this year and a reduced £N in tax next year. So only with discounting does the tax work. If the tax is expected to be abolished next period, it will have its maximum impact.

An Efficiency-Wage Model

Clearly firms choose their wages with more than quitting behavior in mind. Morale is also important, since it affects productivity. And morale may depend on relative incomes. Thus output per worker might be

$$\gamma e = \gamma e\left(\frac{W}{\overline{W}} X\right) \qquad (e' > 0, \ e'' < 0) \ .$$

Thus unemployment serves as a device to discipline workers (Shapiro and Stiglitz 1983). In this case it is easy to see that the inflation tax will reduce unemployment, even if quitting is independent of wages. Assuming quitting is zero, the firm's present value is

$$PV = \sum_j N_j \left[\gamma e\left(\frac{W_j}{\overline{W}_j} X_j\right) - W_j(1 + t) + tW_{j-1} + S \right](1 - \delta)^j \ .$$

The optimal choice of wage requires

$$-(1 + t)\overline{W} + \gamma e'X + t(1 - \delta)\overline{W} = 0$$

with second order conditions requiring $e'' < 0$. This is similar in form to equation (6.3") for the model with quitting. If it is combined with the zero profit condition and government budget balance ($T = 0$), we find that

$$e'(X)X - (1 + \delta t)e(X) = 0 \qquad (6.5)$$

and

$$\frac{\partial X}{\partial t} = \frac{\delta e}{e''X - \delta te'} < 0 \ .$$

Once again the tax reduces unemployment by reducing real wages and making more employment profitable until this reduces efficiency too far.

A Model with Quitting, Hiring, and Vacancies

Finally we can look at firms' behavior in a rather more sophisticated way, with wages affecting hiring as well as quitting.[7] Firms hire by advertising genuine vacancies. That is, they stand ready to fill any vacancy if a suitable applicant appears. And in general they will not wish to employ a worker unless there is a work place for him to work at.[8] Hence the present value of the firm's profits is

$$PV = \sum_j N_j \left[\gamma - (1 + t)W_j + tW_{j-1} + S - \gamma\phi \left(1 + \frac{V_j}{N_j} \right) \right] (1 - \delta)^j$$

where $\gamma\phi$ is the cost per work place ($\phi < 1$), V_j is vacancies, and $(N_j + V_j)$ is the number of work places. Profit is maximized subject to the firm satisfying its flow of labor constraint. For simplicity we shall assume that employment does not change between periods.[9] Hence the firm's quits equal its hires:

$$QN = PV$$

where P is the proportion of vacancies filled per period. We shall assume, for our present purposes, that quits can be written as $Q\left(\dfrac{W}{\overline{W}}, \dfrac{U}{V/N}\right)$ and that the proportion of vacancies that a firm fills is $P\left(\dfrac{W}{\overline{W}}, \dfrac{U}{V/N}\right)$—it depends on the relative wage and on the aggregate ratio of unemployed to vacancies in the economy. Thus the firm's maximand is

$$PV = \sum_j N_j \left[\gamma - (1 + t)W_j + tW_{j-1} + S - \gamma\phi \left(1 + \frac{Q_j}{P_j} \right) \right] (1 - \delta)^j \ .$$

If the firm reduces its wages, it reduces its wage bill. But, by reducing its ability to retain and hire labor, it also raises its vacancy rate. The optimal wage involves a balancing of these effects. This requires

$$- (1 + t) - \frac{\gamma\phi}{p^2} \left(P \frac{\partial Q}{\partial R} \frac{1}{W} - Q \frac{\partial P}{\partial R} \frac{1}{W} \right) + t(1 - \delta) = 0$$

where $R = W/\overline{W}$, the relative wage. If η_{QR} is the absolute elasticity of quits with respect to the relative wage and η_{PR} is the absolute elasticity of hiring with respect to the relative wage, this implies that (setting $W = \overline{W}$)

$$- (1 + t) W + \gamma\phi \frac{Q}{P} (\eta_{QR} + \eta_{PR}) + t(1 - \delta) W = 0$$

or

$$(1 + \delta t) W - \gamma\phi \frac{V}{N} (\eta_{QR} + \eta_{PR}) = 0 . \qquad (6.6)$$

But zero profit and government budget balance $(T = 0)$ imply that

$$\gamma - W - \gamma\phi \left(1 + \frac{V}{N} \right) = 0 . \qquad (6.7)$$

Substituting into (6.6) for W (taken from (6.7)),

$$\frac{V}{N} = \frac{1 + \delta t}{1 + \delta t + \eta_{QR} + \eta_{PR}} \cdot \frac{1 - \phi}{\phi} .$$

Thus

$$\frac{\partial V/N}{\partial t} > 0 .$$

Hence a rise in the tax will raise vacancies. It will also reduce real wages (see (6.7)).

But what happens to unemployment? At the whole economy level the flow equilibrium condition is

$$Q\left(1, \frac{U}{V/N} \right) = P\left(1, \frac{U}{V/N} \right) \frac{V}{N} = f\left(U, \frac{V}{N} \right) \qquad (6.8)$$

$$(Q_2 < 0, f_1 > 0, f_2 > 0) .$$

Hence if vacancies rise, unemployment falls.

The overall mechanism here is quite similar to that in the earlier models. The tax reduces real wages. This makes it profitable to expand vacancies, and this reduces unemployment.

Models Where Unions Set Wages:
A Wholly Unionized Economy

Some of us come from countries where unions are important, and one naturally asks whether the tax would be effective in that situation. We shall show that it would. In fact the effects would be the same whether the tax were levied on firms or workers, but it is more politically feasible to levy it on firms.

We shall assume that the unions fix the real wage, but the firms fix employment. The tax works by altering the trade-off between employment and wages that the unions face. Above the norm a wage increase in the pockets of the union reduces employment more when there is a tax than when there is not—because it raises labor cost by more than it raises wages. Similarly a wage reduction raises employment more with the tax than without it. Hence the tax makes the demand curve faced by the individual union (as a function of the wage paid) more elastic. It thus encourages a higher level of employment.

Let us be a bit more formal. The economy consists of a set of equal-size sectors within each of which the union sets the sector real wage, taking the outside real wage as given. In doing so it takes into account the fact that the sector level of employment (N) depends negatively on the sector real labor cost:[10]

$$N = N(W + T) \ .$$

In setting wages, unions maximize some objective function, subject to the firm's demand function for labor. Many objective functions have been proposed for unions. Clearly unions care both about wages and about jobs for their members. Since members continually leave, one might expect the unions to raise wages repeatedly to at least as high as the demand price for the surviving members. But this overlooks the fact that unions cannot prevent other members from continuously joining. Therefore, the union maximizes the interests of a stable but constantly revolving population. This dynamic problem is analyzed reasonably fully in Jackman, Layard, and Pissarides (1983), but here we shall present a much simpler and less rigorous analysis that leads to similar conclusions.

Each union is concerned with the long-run welfare of a group consisting of M people. Of these people, N are employed in the union's sector. The remaining $M - N$ are either employed elsewhere in the economy, with probability $(1 - U)$, or unemployed. If employed they get the general wage $\overline{W}$. For simplicity we shall ignore unemployment benefits and assume that utility is linear in income. The union's objective in period j is thus the expected income of its M members in period j, which is

$$Z_j = N(W_j + T_j)W_j + [M - N(W_j + T_j)] \ (1 - U)\overline{W}_j$$
$$= N(W_j + T_j) \ [W_j - (1 - U)\overline{W}_j] + \text{constant} \ .$$

The union thus cares only about the sum of the rents (or surpluses) obtained by its members. (Note that the size of the membership M, which might appear difficult to determine in advance, does not affect the maximimization result.)

In the multiperiod context the union maximizes

$$PV = \sum_j N\left[(1 + t)W_j - tW_{j-1} - S\right] \left[W_j - (1 - U)\overline{W}_j\right] (1 - \delta)^j .$$

For simplicity, we shall assume that there is no economic growth.[11] It then follows that in general equilibrium (with $W = \overline{W}$), the union's wage behavior implies that

$$U = - \frac{N}{N'W} \frac{1}{(1 + \delta t)} .$$

Since budget balance requires that ex post $T = 0$, this can be written as

$$U = \frac{1}{\eta} \frac{1}{(1 + \delta t)} \qquad (6.9)$$

where η is the sector-specific elasticity of demand for labor.

This analysis makes excellent sense. Unemployment is higher the less elastic the sector-specific elasticity of demand for labor. But if an inflation tax is imposed, this increases the elasticity of labor demand with respect to the wage, since labor cost now rises faster than wages. And this higher elasticity of demand for labor leads to higher equilibrium employment. The story is illustrated in Figure 6-2. The original demand curve is DD and the final one $D'D'$. The equilibrium shifts from E to E' (which has to lie on the original demand curve due to the requirement of budget balance).

A Partially Unionized Economy

A wholly unionized economy may be a reasonable description of Britain but certainly not of the United States. Suppose that only part of the economy is unionized, the wage being chosen by unions. Elsewhere (in the "competitive sector") the wage is determined by supply and demand.[12] The supply of workers at the level of wages prevailing in the competitive sector is elastic with respect to the wage. We consider that part of the population not employed as unemployed. In these circumstances a rise in the union mark-up will push workers into the competitive sector, reducing its wage and increasing unemployment. Equally a fall in the union mark-up will reduce unemployment. But TIP will reduce the chosen mark-up and thus reduce unemployment.

First we shall show how TIP affects the mark-up and then how the mark-up affects unemployment. Let the union wage (W_u) equal the nonunion wage (W_c)

Figure 6-2. Sector-Specific Employment in a Union Model.

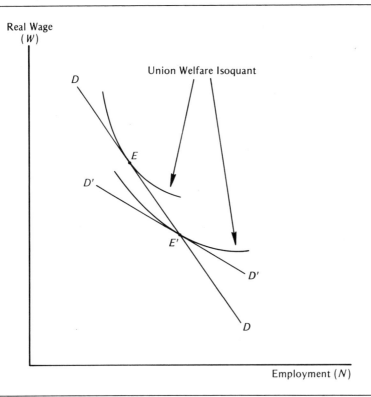

times μ. The union maximizes the present value of the expected rents of its members, which, assuming zero growth, is

$$PV = \sum_j N_j \left((1 + t) W_c \mu_j - t W_c \mu_{j-1} - S\right) W_c (\mu_j - 1)(1 - \delta)^j$$

Assuming a balanced budget, the optimum mark-up $(\mu - 1)$ is given by

$$\mu - 1 = \frac{1}{\eta(1 + \delta t) - 1} .$$

A rise in the tax reduces the mark-up.

But how does the mark-up affect unemployment? We assume that the whole population L is willing to work at the union wage. The proportion of them who get work in the union sector is $D_u(W_c \mu)/L$ where $D_u(W_c \mu)$ is demand in the union sector. The number of people who are willing to work at the competitive wage is $S(W_c)$. Of these only a proportion, $1 - D_u(W_c \mu)/L$, supply themselves to the competitive sector, since the rest have jobs in the union sector. Thus equality of supply and demand in the competitive sector requires

$$D_c(W_c) = \left(1 - \frac{D_u(W_c\mu)}{L}\right) S(W_c) . \qquad (6.10)$$

From this one can see that a rise in the mark-up lowers the competitive wage, by flooding the competitive sector with workers. For, from equation (6.10),

$$(D'_c - (1 - D_u/L)S' + D'_u \mu S/L)dW_c = (-D'_u W_c S/L)d\mu .$$

The resulting change in employment is given by[13]

$$
\begin{aligned}
dN &= (D'_u \mu + D'_c)dW_c + D'_u W_c \, d\mu \\
&= \left[D'_u \mu + D'_c - \frac{T}{S} D'_c + (1 - D_u/T)\frac{TS'}{S} - D'_u \mu\right]dW_c \\
&= \left[D'_c\left(1 - \frac{T}{S}\right) + \left(1 - \frac{D_u}{T}\right)\frac{TS'}{S}\right]dW_c .
\end{aligned}
$$

Hence

$$\frac{\partial N}{\partial W_c} > 0 .$$

Thus, if the mark-up (μ) rises, the competitive wage falls and employment falls. By using TIP this process can be put into reverse: The mark-up will be reduced and employment will rise.

CONCLUSION

There are many more issues that could, and should, be discussed in connection with the theory of TIP. As we stated above, our theory does not allow us to distinguish between a tax on the level of wages and on wage inflation. According to the theory, exactly the same results can be achieved by operating a self-financing tax/subsidy scheme in which the firm pays the following tax per worker:

$$T = tW - S .$$

The wage tax will have exactly the same force whether it is a tax on wage *growth* or the wage *level*, provided it is accompanied by a substantial per capita subsidy. With TIP the main per capita subsidy element comes from the norm and is represented by the term tW_{-1}. But in each case it is the combination of the proportional tax with the per capita subsidy that produces the twist in the terms on which wage-setters make their decisions.

Thus another way to reduce the NAIRU would be to reconstruct employers' taxes on labor so that there were a higher proportional tax, offset by a per capita subsidy.[14] Is there any point in using a tax on wage *inflation* at all, if the same result could be got by a tax on the *level* of wages? There are two arguments for using it. First, we do not really know with any certainty how the natural rate is determined. The models offered above are, we hope, quite well grounded in microeconomic theory. But all we know from empirical observation is that inflation has a tendency to rise when unemployment gets below a certain level. Thus the problem in reducing unemployment *is* inflation. It therefore seems natural to address at least one of our policies directly to that problem. It may work by the mechanism we have specified. But, even if all our models are irrelevant, there could be a hope that it would work by some other mechanism.

A second argument in favor of an inflation tax is that it could help not only to reduce the natural rate of unemployment (at constant inflation) but also to reduce inflation (if one wanted to) with less unemployment than would otherwise be required. In practice disinflation normally requires that wage-setters set wages below the level at which they expect the general level of wages to be set. It is easy to check in our models that if this occurs (with $W = (1 - \lambda)\bar{W}$ where $\lambda > 0$), unemployment will be higher than otherwise. An inflation tax could offset this. These are good arguments for operating a TIP as well as other measures to maintain employment. Thus, while our model may not fully capture the effects, we believe that the case for TIP is strong.

NOTES TO CHAPTER 6

1. For evidence that employment is affected by real wages see Nickell and Andrews (1983). If there is imperfect competition, aggregate demand can exert an influence only in the short-run, but in the long-run the level of aggregate demand is constrained to be consistent with the NAIRU.
2. The change in real wages is

$$d\left(W(1 - t)\right) = dW\left(1 - t - W\frac{dt}{dW}\right)$$

where t is the tax rate and W the gross wage rate. Hence if $dW < 0$, real wages rise if

$$1 - t < W\frac{dt}{dW}.$$

Assuming no change in the budget deficit, the government budget constraint is

$$tWN - (1 - N)B = \text{constant}$$

where N is employment and B is unemployment benefit. Differentiating the budget constraint yields

$$\frac{dt}{dW} W = -\frac{dN}{dW} \frac{W}{N} \left(t + \frac{B}{W} \right) - t .$$

So real wages rise if

$$-\frac{dN}{dW} \frac{W}{N} > \frac{1}{t + \dfrac{B}{W}} = \text{(say) } 1.1 .$$

Current work at the Centre for Labour Economics gives labor demand elasticities of this order of magnitude.

3. Chapter 7 by Pissarides analyzes the general case where this is not necessarily done.

4. Even in a supply and demand world some self-financing policies can change the NAIRU — for example, a marginal employment subsidy.

5. See Calvo (1979) and earlier papers by Salop, Stiglitz, and others.

6. Allowing γ to alter exogenously over time does not affect the results. Introducing fixed capital and nonzero profits does not lead to substantially different conclusions.

7. For a more elaborate treatment see Jackman, Layard, and Pissarides (1983).

8. If an establishment is very large and employs large numbers of the same type of workers it may be worth its while declaring more vacancies than it has vacant work places, in order to attract more workers, even if occasionally it will have no place where an appointee can work.

9. Strictly the steady state should only be assumed after we have taken the first-order conditions. However, this complicates the analysis without affecting our qualitative conclusions.

10. This relationship depends on both the marginal productivity conditions and the demand conditions for the sector's output. Marginal productivity implies that in the ith sector

$$N_i = f\left((W_i + T_i) \frac{p}{p_i} \right) \qquad (f' < 0)$$

where real labor cost $(W_i + T_i)$ is measured relative to the general price level (p) and p_i is the price of sector output. Product demand gives a relation between sector employment and relative price:

$$\frac{p_i}{p} = g(N_i) \qquad\qquad (g' < 0) .$$

Hence, combining the two equations,

$$N_i = h(W_i + T_i) \qquad\qquad (h' < 0) .$$

11. If we allowed economic growth of the form that $N = N\left(\dfrac{W + T}{A}\right)$ where A is the level of technical progress, then equation (6.9) would still hold, since, if we assume U constant, $(W + T)/A$ must be constant.

12. This model is a modified version of Minford (1983).

13. Since we are assuming zero growth, $T = 0$ in each sector. If we allowed for growth, T would only equal zero in *each* sector if we made the subsidy proportional to wages rather than a per capita payment.

14. Moves toward greater progressivity in employment taxes, either by this method or TIP, would have even greater advantages when one allows for the existence of heterogeneous labor (Jackman and Layard 1980; Johnson 1980).

7 EQUILIBRIUM EFFECTS OF TAX-BASED INCOMES POLICIES

Christopher A. Pissarides

If an economy needs an anti-inflation plan, it needs it most when conventional monetary policies do not work smoothly to bring inflation down without excessive output loss. If the macroeconomy functioned in the way that new classical economics claims, anti-inflation plans would, at best, have no effect on the economy. More likely, they would distort the resource allocation function of an efficient price system.

Recent experience with monetary policy, however, both in the United States and in Britain, has shown that bringing down inflation involves considerable output costs (Gordon and King 1982; Perry 1983; Buiter and Miller 1983a). Market anti-inflation plans have been put forward both as policies that would reduce the output loss during the transition to lower inflation (Lerner and Colander 1980, 1982; Colander 1980; Seidman 1978, 1979; Meade 1982; Layard 1982a, b) and as policies that will lower the natural rate of unemployment. In this paper we consider the effects of two stylized plans on unemployment in continuous nonstochastic rational expectations equilibrium, by making use of a model that has no explicit inflation and no short-term adjustment dynamics.

To see the relevance of this analysis for anti-inflation policies consider the argument first put forward by Friedman (1968). Changes in the rate of inflation swing the economy around a "natural" equilibrium, or more accurately around a nonaccelerating-inflation unemployment rate. The economy's natural equilibrium is influenced by relative prices, not by the rate of inflation (except for such "effects" as the Tobin-Mundell effect). But anti-inflation plans are supposed to work in the labor market by influencing incentives that firms and workers face—

that is, by inducing a change in relative prices. So, whatever the effect of the anti-inflation plans on the speed of transition to noninflationary equilibrium, there is a good chance that the natural unemployment rate will be affected by the plans. As a result the economy will swing around a different natural rate during inflations and disinflations when anti-inflation plans are in operation.

The effect of the plans on the natural unemployment rate may or may not be the main channel through which they are supposed to ease the transition to noninflationary equilibrium. The early literature is not very clear on the issue, though Layard's (1982a, b), Seidman's (1979), and Lerner and Colander's (1982) discussion is certainly consistent with it (by contrast, Lerner and Colander (1980) emphasize mainly the effect of the policy on expectations). The later literature has emphasized this point (for example Colander 1985a). The model of this paper is agnostic on this issue, since it does not consider the adjustment to equilibrium. But influencing the natural rate is certainly a potential channel through which the anti-inflation plans would work, since the very idea of a market-based plan is that to be effective, the plan has to change the relative prices that people face. Thus there cannot be a complete analysis of the effects of the plans without a study of their effects on the economy's natural equilibrium.

The model that I use to study these effects draws heavily on work that we have done at the Centre for Labour Economics, L.S.E. The main references are Layard (1982a), Jackman and Layard (1982a), Nickell and Andrews (1983), Jackman, Layard, and Pissarides (1983), and Pissarides (1985a, b). It is a model where the firm bargains with its workers about the wage rate and maintains the "right to manage"—that is, to choose employment in any way that it pleases. Naturally, it chooses employment to maximize profits, so what we have is a model of Nash wage bargaining combined with a labor demand curve. The wage bargain is flexible enough to contain the monopoly union as a special case. The monopoly firm is also a special case, but it is not an interesting one in the context of this model because we do not consider the possibility of attracting more workers by raising the wage rate. Also, the restriction that employment is given by a point on the labor demand curve is not important for the equilibrium solution for unemployment, though it does influence the real wage outcome. This rather peculiar property of the model depends partly on some special assumptions and it is derived in the appendix to this chapter. Because of it, the effect of the anti-inflation plans on unemployment is the same both in a labor demand curve model and in an efficient employment contract model.

I consider two kinds of anti-inflation plans. First, a tax is imposed on nominal wage increases, and the revenue is used to subsidize employment (referred to as WIP). I show that there is a one-to-one correspondence between the tax on nominal wage increases and a tax on the real wage, so the policy is equivalent to one where wage taxes are used to finance employment subsidies. Second, I consider a policy that taxes value added and, as with WIP, uses the revenue to subsidize employment (VAP). This policy bears a close relation to Lerner's and Colander's (1980) MAP, where the firm can raise its price of output by, say, 1 percent only if it has a tradable coupon. Then, the coupon credits that the firm gets at the beginning of the period correspond to the lump-sum subsidy and the coupons that have to be given up to raise price correspond to the tax on (nominal) value added. The fact that there is a free-market price for these coupons ensures that both the tax and the subsidy are positive.

Both the wage and value-added policies reduce equilibrium unemployment because of the subsidy element. WIP reduces equilibrium unemployment through two routes: by increasing the elasticity of the demand for labor and by tilting the sharing of the rents from employment in favor of firms. VAP has no effect on the sharing rule, but it increases the elasticity of the demand for labor and so also reduces equilibrium unemployment. A comparison between the two policies shows that VAP is more effective than WIP, despite the effects of the latter on the sharing rule, because VAP makes the labor demand curve more elastic than WIP. It would appear, then, that as far as the equilibrium effects of the policies are concerned, the most effective way of shifting the adjustment paths of an economy in a favorable way is to tax value added and use the revenue to subsidize employment.

THE MODEL

There are three unknowns that are determined by the model: real wages, unemployment, and vacancies. The capital stock, both at the level of the firm and in the economy as a whole, is fixed, and so is the total labor force. Real wages are determined by a Nash bargain between the individual firm and its labor force. With the wage determined, the firm chooses its vacancy rate and its level of employment. The choice of wage is "rational" in the sense that both the firm and its workers realize that their chosen wage will influence the firm's choice of vacancy rate and employment; the firm chooses vacancies and employment to maximize its profits, given the Nash wage.

Thus, there is no bargaining over employment (or more correctly over job slots) and the outcome will not in general be efficient. Workers could offer to work more at the going wage rate with benefits to both the firm and the worker. We adopt this assumption on the grounds of realism (Nickell and Andrews 1983; Oswald 1984b). The alternative of efficient bargaining over employment does not seem to correspond to what is going on in labor markets. Perhaps with many small firms it would be difficult for a labor union to monitor accurately the number of job slots chosen by each firm. Alternatively, there could be circumstances where letting firms maximize profits conditional on a bargaining outcome for the wage is efficient. It is interesting that in the model of this paper the standard case that we consider gives the same outcome for aggregate unemployment in both profit maximizing and efficient employment bargaining. The outcome for each individual firm, given the behavior of the rest of the market, is different in each case, for the usual reasons. But when all individual outcomes are put together macroconsistency requires that unemployment be the same in each case, though the real wage rate will in general be lower if there is bargaining over employment. This result (which may not hold in more general models) is demonstrated in the appendix to this chapter.

The rate at which workers arrive at a firm to take jobs depends on the number of genuine job vacancies that the firm has. A genuine job vacancy is one that represents a job slot with as much capital as one that is occupied and actively producing output. Thus, the firm allocates the same capital to all its job slots, regardless of whether they are occupied or not, and it is always willing to take on as many additional workers as the number of job vacancies that it has. If vacancies did not represent genuine labor needs, the firm would be turning down workers applying for some of its advertised vacancies. Soon this policy would become known, and the firm would lose its reputation as one that would advertise only when it had genuine needs. Workers would then stop responding to its advertisements, and long-run profits would suffer (see Jackman, Layard, and Pissarides, 1983).

Suppose then, that if the firm's capital stock is K, and if it has n_i employees and v_i vacancies, its capital per job is $K/(n_i + v_i)$. Hence total output is $F(n_i, n_i K/(n_i + v_i))$, where $F(\cdot)$ is the production function. The rate at which workers arrive to the firm is pv_i, where p is a number less than 1, depending positively on the aggregate unemployment/vacancy (u/v) ratio. The functional form of p depends on the "technology of search." For the purposes of this paper we simply postulate that the more job searchers there are in relation to job vacancies, the more likely is a job vacancy to be searched. The firm cannot control the rate at which workers arrive at individual vacancies, so there are no reputations concerning high-wage and low-wage firms. Since in equilibrium all firms will negotiate the same wage, this does not seem particularly restrictive.

Workers leave the firm at the constant rate s. Assuming that s depends on the u/v ratio, like p but in the opposite direction, would be a trivial extension not worth pursuing. Assuming that s depends on the negotiated wage rate would be a more substantial extension. However, the extension would not alter significantly any of the results, since a model with endogenous quits produces similar conclusions (Johnson and Layard 1984). Moreover, the extension is not so compelling in the model of this paper, since the wage rate is determined after bargaining and not by a firm with monopsony power. It seems more straightforward to assume that the firm's labor force is characterized by "natural wastage" at the constant rate s.

Thus, workers come to the firm at the rate pv_i and leave at the rate sn_i, with both p and s outside the control of the firm. A firm that is neither expanding nor contracting will experience, on average, equality between these two rates. We shall impose this equality as a constraint on the firm's behavior, though in a stochastic world it will not be satisfied at all times. The results that we derive are ex ante steady-state results that describe average behavior for a typical firm.

We incorporate the constraint in the firm's maximization problem by using it to solve for the firm's vacancies v_i:

$$v_i = \frac{s}{p}\, n_i \tag{7.1}$$

A relationship like equation (7.1) will also hold in the economy as a whole, where we also have $p = p\,(u/v)$ and $n = \ell - u$, with ℓ denoting the fixed labor force. So (7.1) for the economy as a whole becomes the u, v locus

$$v = \frac{s}{p\,(u/v)}\ (\ell - u) \tag{7.2}$$

This locus in u, v space is convex to the origin and downward sloping, provided we impose the reasonable restriction that the elasticity of p with respect to u/v is less than 1 (see Pissarides 1985a, b).

With equation (7.1), the firm's production function becomes $F(n_i, pK/(s+p))$, with $pK/(s+p)$ parametric. We assume that this function is Cobb–Douglas

$$F(\ ) = A\left(\frac{pK}{s+p}\right)^{\alpha} n_i^{\,1-\alpha}, \qquad 0 < \alpha < 1$$

Denote the first two terms by k; hence output for the typical firm is simply

$$F(\ ) = kn_i^{\,1-\alpha}$$

The firm chooses n_i to maximize real profits, given the wage. Let q_i be the real price of the firm's output and w_i be the real wage rate. Then profits are

$$\Pi = q_i kn_i^{\,1-\alpha} - n_i w_i \tag{7.3}$$

Employment is therefore given by the demand equation

$$(1 - \alpha)q_i kn_i^{\,-\alpha} - w_i = 0 \tag{7.4}$$

At the optimum point the firm's profits are most conveniently written as

$$\Pi = \frac{\alpha}{1 - \alpha}\ w_i n_i\,, \tag{7.5}$$

that is, they are a fraction $\alpha/(1 - \alpha)$ of the wage bill.

Since there are constant returns to scale, we can think of these profits in equilibrium as the return to capital. Then, we can also think of the entrepreneur as the owner of capital (or as someone bargaining with labor on behalf of the owners of capital). The bargain is over the wage rate w_i, with both parties acknowledging that employment will be given by equation (7.4). The Nash bargaining solution may be derived by maximizing the function (see, for example, de Menil 1971)

$$B = (U - U_o)^\beta (\Pi - \Pi_o)^{1-\beta}, \qquad 0 \leqslant \beta \leqslant 1 \qquad (7.6)$$

where U and Π are the workers' and firm's expected returns from agreement, and U_o and Π_o are their returns when there is disagreement (threat points). β indicates bargaining strength; if $\beta = 1$ the outcome is one of monopoly union maximizing subject to the demand curve, as in Jackman, Layard, and Pissarides (1983). If $\beta = 0$, the firm chooses the wage to maximize profits as a monopsonist. Given our assumptions about the supply of labor to the firm (the form of the $p(\ )$ function) the case $\beta = 0$ is not very meaningful: The firm will be able to reduce the wage down to the level of the utility from leisure without any effect on the supply of labor. However, the model can easily be generalized to one where the firm has some monopsony power by being able to influence the $p(\ )$ function. A variant of this model was also analyzed by Jackman, Layard, and Pissarides (1983). Finally, if $\beta = \frac{1}{2}$ we have the symmetric Nash solution, where one party will get a bigger share than the other only if it has a stronger threat point.

The firm's profit from agreement is given by equation (7.5), with n_i obtained as the solution to (7.4). We assume that its profit when there is disagreement is zero. The workers' utility from agreement is simply the wage bill $w_i n_i$, whereas their return when there is disagreement is average income elsewhere in the market, $(1 - u)w + ub'$; b' is real income (psychic or actual) during unemployment. It is reasonable to assume that b' is less sensitive to shocks in the short run than the value of output and the market wage, and this assumption is critical in some short-run models (McDonald and Solow 1981; Pissarides 1985a). However, it is less compelling to assume so in steady-state equilibrium models and in the model of this paper the assumption of a rigid b' is not particularly important. It simplifies the results considerably if we assume instead that the "replacement ratio" is constant — that is, write $b' = bw$, with b constant. We shall pursue this simplification in the formal model and point out informally the implications of relaxing it (see also Johnson and Layard 1984). Hence we write

$$U - U_o = n_i \left[w_i - (1 - u + ub)w \right] \quad 0 \leqslant b < 1 \qquad (7.7)$$

In this utility function, workers who do not get a job with the firm receive the mean return elsewhere in the market. Also, new employees with the firm are afforded the same weight in the wage bargain as existing employees, so the fact that the firm's labor force is subject to continuous turnover does not influence the workers' objective function. These assumptions may not be so realistic in cases where the bargaining is carried out by a trade union on behalf of the firm's workers, for example, when bargaining unions may attach greater importance to the rewards of existing senior members than to newcomers. We shall not model these extensions here though they could give rise to different wage equations (see Nickell and Andrews 1983 and Oswald 1984a). They are, however, unlikely to change the predictions concerning the effects of taxes and subsidies on unemployment.

Maximizing the equation (7.6) with respect to w_i we obtain the first-order condition

$$\beta \Pi \left(n_i + \frac{\partial n_i}{\partial w_i} \frac{U - U_o}{n_i} \right) = (1 - \beta)(U - U_o) n_i \qquad (7.8)$$

But from equation (7.4),

$$\frac{\partial n_i}{\partial w_i} \frac{1}{n_i} = - \frac{1}{\alpha w_i} \qquad (7.9)$$

so, substituting from (7.5), (7.7) and (7.9) into (7.8), we get

$$w_i = \frac{\beta + (1 - \alpha)(1 - \beta)}{(1 - \alpha)} (1 - u + ub)w \qquad (7.10)$$

Equation (7.10) gives the negotiated wage rate when wages elsewhere are taken as given. The wage rate is higher when:

1. Workers' bargaining strength, as measured by β, is higher, reaching its maximum in the monopoly union case $\beta = 1$ (note also that if $\beta = 0$ the only solution consistent with $w_i = w$ is $b = 1$, otherwise $w_i < w$);

2. The share of capital α is higher because then the wage elasticity of the demand for labor, $1/\alpha$, is lower;

3. The replacement ratio b and wages elsewhere w are higher because then the workers' threat point in the bargaining is strengthened;

4. Unemployment is lower because it reduces the value of the workers' threat point.

For any exogenous expectation of w, the model is solved as follows. Assume each firm in the economy has the same capital/labor ratio, and substitute w_i from equation (7.10) into (7.4). Then by summing over i (7.4) becomes an equation in two unknowns, v and u: Both of these enter via p, and for a fixed labor force $n = \ell - u$. Equation (7.2) is also an equation in the same unknowns, so they can be simultaneously solved for v and u. Substitution of u into equation (7.10) yields the solution for the wage. However, in an equilibrium model it is more reasonable to solve this system under endogenous and correct perceptions—that is, to assume that changes will take place in the economy until $w_i = w$. Then equation (7.10) becomes an equation in unemployment. Since the only endogenous variable that enters the relationship between w_i and w is u, it is u that will have to change until $w_i = w$. Moreover the unemployment rate obtained from (7.10) under the condition $w_i - w$ corresponds exactly to the definition of the natural unemployment rate, since if $w_i \neq w$ there will be real-wage dynamics in the economy. For example, suppose that for the typical firm $w_i > w$—that is, unemployment is "too low." Firms then will try to beat the average wage in the market, something that they cannot do collectively. The result will be a continuous increase in real wages, as firms try to beat each other by offering more in real terms. Hence, if unemployment is below its "natural rate," money wages in the market as a whole will rise faster than prices. By a similar reasoning, money wages will rise more slowly than prices if unemployment is above its natural rate.

Thus, the natural rate of unemployment is the unique rate that solves (7.10) when $w_i = w$. Putting $w_i = w$ in equation (7.10), we obtain

$$ u = \frac{\alpha\beta}{\beta + (1 - \alpha)(1 - \beta)} \frac{1}{1 - b} . \tag{7.11} $$

Unemployment is higher when the share of capital is higher, the bargaining strength of labor is higher, and the replacement ratio is higher, all because they raise the wage rate and hence require higher unemployment to offset the gain to the workers. The model is consistent, in that the higher wage rate will induce firms to move down their labor demand curves, providing the higher unemployment. Thus, the way the model is solved now is by substituting u from equation (7.11) into (7.2) to obtain v, and then with knowledge of v and $n = \ell - u$, (7.4) gives the average wage rate. Equation (7.11) is our equation for equilibrium unemployment. We shall use it to examine first the effects of WIP and subsequently the effects of VAP.

WIP

The model of this paper is entirely in real terms, yet WIP consists primarily of a tax on nominal wage increases. However, there is a well-defined relationship between the tax on nominal wage increases and a tax on the real wage rate.

Consider two adjacent periods, τ and $\tau + 1$, for given nominal wage rate in $\tau - 1$, denoted $w'_{i\tau-1}$. WIP taxes nominal wage increases above a certain norm. Let the norm be π_0 and the rate at which the nominal wage increase is taxed be t'; t' may be quite a high rate—100 percent ($t' = 1$) or even higher. Then if the firm and its workers choose nominal wages $w'_{i\tau}$, $w'_{i\tau+1}$, the tax they pay in nominal terms is

$$\text{period } \tau \text{ tax } = t'(w'_{i\tau} - w'_{i\tau-1}(1 + \pi_0))$$

$$\text{period } \tau + 1 \text{ tax } = t'(w'_{i\tau+1} - w'_{i\tau}(1 + \pi_0))$$

Suppose now there is expected inflation in period τ of π and the real rate of interest is r. The firm that raises its nominal wage in period τ by a small amount has to pay tax now at the rate t', and receive a nominal benefit next period at the rate $t'(1 + \pi_0)$. But from the firm's point of view prices are given, so the nominal tax in τ is also a real tax, whereas nominal benefits next period should be discounted at the nominal rate of interest—that is, in the period analysis in this section, they should be divided by $(1 + r)(1 + \pi)$. A small increase in the wage in period τ, given the price level, leads to a net tax burden of

$$t' - t' \frac{1 + \pi_0}{(1 + r)(1 + \pi)}$$

Hence, the tax on nominal wage increases is equivalent to an implicit tax on real wages at the rate

$$t = t' \frac{r(1 + \pi) + \pi - \pi_0}{(1 + r)(1 + \pi)} \qquad (7.12)$$

If second-order effects are ignored, this formula simplifies to

$$t = t' \frac{r + \pi - \pi_0}{1 + r + \pi}$$

As an illustration, suppose $\pi = \pi_0$—that is, the norm is equal to expected inflation. Then the tax on real wages corresponding, say, to a 100 percent of inflation tax is a fraction $r/(1 + r)$, or if the real interest rate is small, it is approximately equal to the real rate. If, alternatively, π is high, say 10 percent, and the norm is fixed at 5 percent, the tax on real wages corresponding, say, to $r = .02$ and $t' = 1$ is $t = .06$. Two comments might be made in this connection. First, at the rates of inflation and real interest that have been experienced recently in Britain and the United States, the tax on real wages is approximately equal to the WIP tax rate multiplied by the real rate of interest plus the inflation target reduction $\pi - \pi_0$. Second, $r + \pi - \pi_0$ is likely to be quite small: For example it is doubtful whether a government could fix a norm much below the expected inflation rate. In view of this, the same effect on the real system as the one implied by a substantial WIP policy could be obtained at quite low taxes on real wages. For example, a payroll tax of 2 percent (such as the national insurance surcharge in Britain) would have the same effect on employment as a very substantial tax on nominal wage increases.

Of course, if WIP consisted only of a tax it is doubtful whether it would have beneficial effects on employment. Associated with the tax, however, there is a rebate in the form of an employment subsidy paid to the firm. The typical firm behaves as if it paid tax $tw_i n_i$ in real terms; under a full WIP scheme it would receive an implicit subsidy of an_i, and if there was budget balance and all firms were identical, $tw_i = a$ (see Layard 1982a). The employment subsidy a is not equal to the amount of subsidy that the firm actually receives under the scheme, just as the tax rate t is not what the firm actually pays. Both a and t are implicit rates that affect real behavior, given the structure of the WIP package. We have already derived the relationship between t and the WIP tax rate t'. We can derive a similar expression for the subsidy.

Let a' be the real subsidy that the firm actually receives. Then, the net transfer from the authorities to the typical firm in period τ, in real terms, is

$$a' - t'w_{i\tau} + t'w_{i\tau-1} \frac{1 + \pi_o}{1 + \pi}$$

If, ex post, all firms negotiate the same wage rate and there is no real wage growth, the net transfer to the typical firm under budget balance must be equal to zero. Hence, dropping the subscripts on w, a' must be equal to

$$a' = t'w \left(1 - \frac{1 + \pi_o}{1 + \pi}\right)$$

By making use of equation (7.12) we can express a' in terms of the implicit tax rate on the real wage rate,

$$a' = tw \frac{(1 + r)(\pi - \pi_o)}{r(1 + \pi) + \pi - \pi_o}$$

Hence, if $\pi \neq \pi_o$, the implicit subsidy that the firm uses in making its decisions is related to the actual payment a' by the formula

$$a = a' \frac{r(1 + \pi) + \pi - \pi_o}{(1 + r)(\pi - \pi_o)}$$

If $\pi = \pi_o$ then the authorities have no revenue, so there is no subsidy payment. But the firm still behaves as if there is a real subsidy, since from equation (7.12) we get that $t = t'r/(1 + r)$, so

$$a = wt' \frac{r}{1 + r} > 0$$

Thus, when there is a WIP in operation, the firm behaves as if there is a proportional tax on the real wage, and a lump-sum employment subsidy, both of which are positive even in the case where there is no money changing hands between the firm and the authorities. The reason for this is that the tax-subsidy transfers depend on wages in adjacent periods, and the firm discounts the future, whereas the money changing hands does not depend on the discount rate. In what follows, we shall work with the implicit real tax rate and subsidy t and a, as if these were the actual transfers. It is instructive to begin the analysis by considering the effects of taxes and subsidies without imposing budget balance and return to it at a later stage.

We return to equation (7.3) and add to the firm's profit the WIP taxes and subsidies

$$\Pi = q_i k n_i^{1-a} - n_i w_i (1 + t) + a n_i \qquad (7.13)$$

Hence the demand for labor now satisfies

$$(1 - \alpha) q_i k n_i^{-a} - w_i (1 + t) + a = 0 \qquad (7.14)$$

As before we shall need the expression

$$\frac{\partial n_i}{\partial w_i} \frac{1}{n_i} = - \frac{1 + t}{\alpha [w_i (1 + t) - a]} \qquad (7.15)$$

Also, profits at the optimum satisfy

$$\Pi = \frac{\alpha}{1 - \alpha} n_i [w_i (1 + t) - a] \qquad (7.16)$$

The workers' return is, as before, given by equation (7.7), and the objective function is (7.6), so maximizing now by taking into account (7.13) – (7.16) and going through the same substitutions as before, we obtain the new wage equation, corresponding to (7.10),

$$w_i = \frac{\beta + (1 - \alpha)(1 - \beta)}{1 - \alpha} (1 - u + ub)w - \frac{\alpha\beta}{1 - \alpha} \frac{a}{1 + t} \qquad (7.17)$$

Equation (7.17) suggests that for given w and if $a = 0$ (that is, if there is no subsidy) the tax is absorbed entirely by the firm. If $a > 0$, then the subsidy reduces wages, whereas the tax part of the policy increases them. These results may appear counterintuitive and indeed they should not be taken too seriously. The reasons for them are the high elasticity of labor demand with respect to wage changes, evident in equation (7.15), and the fact that a decrease in employment makes the workers worse off but has no effect on the firm's profits, by the envelope theorem. Thus, the results in equation (7.17) depend crucially on employment changes, and so unemployment should not be treated as constant when doing the comparative statics of the WIP instruments.

Consider therefore the equilibrium condition $w_i = w$, which gives unemployment. Imposing the condition in (7.17) we derive

$$u = \frac{\alpha\beta}{\beta + (1 - \alpha)(1 - \beta)} \frac{1}{1 - b} \left(1 - \frac{a}{w(1 + t)}\right) \qquad (7.18)$$

Thus, if $a = 0$, we have the same equation as before, (7.11). Unemployment is unaffected by the tax and so, from the labor demand equation (7.14), the wage tax must be passed on entirely to workers—that is, w falls by the full amount of the tax. By the assumption of a constant replacement ratio b, this has no effect on unemployment or vacancies; if the decrease in the wage raised the replacement ratio there would be a negative effect on unemployment (that is, unemployment would rise) (see also Pissarides 1985a). Thus, if there is any beneficial effect of the WIP package, it is from the subsidy that it is derived and not from the tax.

The subsidy reduces unemployment by increasing the demand for labor. In equilibrium wages will be higher and vacancies will also be higher as a result of the subsidy. Imposing the financing condition $tw = a$, we derive the unemployment equation

$$u = \frac{\alpha\beta}{\beta + (1 - \alpha)(1 - \beta)} \frac{1}{(1 - b)(1 + t)} \qquad (7.19)$$

Hence unemployment falls when t is positive. Imposing also budget balance on the demand for labor curve equation (7.14) we find that the higher employment requires a lower real wage. Also, from the u/v curve, equation (7.2), the lower unemployment brings about a higher vacancy rate.

Although one might be tempted to conclude from this that when a subsidy and a tax are combined the effect of the subsidy dominates, such an inference would be misleading. When there is bargaining over wages, the tax on wages has two effects. First, there is an average effect. By taxing away tw_i, the authorities reduce the firm's payoffs from a wage agreement by tw_i. Second, there is a marginal effect. When all the effects of wage changes during negotiations have been taken into account, the tax on wages introduces an extra effect that biases the outcome in favor of the firm: A small decrement to the wage saves the firm some tax, at no extra cost to the worker. This strengthens the firm's hand in the bargaining, giving it a slightly bigger share of the surplus. By contrast, the subsidy has only an average component. The introduction of the subsidy does not affect the relative payoffs from changes in the wage rate during negotiations, but it affects the firm's payoff from agreement by giving it an extra revenue an_i. Since the average component of the tax made the firm worse off by an amount $tw_i n_i$, under budget balance the average effects cancel each other out, leaving only the effect of the marginal tax rate on the equilibrium outcome. This helps to reduce wages by strengthening the firm's hand in bargaining, and so it increases vacancies and employment.

This discussion has ignored the effects of the WIP instruments on the elasticity of the demand for labor. Even if $\beta = 1$, when workers get the entire surplus from employment, WIP with budget balance reduces unemployment (see Jackman and Layard 1982a, b). The reason for this is that WIP changes also the elasticity of the demand for labor. An increase in the elasticity makes labor worse off in the bargain, leading to lower wages. As with the argument of the preceding paragraph, the tax has two effects on the elasticity, a marginal effect and an average effect. The marginal effect is shown in the elasticity expression in equation (7.15) by the inclusion of t in the numerator: This increases the elasticity. The average effect works through the term $w_i t$ in the denominator. This reduces the elasticity, and if $a = 0$ the two effects offset each other. But the subsidy also has an average effect that increases the elasticity. If $a = tw_i$ the two average effects offset each other, leaving the marginal effect of the tax as the only effect on the elasticity. This increases the elasticity, making the firm better off during bargaining and leading to a further reduction in the wage rate. This is the reason that the tax reduces unemployment even in the monopoly case $\beta = 1$. If we ignored the marginal effect of the tax on the elasticity of the demand for labor, the unemployment equation would be modified to

$$u = \frac{\alpha\beta}{\beta + (1 - \alpha)(1 - \beta)(1 + t)} \frac{1}{1 - b} \tag{7.20}$$

Then, the tax would work only in the case $\beta < 1$, when, because of the flexibility in β, the firm gets more of the surplus by becoming more aggressive in the bargaining process. The marginal effect of the tax on unemployment obtained from equation (7.20) is smaller than the effect obtained from equation (7.19) because both the elasticity effect and the sharing effect of the policy work in the same direction in (7-19).

VAP

Under VAP the authorities tax nominal value added. For reasons similar to those of WIP we can take the tax to be on the firm's relative price q_i. If we also assume budget balance—that is, assume that any revenue is returned to firms as an employment subsidy—there is also a subsidy side to the policy. Thus, if we denote the proportional tax rate by t, budget balance for the typical firm requires

$$t q_i k \, n_i^{1-a} = a n_i \tag{7.21}$$

As with the analysis of WIP, we return to the profit expression in equation (7.3) and add the tax and subsidy. Hence, the firm's profit becomes

$$\Pi = (1 - t)q_i k n_i^{1-a} - n_i w_i + a n_i \qquad (7.22)$$

The demand for labor now satisfies

$$(1 - \alpha)(1 - t)q_i k n_i^{-a} - (w_i - a) = 0 \qquad (7.23)$$

This demand satisfies

$$\frac{\partial n_i}{\partial w_i} \frac{1}{n_i} = - \frac{1}{v\alpha(w_i - a)} \qquad (7.24)$$

The firm's profits at the optimum point are given by

$$\Pi = \frac{\alpha}{1 - \alpha} \; n_i(w_i - a) \qquad (7.25)$$

Maximizing the objective function, equation (7.6), with respect to w_i by taking into account (7.7) and the new expressions for the firm, equations (7.22) – (7.25), we derive

$$w_i = \frac{\beta + (1 - \beta)(1 - \alpha)}{1 - \alpha} \; (1 - u + ub)w - \frac{\alpha\beta}{1 - \alpha} \; a \qquad (7.26)$$

Imposing the equilibrium condition $w_i = w$ and solving for u we obtain

$$u = \frac{\alpha\beta}{\beta + (1 - \alpha)(1 - \beta)} \; \frac{1}{1 - b} \left(1 - \frac{a}{w}\right) \qquad (7.27)$$

Comparing equation (7.27) with (7.18), we find that the difference between VAP and WIP is that the tax rate in VAP does not influence unemployment directly, even if there is a subsidy. The reason is that the tax rate in VAP has no effect on the sharing of the surplus from employment between the firm and the worker. The tax rate in VAP has only an average effect, and if $a = 0$, the equilibrium conditions are such that it is passed entirely on to wages. If we put $a = 0$ in (7.27) we get the same unemployment rate as without the policy, so the wage rate obtained from the labor demand curve is reduced by the full amount of the tax.

If there is a rebate of the revenue from the tax in the form of an employment subsidy, the equilibrium unemployment outcome will be affected. The ratio a/w in equation (7.27) may be expressed in terms of the parameters of the model and the tax rate by making use of budget balance (7.21) and the labor demand curve (7.23). Thus, substitute $q_i k n_i^{-a}$ from (7.21) into (7.23), to obtain

$$\frac{a}{w} = \frac{t}{1 - \alpha + \alpha t} \qquad (7.28)$$

Hence, substituting from (7.28) into (7.27) we obtain

$$u = \frac{\alpha\beta}{\beta + (1 - \alpha)(1 - \beta)} \frac{1}{1 - b} \frac{(1 - \alpha)(1 - t)}{1 - \alpha(1 - t)} \tag{7.29}$$

An increase in the tax, combined with a subsidy, reduces unemployment.

The effect of VAP under budget balance works entirely through the elasticity of the demand for labor. The tax itself does not influence the elasticity, as equation (7.24) makes clear. But the subsidy raises the elasticity, reducing the power of labor in the wage bargain. As a result, although the firm does not pay any tax ex post, the negotiated wage rate is reduced and employment is increased.

If the firm had some monopoly power in output markets the results would be the same, since it would not be negotiating price setting with labor. For as long as marginal wage adjustments do not influence the tax that the firm pays, other than through the accompanying employment adjustments, a combined tax-subsidy policy can influence the equilibrium unemployment outcome only through the elasticity of the demand for labor. If there is a marginal wage tax, there is a second channel through which the policy influences the outcome, the sharing rule that the firm and labor employ.

Because WIP works through two channels whereas VAP works only through one, it might be tempting to conclude that WIP has a bigger effect on unemployment than does VAP. However, this conclusion would be incorrect because WIP and VAP affect the elasticity of the demand for labor differently. VAP increases the elasticity by more than WIP, and this extra effect is strong enough to outweigh the second effect of WIP, making VAP a more effective policy.

Thus, from equation (7.15) it follows that WIP increases the elasticity of the demand for labor by a factor $(1/(1 - a/w(1 + t)))$. Equation (7.24) implies that VAP increases the elasticity by a factor $1/(1 - a/w)$, which is greater than the WIP factor in the neighborhood of equilibrium. The effect of this difference on unemployment is sufficiently great to offset the apparent advantage of WIP, which derives from its effect on the share of labor in the wage bargain. Thus, differentiating the WIP unemployment equation (7.19) with respect to t and evaluating at $t = 0$, we obtain

$$\frac{\partial u}{\partial t} = -u$$

Differentiating also the VAP unemployment equation (7.29) with respect to t and evaluating again at $t = 0$, we obtain

$$\frac{\partial u}{\partial t} = - \frac{u}{1 - \alpha}$$

Since $\alpha < 1$, VAP has a greater effect on unemployment than WIP.

CONCLUSIONS

The purpose of this paper has been the modest one of investigating the equilibrium effects of two anti-inflation plans, WIP and VAP. WIP taxes nominal wage
increases and uses the revenue to subsidize employment. VAP taxes value added
and also uses the revenue to subsidize employment. Since both policies alter the
incentives that firms and workers face we would expect them to have some
effects on equilibrium unemployment and real wages. Indeed both policies reduce equilibrium unemployment and equilibrium real wages, with VAP having
the bigger effect. VAP achieves this effect by increasing the elasticity with which
employment responds to changes in real wages. WIP also increases the wage elasticity of employment but by less; although WIP also makes firms stronger in the
wage bargain, the combined effect is not as big as the effect of VAP.

Of course, the equilibrium effects of WIP and VAP are not the only ones
through which the policies are supposed to work. If they were, the results of this
paper would be largely negative. Although the equilibrium effects work in the
"right" direction, they could also be achieved by modest taxes on real wages or
real value added, and modest employment subsidies. For example, at current
inflation rates a 100 percent tax rate on nominal wage increases would produce
the same effect as a 2 to 3 percent tax on real wages, when both are combined
with an employment subsidy. But if WIP and VAP have the desirable effects on
expectations, nominal inertia, and general adjustment processes that their proponents have advocated, our results in this paper indicate that they would also
have a favorable effect by reducing the "natural" rate of unemployment.

APPENDIX 7-A

In the text we considered an efficient wage bargain combined with a labor demand curve. Consider instead efficient wage and employment bargains—that is,
the objective function (7.6) is maximized with respect to both n_i and w_i, and
the demand function (7.4) does not constrain the maximization. Consider the
case of WIP, the one with VAP following easily.

The two maximization conditions are (for w_i and n_i respectively)

$$\beta\Pi - (1 - \beta)(1 + t)(U - U_o) = 0 \qquad (7.\text{A}1)$$

$$\beta\Pi + (1 - \beta)[(1 - \alpha)kn_i^{1-a} - n_i w_i(1 + t) + n_i a] = 0 \qquad (7.\text{A}2)$$

Equation (7.A2) and the profit expression for the WIP model imply

$$[\beta + (1 - \beta)(1 - \alpha)] kn_i^{-a} - w_i(1 + t) + a = 0 \qquad (7.\text{A}3)$$

Equation (7.A3) replaces the demand function (7.14). For $\beta = 0$ – that is, when firms act as pure monopsonists and maximize profits—we get (7.14), but for $\beta > 0$ the employment derived from (7.A3) is higher than that derived from (7.14) for given w_i: The efficient contract is to the right of the demand curve. For $\beta = 1$ unions act as monopolists so they choose employment subject to a zero-profit condition.

Substituting Π from (7.A2) into (7.A1), and $U - U_o$ from (7.7) into (7.A1), and making use of (7.A3), we derive

$$w_i = \frac{\beta + (1 - \alpha)(1 - \beta)}{1 - \alpha} \ (1 - u + bu)w - \frac{\alpha\beta}{1 - \alpha} \ \frac{a}{1 + t} \qquad (7.A4)$$

Thus, the wage equation is the same as in the model of the text, (7.17).

The interesting property of this model is that since the wage equation gives uniquely equilibrium unemployment, equilibrium unemployment in the two models is the same. Putting $w_i = w$ in equation (7.A4) we derive the WIP unemployment equation (7.18), and if there is budget balance we derive (7.19). But substituting unemployment into (7.A3) we derive a lower wage rate now. The effect of the efficient contract under macroconsistency conditions is to reduce the real wage but leave unemployment unchanged. One might speculate whether this is one of the reasons that trade unions do not bargain over employment. If they let firms manage as they wish, their members will end up with higher real incomes ex post.

8 ON THE THEORY OF INCENTIVE ANTI-INFLATION PLANS

David C. Colander

Elsewhere (Colander 1982, 1985a; Colander and Olson, 1984), I have stated in general terms the way in which I see incomes policies working. The central theme of my analysis of incentive anti-inflation plans has been that competition in our economic system is of a classical, not neoclassical, type, in which individuals are continually attempting to monopolize, cartelize, or otherwise restrict entry into their fields, only to have their monopolies, oligopolies, or cartels broken down by other competing coopolists. (Hereafter, to avoid stating "monopolies, cartels, and oligopolists," I use the terms *coopolists* and *coopoly*. I define *coopoly* as a coalition of individuals that is formally or informally organized to restrict entry and thereby increase its rent. I choose this term because it emphasizes the coalitional aspect of the approach and because all other terms, such as *monopoly, oligarchy,* or *cartel*, have been tainted by previous use.) In this paper I will briefly outline my understanding of how incentive anti-inflation plans work and relate it to the models presented in Chapters 5, 6, and 7 of this volume.

In this chapter I first discuss what I call the coopoly theory of pricing, which adds some intuition to the formal models presented in this volume; then I demonstrate how an incentive anti-inflation plan changes the costs of coopolizing and thereby changes the partial equilibrium of a market. Next I discuss why that result carries over to general equilibrium and how it has a stochastic interpretation. Finally, I relate my approach to the theoretical analyses of Koford and Miller (Chapter 5); Jackman and Layard (Chapter 6); and Pissarides (Chapter 7). My discussion will be less rigorous than theirs and is designed to provide the intuition needed to interpret those formal models.

THE COOPOLY MODEL

In its most abstract form the coopoly theory of pricing outlined in this chapter is exceedingly general and can be adapted to describe a wide variety of market structures, including monopoly, all forms of oligopoly, and perfect competition.[1] It assumes all individuals to be wealth maximizers and has all the same assumptions of the competitive model except that market structure (degree of coopoly) is endogenous and is chosen by profit-maximizing individuals. The general model has an infinite number of possible outcomes; by incorporating assumptions that reflect the technology and political and institutional realities of western economies, a stylized model can be designed that arrives at a unique equilibrium. Combined, these assumptions provide a stylized model that corresponds to many sectors of our economy, in my view far better than does the traditional competitive stylized model.

A key institutional reality of our economy is that it is easier for suppliers than for demanders to organize into a coopoly. This means that if the economy has a bias, it is toward supplier, not demander, coopoly. Any model of incomes policy that is to show a positive effect of incomes policies must incorporate this institutional reality, for it is this institutional reality that an incomes policy is designed to correct, since the purpose of an incomes policy is to reduce the level of coopoly in the system. There are numerous ways to incorporate supplier dominance in a model, but the most tractable way to capture this reality is to avoid problems of bilateral coopoly by assuming that demanders operate as price takers.[2] Given this assumption, the problem facing the supplier coopolist is similar to that facing a monopolist—to maximize profits subject to a given demand curve.

The textbook approach to analyzing the pricing and output decisions of firms is to separate factor and product markets and analyze each market separately. This is unfortunate. It is unnecessarily messy; it presents analytical difficulties and leads to a variety of results that are not consistent with reality. To avoid such problems it is much neater to combine the factor markets and product markets rather than analyze them separately. To do so one merely assumes that production results from a coalition of suppliers; how the suppliers in fact divy up the proceeds need not be addressed.[3] If one follows this route, one has a one-factor model with no separate factor and goods markets, and the "costs of production" are merely the intermediate inputs of other coopolists. Thus the model avoids any issues concerning distributional fights between profits and wages and eliminates too high a real wage as the cause of unemployment.

The intuition of the model is the following: Suppliers coopolize until the marginal costs of coopolizing equal the marginal benefits. The major difference between this model and the traditional model is that in this model, the degree of coopoly is determined endogenously to the model; in the mainstream model, market structure must be imposed by assumption. Because of this difference, assumptions must be made about the costs and benefits of coopolizing because these costs determine the degree of monopoly in the system. To save space, I list them without comment:

1. All producers are assumed to have constant costs of production, so that production costs are independent of the market structure.
2. In the absence of any artificially imposed barrier, individuals are assumed to face a zero cost of entry.
3. The costs of restricting entry begin at zero and rise at an increasing rate.

These assumptions are sufficient to determine an equilibrium of such an economy. In this chapter I consider the nature of the equilibrium that is arrived at in a model with the above characteristics and how an incomes policy can change that equilibrium.

THE COSTS AND BENEFITS OF COOPOLIZING

The set of assumptions listed above is, by design, similar to those of the standard model except that the degree of coopoly in the system is indeterminant. That amount of coopoly depends on the cost and benefit of coopolizing.

The benefits are assumed equal for all suppliers and can be seen in the standard monopolist model shown in Figure 8-1. In the absence of any coopolistic behavior, price would equal cost (P_o), and coopolists' profits would be zero. The benefit for excluding $n - a$ individuals' production is determined by the marginal revenue gained, plus the gain of having to divide the "profits" among only a individuals, where n is the number of suppliers in the perfectly competitive coalition. The former is measured by the distance between the marginal cost curve and the marginal revenue curve, and the latter (the gain from the reduction in the number) is given by the distance between the marginal revenue curve and a curve parallel to the demand curve. Thus in Figure 8-1 the marginal gain to a individuals of excluding $n - a$ individuals is $r_1 + r_2$.

The cost of the coopolization function is determined by the cost of maintaining that coopoly in a steady state equilibrium. If these costs equal the gain from the reduction, the model reduces to the standard monopoly model. If these costs are zero, production approaches zero; if these costs are sufficiently large, no coopoly will occur and perfectly competitive situations will result. These are, however, polar cases. In the standard case the costs are rising with reductions in output. To determine the net marginal revenue, these costs must be subtracted from the benefits. Doing so in Figure 8-2 we derive the net marginal revenue curve (NMR_1). Production is determined where the net marginal revenue equals the marginal cost of production. This situation is graphed in Figure 8-2; equilibrium output is q^1 and equilibrium price is p^1.

Figure 8-1. The Benefit of Coopolizing.

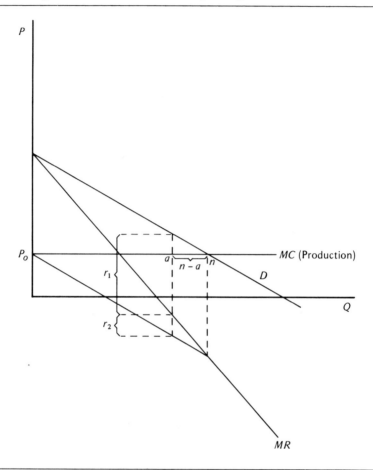

At this output, the coalition a has excluded $n - a$ other participants from the market. Profits are possible in equilibrium because of the assumed differential costs of coopolizing.

INCENTIVE ANTI-INFLATION PLANS
AND AN INDIVIDUAL MARKET

The coopoly model of pricing provides a quite different view of equilibrium in a market, a view in which the market structure or degree of coopoly reflects the underlying costs of coopolizing. It also provides a different view of the way in which an incomes policy works and how an incomes policy can affect the struc-

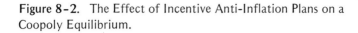

Figure 8-2. The Effect of Incentive Anti-Inflation Plans on a Coopoly Equilibrium.

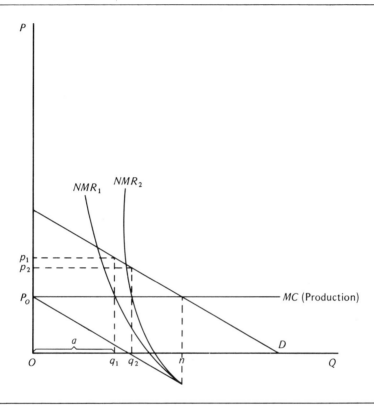

tural bias toward supplier coopoly. An incomes policy operates by changing market structure and making the market more competitive. We can see this by considering how an incomes policy affects the cost of coopolizing. Incentive anti-inflation plans raise the cost of coopolizing and thereby unambiguously lower price and raise output. The plans tax the process of coopolizing and require coopolies to make a payment when they raise price. In so doing they shift up the marginal cost of coopolizing or raising price. In Figure 8-2 we can see this effect; the incomes policy shifts up the net marginal revenue curve to NMR_2 which includes the cost of raising price (subsidy to lowering price). The new equilibrium output is $q^2 > q^1$ and the new equilibrium price is $p^2 < p^1$. Thus in this model an incomes policy unambiguously raises output on lower price.

An intuitive sense of how the plans work can be gained by considering a market which is initially in equilibrium; firms have settled on their relative pricing structure within the industry wage strategy. Now the incentive anti-inflation plan is instituted, and the choices facing the firm change: The high price strategy becomes less desirable and the low price strategy becomes more desirable. Many firms will not respond, but one starts pushing for additional volume and is willing to accept a lower profit per unit output, calculating that with the revenue the plan provides it for lowering price, it can increase its profit by breaking ranks with the oligopoly. It simultaneously has an incentive to be more aggressive in holding down wages. If the other firms do not immediately follow, they will lose sales, and so what was a profitable strategy will no longer be. Eventually they also will be forced to take the low price strategy. As they do, the first firm will be under strong pressure to be even more aggressive in its pricing and wage policy. The cumulative force of these changes restructures the industry much as Freddy Laker and deregulation restructured the airline industry.

STOCHASTIC EQUILIBRIUM

The above discussion and model has two problems for discussions of incomes policies; it is a partial equilibrium, static model. The model becomes far more realistic when given a stochastic interpretation. The normal supply/demand model can be given a stochastic interpretation by recognizing that even at equilibrium in a stochastic world, some demanders and some suppliers will not conclude a trade. Stochastic equilibrium concerns a relationship between excess supplies and demands. Since some excess supply and demand will always exist, the quantities actually traded will always be less than the smaller of the quantity supplied and demanded. Figure 8-3 demonstrates a stochastic model.

The EE line measures the quantity actually traded at given prices; for example, at price p_1, excess demand is x_1 and excess supply is x_2. A stochastic supply/demand equilibrium obtains when upward pressure on price from excess supply equals the downward pressure on price from excess demand. Following the standard dynamic price adjustment assumptions, equilibrium obtains at price p_o and quantity q_o. (See Colander 1986.) At higher prices, excess demands increase and excess supplies decrease; at lower prices excess supply decreases and excess demand increases.

The coopoly model can be given a dynamic interpretation by incorporating the static model of coopoly with the stochastic interpretation. Equilibrium is determined as before where the dynamic pressures on price affect each other; the difference is that it does not obtain at p_o; it obtains at p_1 where excess supply is significantly above excess demand. In the labor market, the excess supply represents job searchers and in the goods market, it represents potential producers who are not producing; excess demand represents job vacancies and potential consumers who cannot find the product.

Looking again at the intuitive example described above, say at the initial equilibrium, most firms felt that if they could increase sales they could increase profits. Thus they were devoting significant efforts to advertising and sales. Simi-

Figure 8-3. Dynamic Equilibrium.

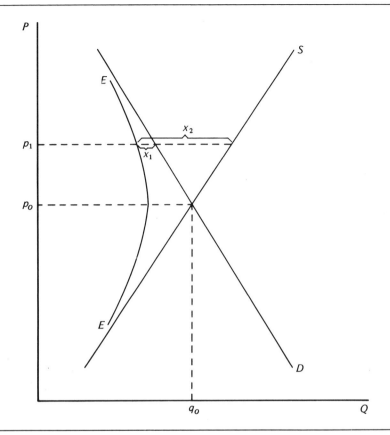

larly, workers were queuing for jobs, and although there was some turnover, new jobs usually went to friends or relatives of people who knew about them. After the plan's introduction, the industry's relative price will fall; excess supply of the good will be less, and it will be less advantageous for the firms to advertise. Similarly, as the relative wage falls, the queue will decrease, and being in the know will be less important since many firms are hiring.

GENERAL STOCHASTIC EQUILIBRIUM

Before the analysis can be applied to incomes policies, one further step must be taken; an incomes policy is designed to control the general price level, not relative prices, and thus the analysis must be applied to the general price level, not to relative prices. The above model was a partial equilibrium model and hence is concerned with relative prices and misallocated, not necessarily unemployed, resources. Monopoly merely causes people to move into unmonopolized sectors. Equally generalized monopoly does not distort resource allocation. If one non-monopolized activity existed (such as selling apples on a street corner), all "excess supply" would gravitate to that activity.

The non-monopolized activity that all equilibrium unemployment models allow is searching and waiting for a job. If that is the single non-monopolized sector, the partial equilibrium results can be transferred to general equilibrium and incomes policies. When individuals are shut out of the generalized market monopoly, they enter nonmarket activities; the choice of these nonmarket activities depends on the relative price of nonmarket activities. Unemployment insurance lowers the relative price of nonmarket activities (it subsidizes the activity of being unemployed; taxes on market activity also do, as do the restrictive barriers set up by seller coopolies). Thus, coopolies increase the level of equilibrium unemployment and excess supply, making the NAIRU higher than the natural rate. Given current institutions, that excess supply cannot be permanently reduced by expansionary aggregate demand policy because that excess supply provides potential competition and its existence is necessary to prevent the change in the price level from accelerating.

By assuming that the above captures a stochastic process where in each time period some portion of the coopoly is breaking down and must be built up again, it can be easily seen how this model can be integrated with the Phelps Island model, increasing the level of unemployed resources in equilibrium. Elsewhere (Colander 1985a) I have argued that the coopolization process determines a NAIRU equilibrium rather than a natural rate equilibrium. An incentive based incomes policy operates by reducing the amount of equilibrium coopoly in the economy. It decreases the equilibrium ratio of excess supply to excess demand, thereby moving the NAIRU closer to the FERU.

Once again the intuition carries through, only this time the same story is told of what happens among industries, not what happens within an industry. As one industry becomes more competitive, other industries are forced to follow suit or lose sales. As they do follow suit, there is less upward pressure on the price level and less unemployment and excess supply in steady state equilibrium.

INCOMES POLICIES, THE REAL WAGE, AND THE REAL PRICE

Previous discussions of incomes policies have always seemed to focus on *wage* income—almost as if there were no other income except wages. For example, Sidney Weintraub's wage-cost markup theory and Layard's and Jackman's theory (Chapter 6) require the real wage to fall to increase employment. The model discussed in this chapter is closer in spirit to that of Koford and Miller (Chapter 5).

It is not the wage that is too high; it is the real price – the price of all market activities vis-à-vis nonmarket activities that include waiting and searching. Thus, in my model, unlike the Jackman and Layard model, the real price, not the real wage, is too high. One way of lowering the real price is to lower the nominal wage, but that is not the only way.

To argue that the real price is too high is not to say that the price level divided by the price level is too high; that is always unity. In an equilibrium unemployment model, however, there are at least three prices: the price of search and waiting (unemployment); the price of capital or entrepreneurship; and the wage or the price of labor. In a dynamic model, to say that the real wage is too high is ambiguous: Is it the wage relative to the price of capital, or is it the wage relative to price of searching (the reservation wages)? To say the real price is too high is not ambiguous. It simply states that the combination wage and price of capital is too high relative to the reservation price. The reservation price – the price of searching and waiting – is a shadow price, since these are nonmarket activities and do not enter into the determination of the price level and hence the concept "real price" is meaningful.

RELATION OF THE COOPOLY MODEL
TO OTHER PAPERS

The above whirlwind overview was not meant to be self-standing; it was meant to justify and provide interpretations of the formal models of Layard and Jackman, Pissarides, and Koford and Miller. The Layard and Jackman and Pissarides models need interpretation because both analog the plans with a tax on wages or value added with the proceeds used as a subsidy for employment. Their models have no inflation. In those models it is unclear why a direct tax of wages and subsidy for employment are not equally good as incentive anti-inflation policies. My discussion provides an answer.

The higher than optimal NAIRU is caused by monopolization, and the natural method of dealing with it is by taxing the process of monopolization. That is precisely what TIP and MAP do. In the Layard and Jackman and Pissarides models, the gain comes from the subsidization of employment; the wage tax merely provides the revenue to finance that subsidy.

TIP and MAP work differently; they do not directly subsidize employment. They subsidize lowering prices. Those lower prices increase the quantity demanded, requiring increased employment of capital and labor. Thus the results of the subsidy are the same, but the process is different. The difference between the way the policy works in the Jackman and Layard and Pissarides models, and the way I see it working, comes on the revenue generating side. In their models, the tax on wages or value added has no positive effect; in my model the tax on wage increases, or value added increases, directly affects the net marginal revenue function, increasing employment as coopolies increase prices.

A second role of the intuitive discussion is to suggest that the results of the partial equilibrium static analysis carry over to an economywide stochastic model. Thus it attempts to answer the criticism of the Koford-Miller chapter that it does not consider dynamics. The argument in their chapter is that monopoly can be reduced by MAP. Whereas monopoly is merely imposed from the outside in their model, in this model it is the steady-state result of a dynamic process.

To relate the above analysis to the actual practice of incomes policies and the other chapters in the volume, a few final comments are in order. First, my discussion is in terms of excess supply and demand in a composite market. In the labor market excess supply and demand relate directly to vacancies and unemployment, but not in a monotonous manner. Second, the model parallels the Pissarides model; the incomes policy works, not by affecting the real wage, and hence the degree of monopoly in the labor market relative to the goods market, as it is normally conceived, but by reducing the generalized degree of monopoly in the economy.

CONCLUSION

To say that an incomes policy works by making it more difficult to monopolize and easier to break down monopolies is an entirely new way to look at incomes policies. Looking at incomes policies this new way provides much more insight into their possible workings than previous analyses do. While this paper has only touched on some of the implications, it has, I hope, stimulated sufficient interest to encourage others to develop more formal models of the process.

NOTES TO CHAPTER 8

1. The coopoly model described here is not rigorously developed. It is a game theoretic concept, and full specifications of the model are exceedingly complicated. However, the intuition behind the model is strong, and it is that intuition that is currently lacking in most considerations of incomes policies.
2. This assumption clearly is not true for all markets, but it can be modified without changing the qualitative results of analysis. Those modifications would, however, make the analysis far more difficult and ambiguous.
3. When the internal distributional question is separated from the pricing question, the analysis is left at a very general level. For instance, it is generally agreed that corporation decisions are poorly captured by models of profit maximizing firms. By avoiding the distributional question, the coopoly model can be applied to all firm structures.

III ADMINISTRATIVE FEASIBILITY

9 IS TIP ADMINISTRATIVELY FEASIBLE?

Richard Jackman
Richard Layard

In Chapter 6, we argued that there was a sound economic case for TIP. For it to be good policy, it must also be administratively feasible. We believe that a fair and workable program can be designed, and in this chapter we outline a scheme that has been fairly fully discussed in Britain.[1] Having outlined it, we shall discuss some of its problems, concluding that the costs are worth the candle.

THE TAX BASE

For the tax to be workable, the tax base must not be too subtle. Previous schemes have in part foundered on the rock of subtlety.[2] We therefore propose no allowance for changes in the occupational or age structure of the work force. But some subtlety is needed. It is no good taxing firms on their basic rates of pay, since they will simply put more pay into bonuses. The tax must be on average earnings. And we must take into account the firm's hours per worker, making hourly earnings the tax base. If instead we used earnings per worker, we should penalize an employer who increased overtime and provide an incentive for employers to dilute their tax base by hiring many very part-time workers—perhaps some who did practically no work at all.

EARNINGS

Earnings would be defined as for income tax purposes, so that they would be exactly the same as the base for which the employer deducts income tax at source (pay as you earn—PAYE). This includes whatever fringe benefits are

141

included in income tax. It excludes employers' contributions to superannuation funds, as well as employers' social security contributions. Either none or both of these would have to be included, and to include both would lead to cries of double taxation.

HOURS

The main problem with the tax base would therefore be the measurement of hours. For the 90 percent (or so) of workers whose pay is time-related there is no major difficulty. Hours would be hours worked (clock hours), since it is total earnings per hour worked that affects labor costs. For workers whose pay is time-related, hours worked are recorded by nearly all firms. This applies to piece-workers as well as workers on straight-time rates.

The next category of workers is those with contractual hours that are fixed. Here the main variation of hours worked comes through sickness, absence, and changes in holidays. Sickness (and other) paid absence could be disregarded. Firms could be asked to attribute to a worker in each quarter one-quarter of the annual hours he would work if he had his full quota of holidays and no sickness or other absence.

Finally there are workers with no contractual hours—above all, salesmen, but also many managers, academics, and so on. Here the employer could be asked to put in whatever approximate figure she considered most appropriate. The exact figure would not matter greatly, provided it were not arbitrarily altered from year to year.[3]

To monitor what was happening, firms would be required to submit with their tax checks a statement of earnings, number of employees, and assessed hours, separately for the three categories of employee. An increase in contractual hours for nontime-paid staff would be possible only if a satisfactory explanation was provided by the firm. For hourly paid workers, a firm that greatly increased its hours per worker would be a likely candidate for audit.

METHOD OF COLLECTION

It is very desirable that the tax be paid quickly after the corresponding wage payment. The tax would therefore be paid quarterly and self-assessed by the firm (as in the case with the firm's payment of PAYE and social security contributions). The firm would send a tax check quarterly to the relevant computer center. It would be subject to spot audits at one week's notice (as with PAYE and social security contributions). At present in Britain the audit of the whole PAYE and social security contributions at the firm's end requires fewer than 500 inspectors, and so there is no reason why the audit of the TIP should require more than 100 or so. Apart from a small amount of additional work at the two computer centers and the cost of designing the tax, this would be all the additional administrative cost to the government.

COVERAGE

To reduce the collection costs, the tax should be confined to companies employing more than 100 workers. In Britain, this would mean that fewer than 20,000 companies were involved, compared with nearly a million pay-points for PAYE. This would save greatly on administrative cost both to government and to firms. Most of the firms affected have computerized payrolls and record the clock hours of their hourly paid workers in a mechanical fashion. Moreover, in large firms cheating is less likely both because firms value their reputations and because the manager who cheated would be less likely to gain personally from the firm's cheating.

One might think at first blush that if small firms were exempt this would lead to everyone wanting to become a small firm. But this would not happen provided that whatever subsidy was paid out applied only to firms that were liable for the inflation tax.

STRUCTURE OF THE TAX

Because the effective tax rate is (in a permanent scheme) δt, the tax rate (t) would have to be quite high—say, 100 percent. The alternative is to have the tax liability relating to a fixed base. For example, one could say that until further notice the tax will be levied on the excess of wages over their level when the tax was first announced. At some point the base would have to be changed, but if this was done in an unpredictable way, it would discourage firms from thinking that they could derive any future tax benefit from a current wage increase. However, a fixed-base procedure would after a time heavily penalize firms that had upgraded their skill level.[4] So it could be followed for only a few years—at most the duration of a Parliament. We are doubtful whether this would be desirable, and favor a tax on annual wage growth levied at a high tax rate, of at least 100 percent.

This assumes that, as is desirable, the tax is not allowable against the corporation tax.[5] (If it were allowable, its impact would be very different on firms that do and do not pay corporation tax.)

The growth of hourly earnings would be calculated over the corresponding quarter in the previous year. This would ensure that a firm's tax liability was similar in each quarter of the year, rather than being concentrated in the quarters when settlements come into force.

We have assumed that there is a negative range of tax. Firms that pay below the norm pay negative tax. Otherwise the tax penalizes those firms where wages grow in jumps relative to those with the same long-run wage growth but having a steadier growth path.[6] However, a negative tax could lead to complaints from workers that their firms were being rewarded for underpaying them. These costs may be worth accepting.

It is important that the rate of subsidy is not changed too often. For, although we have (for analytical purposes) insisted that the scheme should be revenue-neutral, this can lead to confusion in the public mind. People tend to argue that if it is revenue-neutral it can have no effect. This is of course the same as saying that if we increase the tax on smoking and decrease general taxes by an equivalent amount, this can have no effect on smoking. But in view of the misunderstanding, which would be certain to continue, we think that there should be no automatic adjustment of business taxation. Instead the government should, when it announces a TIP, announce that it does not intend to allow this to lead to an increase in business taxation. Discretionary subsidy rates would be used to ensure this. The subsidy could either be treated as part of the tax scheme or be administered through a cut in social security contributions.

IDENTITY OF FIRMS

The tax would be levied on each firm taken as a whole.[7] There are obviously problems connected with mergers and disintegration of firms, but these can be handled provided it is understood that wherever there has been continuous economic activity that activity is deemed to have a past. Thus with a merger, the present firm would be treated as if in the previous year it had consisted of its component firms. And if a firm disintegrated, its present constituents would be treated as if they were a single firm. (The allocation of liability would be a required topic in a disintegration agreement.)

PUBLIC SECTOR

An obvious problem is whether it makes sense for the public sector to tax itself. In a country like Britain it does not (except for the taxation of nationalized industries). Some people have implied that this gravely weakens the whole scheme. But this is based on a misunderstanding of the economics of unemployment. The function of unemployment is to make decentralized wage-setters set the same wages that they expect others to set. TIP reduces the unemployment needed to make them do that. If it does not alter the way in which public sector wages are set, this does not matter. For public sector wages are fundamentally determined (in Britain at least) by comparability with the private sector. This could be reinforced by more explicit formalization. For example there could be a presumption that public sector workers get the norm plus a catch-up equal to the difference between the last year's private sector pay growth and last year's norm.[8] In this way average pay in government and the private sector would grow in line.[9] In the nationalized industries the tax might have an additional effect through the incentive that it provided to employers to resist wage increases (just as in the private sector). This incentive would obviously not hold if it were known that the industry's government-determined "external financing limit" would be increased to pay the tax, and doubtless this would sometimes occur. Thus it may be that the tax would have little direct effect on miners' pay. But it would profoundly affect most of the public sector through comparability.

THE INTRODUCTION OF THE TAX

Of course a key issue is how the tax is introduced, for this will have a big effect on its credibility. For technical reasons the tax could not come into force on the day it was announced as it is a tax on wage growth and can only be levied once firms have been collecting data on appropriately defined wage payments for at least a year. This suggests the following strategy. A government would simultaneously announce a conventional incomes policy (for instance, a percentage limit on wage settlements) to last for perhaps eighteen months plus the fact that after eighteen months it would be replaced by a TIP. When the eighteen months were up, the public would welcome the greater flexibility to adjust differentials and redress anomalies that the TIP permitted. But they would also think of the TIP as a modification of a more familiar type of incomes policy, which would add to the credibility of the tax.

THE EFFICIENCY COSTS OF THE SCHEME

The scheme we have outlined is of course crude. It would therefore have significant efficiency costs that would be justified only if they were (as we believe) outweighed by the benefits of substantially higher employment.

The first problem is that the scheme would damp down the adjustment of relativities in the economy. There are of course a lot of pointless changes in relativities that occur under present arrangements and that get unwound within a few years. If the existence of a norm were to discourage this, it would be all to the good. But there are other changes in relativities that are necessary to the efficient functioning of the economy and that will be discouraged by the tax.

1. Some firms need to increase their relative wages to attract more labor. This is the biggest problem. But firms need to increase relative wages to attract labor only when there is reasonably full employment. And in this case the full employment itself is a major benefit to be set against the efficiency cost of the tax on adjustment.

2. Firms use increases in relative pay as bribes to induce improved working practices (productivity agreements). Such deals are important, but there is no

way of exempting them from the tax without opening up an unpluggable breach in the dyke. We would simply point out that the tax is paid only in the year of the wage improvement. If productivity deals are discouraged, this again is a cost worth bearing.

3. A firm with higher than average productivity growth (not due to better working practices) may wish to share the gains with its work force. The tax will discourage this, and as a result of it workers in this firm will get lower real wages than otherwise (though some relative improvement), and the firm will get lower after-tax profit (because it has given a relative wage increase).

This does not seem to us a major problem, unless it affects the allocation of resources by reducing recruitment, as in 1. If the firm has no need to raise its relative wage, one could argue that in the absence of the tax the efficient thing (from the whole economy point of view) would have been for the firm to reduce its price. That is certainly what does happen in the long-run in the economy, when some industries have more rapid productivity growth than others. By and large, wages grow at the same rate in all industries (due to labor mobility between industries), and prices in the high-productivity growth industries fall relative to prices elsewhere. In the short-run, of course we often see a rise in wages in the high-productivity growth sectors, to attract more labor where this is necessary, and a rise in profits that has the effect of drawing in capital. But in this case we are back to the problem under 1.

There is also of course a problem of motivation and morale. If value added per worker rises, workers reasonably expect a fair share of the increase. However, the tax does not prevent firms choosing to share out the reduced cake (value-added net of tax) in the same proportions that they would have chosen in the absence of the tax.

There are other possible distortions that might be induced by TIP and do not concern the adjustment of differentials. A firm can escape the tax by increasing the proportion of unskilled workers in its work force. For example, if an individual is paid W_i and the firm's average wage is W, the firm can reduce its tax by $(W - W_i)$ times the tax rate by hiring him.[10] Thus in terms of its annual value, the proportional subsidy to employing an unskilled worker is $\delta t (W - W_i)/W_i$ where t is the tax rate and δ the real discount rate per annum (since the tax is paid for a year only). For a 100 percent tax rate and a 5 percent discount rate, the subsidy is about 1½ percent, which is not a major distortion. Many people would in fact say it was desirable, in order to offset the rigidity of relative wages.

Another response a firm might make would be to subcontract some of its skilled work to former employees becoming self-employed and forming small partnerships. Again the subsidy to disemploying a skilled worker is approximately $\delta t (W_i - W)/W_i$—not an enormous subsidy.

Our conclusion is that there are significant costs. But the benefits (of at least 2 percent higher level of GDP) are of a different order of magnitude.

THE PROBLEM OF FAIRNESS

There is also the problem of fairness that we began with. The scheme we have proposed can be attacked as being unfair from two sides. Firms can complain that the tax is levied on them and not on workers, who are "responsible for inflation." On the other side, workers can complain that the tax relates only to wages and not profits. Let us face them in turn.

The tax is paid by firms rather than workers, for three reasons. First, it is politically difficult to tax workers. Second, employees could not be taxed on the basis of their own personal increases in earnings, since this would make it impossible to operate incremental scales and would discourage job mobility and promotion effort. So an employee tax would have to be levied on the basis of increases in group earnings, which would lead to endless arguments about what group an individual belonged to. The only possible definition would be all workers employed by a particular firm. But some workers would then have a legitimate grievance if they were taxed because of extra increases given to other workers in the firm or because of an improvement in the skill distribution of the firm's workforce. Third, and most important, in many quite plausible models of unemployment the employment effects of a TIP levied on workers is not the same as of a TIP levied on firms, especially if, as often happens, unemployment benefit is adjusted to maintain the ratio of benefit to net income in work.[11]

Turning to the treatment of capital income, the prime reason for taxing wages only is that more employment requires lower real wages. But it might be necessary for cosmetic reasons to make some attempt to tax the growth in capital income. Administratively the simplest thing would be to operate a tax on increases in dividends, levied on firms. There could be the same norm for dividend increases, and the same tax rate on increases above the norm. There would also of course have to be a share-out of the tax proceeds, which would be done via reduced social security contributions for firms. An alternative, even more cosmetic, device is a price commission with power to strike down price increases on a selective basis – the power being rarely exercised.

But, whatever is done on that front, the main selling point for TIP is what it will do for employment, and thus for labor. We have to continue sressing this until we are blue in the face.

NOTES TO CHAPTER 9

1. See in particular report of the Liberal/SDP Commission on Unemployment and Industrial Recovery, *Back to Work* (1982), which provided the basis for the Liberal/SDP Alliance adoption of the inflation tax as a part of its economic policy.

2. The French prélèvement conjoncturel, which lasted for eight months in 1975, was an employer tax on the excess growth of value added per unit of factor input above a norm. There are obvious difficulties in the calculation of factor input and obvious planning problems for the firm, since *real* value added per unit of input is sensitive to unpredictable demand factors.

3. To exclude workers working a small number of hours it might be wise to exclude from the measurement of earnings and hours all workers not liable for National Insurance contributions.

4. It would also add to the complexity of taxing "new" firms.

5. Precedents include the petroleum revenue tax and the windfall profits tax on banks.

6. The same would be true of a tax levied at an increasing marginal rate.

7. Companies would be defined as for the corporation tax.

8. This formula could be modified to allow extra increases for government employees whose occupations were in shortage or whose comparator groups had grown faster than the private sector average. Any extra payments of this type would of course be deducted when calculating the catch-up.

9. This is so only if inflation is stable. Rising inflation would hurt public sector workers and vice versa, since in the long-run public and private sector pay grow at the same rate.

10. Let N be the number of workers, t the tax rate, and W_{-1} last year's average wage adjusted for the norm. The firm's tax liability if the worker is not hired is $t(W - W_{-1})N$, and if the worker *is* hired it is $t(WN + W_i - W_{-1} (N + 1))$. The difference is $t(W_i - W_{-1})$. Presumably W_{-1} is approximately the same as W.

11. In the union wage-setting models in Chapter 6, the real effects are independent of which side of the market is taxed, but this is not so of the firms' wage-setting models.

10 DESIGN OF A MARKET ANTI-INFLATION PROGRAM

William Vickrey

DIFFICULTIES WITH SPECIFIC PRICE CONTROLS

Direct price and wage controls, such as have often been used in wartime, tend to be unsatisfactory as semipermanent measures for use under more normal circumstances. In wartime a certain amount of patriotically motivated cooperation is available that tends to be lacking in peace time. If the duration is generally expected to be short, there is less time for prices based on historic patterns to get badly out of line, and the rate of introduction of new products that cause difficulty is less. Where specific items become scarce, rationing can be resorted to.

For use as a long-term peace-time measure, historically based price controls tend to become more and more inappropriate, requiring constant administrative adjustment that is likely to be slow and inaccurate. New products are introduced with a frequency considerably enhanced by attempts to use spurious novelty as a means of defeating the price controls. Any attempt to prevail over these obstacles would require a vast, expensive, and cumbersome bureaucracy. And most important politically, the whole project is likely to be opposed by labor representatives who fear with some justification that wage and price controls would turn out to be considerably more effective in controlling wages than in controlling prices.

Attempts to avoid the bureaucracy by resort to guidelines, exhortation, and "jawboning" have proven to have little effectiveness, except possibly as a short-term expedient. Specific wage and price controls would seem to have little to offer as a long-term solution to the problem of persistent inflationary pressure.

TAX INCENTIVE PLANS (TIPs)

Many proposals have been advanced for applying anti-inflationary pressure in the form of credits or surcharges on existing taxes. These plans also suffer from the difficulty of evaluating a measure of price change that can be used to determine the surcharge or credit. In addition, in many cases they operate somewhat capriciously, depending as they generally do on the existence of a liability for the tax. This is especially true of those TIPs that are based on the corporation income tax, as a fairly large number of corporations will have no net income and no tax liability for any given year. It is of course possible to circumvent this difficulty to some extent by the use of a "refundable" tax credit.

There is a further difficulty not often emphasized, which is that in adding yet another special provision to a tax law already riddled with special provisions it is difficult to predict how the new TIP will interact with these other provisions in various combinations. Ten special provisions can interact in $2^{10} = 1,024$ possible combinations. Tax lawyers and accountants can be relied on to take advantage of these interactions to produce strange and wonderful results not at all consonant with the basic purpose of the TIP. As an example, when charitable gifts of appreciated property were allowed to be deducted at current value rather than at cost, tax practitioners worked out schemes for giving just the gain rather than the entire property, so that frequently the taxpayer came out better off than if he had sold the property and kept the proceeds. It is almost impossible to predict the outcome of adding a new proviso to the tax code.

Finally, a TIP, being basically a tax measure, must, in the United States, be embodied in legislation that is constitutionally required to originate in the House of Representatives and work its tedious way through the Ways and Means Committee, the House, the Senate Finance Committee, the Senate, the House, the Conference Committee, the House again, the Senate again, and finally the White House. As conditions change, the lags between the perception of the need for a change in the rates of the TIP and the effective enactment of the change are likely to be excessively large, even under a speeded up procedure such as was characteristic of the early days of the New Deal.

While in principle it would be possible for the Congress to delegate to the executive branch the authority to adjust the rates in the TIP according to current conditions, much as the Federal Reserve System has enjoyed the power to adjust the rediscount rate, the Congress and especially the House have in the past shown themselves exceedingly jealous of their constitutional prerogative in this matter and are unlikely to assent to such a delegation of authority, even assuming that the Supreme Court would declare such a delegation to be allowable under the Constitution. On the whole the prospects for a workable and effective TIP plan along the lines so far explored appear to be exceedingly slim.

THE CONCEPT OF A MARKET IN RIGHTS
TO RAISE PRICES

One way to assure a specified trend in the general price level without having to guess in advance what level of incentive will do the trick is to arrange for the required level of incentive to be determined in a market. In effect, rights to raise prices (and their opposite, obligations to lower them) could be required to be traded in a market in which the price of these rights would converge to a level such that the balance of increases and decreases in prices would in the aggregate be just what is required to produce the desired overall price level. The equilibrium price of these rights so arrived at would provide just the right degree of incentive to yield the desired result.

However, one difficulty with a MAP scheme defined directly in terms of prices is that like many forms of TIP it requires the determination of by what amount prices have been increased or decreased in the face of changes in quality, proportions, and the ancillary terms of sale. The problems that would be encountered in attempting to administer a program couched in these terms would be formidable, though possibly they could be overcome if the need were sufficiently urgent.

A more fundamental difficulty is that if the program is based solely on sales prices of outputs at all levels, pyramiding problems would occur in that more stringent restraint would be imposed on products that are produced in several stages and pass through several hands on the way to the consumer as compared to those where there are fewer stages or a greater degree of vertical integration. To be sure, this problem might prove transitory if it turned out that the restraining pressure would need to be substantial only during a brief initial period in which the preexisting inflationary expectations were being dealt with. But in any case, once this problem is recognized, it should be possible to come up with a better solution.

IMPLEMENTATION OF A MAP IN TERMS
OF MARK-UPS

A MAP as an Excess Gross Mark-ups Tax

An approach that appears to avoid much of the above difficulty is to formulate a MAP in terms of the relation between *gross mark-ups*, or the excess of gross sales over the cost of inputs other than primary factors. Each agent would be given an entitlement to gross mark-ups based on that agent's past history of gross mark-ups adjusted by changes in the inputs of capital, labor, and other prime factors.

One way to think of the proposal is as an excess value-added tax with transferable entitlements, somewhat analogous to the wartime excess profits tax—the differences being that the base is akin to value added rather than net profits and that the "entitlement" to value added, unlike "normal profits," is capable of being modified by direct purchases from, or sales to, other agents, whereas under the excess profits tax transfers of entitlement to normal profits were possible, if at all, only through mergers or spin-offs. In addition, the entitlement to normal profits was adjusted mainly with respect to investment or disinvestment since the base period, whereas with the excess gross mark-ups tax adjustments would also be made with respect to changes in labor and other prime inputs.

Another way to relate the proposal to existing institutions is to regard it as a modification of the value-added taxes prevalent in the European Common Market. The main additional administrative requirement is the determination of the entitlements to gross mark-ups, which indeed is likely to prove the critical element in the feasibility of the plan.

The term *gross mark-ups* is used in preference to *value added* or *net sales* in order to emphasize the price control effects of the plan, whereas *value added*, to the extent that it is sometimes defined as the sum of prime factor payments, has more of a connotation of income control. But this is a mere matter of euphemistics, which—while it may have political importance in gaining acceptance of the proposal—is not an essential difference.

Ideally the purchases and sales of entitlements to gross mark-ups would be handled through some kind of organized market. Indeed the primary incentive impact of the scheme would be through the market price of entitlements rather than the tax itself, which might raise relatively little revenue, if any. The chief purpose of the tax would be to provide the back-up incentive for firms to provide themselves with an adequate amount of entitlement to cover their operations, and in most cases tax would become payable only as a penalty for failure to comply with the requirement. The strength of the incentive to keep prices down would vary automatically with the market price of entitlement and would not require adjustment by an act of Congress. The exact level of the tax rate or the tax schedule, if it were graduated in some way, would be relatively unimportant, and it could be adjusted, if necessary, at longer intervals without significant change in the adaptability of the scheme to short-term changes in the economic environment.

Indeed, it would be possible to couch the enforcement part of the scheme in terms of requiring any deficiency in entitlement revealed at the end of the accounting period that could not be met in the market (the firms with a shortage of entitlement being in effect "cornered") to be made up by the purchase of additional entitlement issued by some such agency as the Federal Reserve System much as deficiencies in bank reserves can be made up by borrowing at the rediscount window. But whether the Congress would be willing to delegate authority to determine the price to be paid for this "make-up" entitlement remains to be seen.

Still another possibility for dealing with firms with a deficiency of entitlement at the end of the accounting period would be to permit borrowing against future entitlement at a suitable discount rate. In this case it would be necessary to provide some restriction to prevent the scheme being vitiated by indefinitely continued rollovers. It might even be possible to dispense entirely with the explicit tax element of the plan.

But whatever method is used to induce compliance, it is the market price of entitlements that is the decisive element, and the tax, if there is one, is a purely secondary back-up element.

Adjustment of Entitlements for Changes in Capital

For existing firms, entitlement to gross mark-ups would be determined on the basis of starting with the gross mark-ups for some appropriate past period and adjusting this to take account of changes in capital invested in the firm, employment, and possibly other prime inputs. The base period should preferably be one prior to the start of serious consideration of the scheme so that anticipation of the application of the scheme will not lead to a spate of price increases as sellers attempt to establish a higher basis for the computation of future entitlements.

Adjustment for changes in investment is fairly straightforward. One can, indeed, follow the precedents established for the excess profits tax, though there may be reasons for a different treatment in some cases. The chief problems involve the treatment of inventories, depreciation, and distinguishing between purchases of inputs on current account and on capital account. If only the income tax were on a sound basis instead of being full of special provisions such as accelerated depreciation and the like, one could simply take net income minus distributions, plus net receipts from loans and sale of equity, and adjust entitlement by a percentage of this change in investment. As it is, it may become desirable to make adjustments to net income to reflect normal accounting for purposes of determining entitlement.

Adjustment of Entitlements for Employment Changes

How entitlements should be adjusted for changes in employment is one of the more critical problems for a MAP scheme. To adjust entitlement on the basis of changes in total payrolls or labor costs would largely vitiate the scheme, since then there would be no disincentive to raising labor compensation together with prices without limit. At the other extreme, to allow only a flat amount per additional employee hired would involve a rather sharp discrimination against the hiring of the more highly skilled employees. While under current circumstances there would be much to be said for a discrimination in this direction, given the concentration of unemployment among the unskilled, this may be thought of as going too far. It may be satisfactory to adopt some intermediate compromise by allowing a flat amount per additional employee plus a fraction of the payrolls in excess of this fixed amount. Unfortunately there seems to be no clear principle to appeal to as to where this compromise should be struck, leading to a possibility for debate and even filibuster over the issue.

Such a plan would tend to discriminate in favor of shorter hours and part-time employment, again possibly a not undesirable discrimination in the light of the current relative scarcity of part-time employment opportunities. To attempt to eliminate this discrimination would pose formidable administrative problems, given possibilities for disguising shorter hours as simply lax enforcement of flextime, for example. It would, however, be appropriate, where the wage paid is less than would be paid for full-time work at the minimum or standard wage, to limit the adjustment to entitlement to the actual payment.

One should beware of insisting on too sophisticated adjustment to entitlements, given the likelihood that the market price of entitlement would decline rapidly to a very low level as the operation of the scheme reduces inflationary pressures by eliminating inflationary expectations. The degree to which this would occur would depend to some extent on the speed with which an attempt is made to reach full employment.

The Calculation of Gross Mark-ups

The calculation of gross mark-ups, though a simpler matter than the calculation of net income, is not as simple as it might seem at first blush. In principle, purchases and sales of capital assets must be distinguished from purchases and sales on current account and treated as adjustments to investment rather than to mark-ups. The distinction can in some cases be difficult and even arbitrary. Increases in inventory must likewise be excluded and decreases in inventory included in the nonprime factor cost of goods sold. Inventory for this purpose must include not only stocks in storage but work in progress. Depreciation needs to be treated in a similar fashion, with the difference that determination of the appropriate value for depreciation is open to much greater uncertainty than the valuation of inventory changes.

While for income tax purposes errors in evaluating these items may make only a relatively modest difference, since the result in most cases is merely to shift income from one accounting period to another, for MAP purposes the stakes are higher, at least in the initial phase of the scheme, since the market price of entitlement may be expected to fall off rather sharply as inflationary expectations abate. This is not the place to try to specify in detail how these separations are to be made in particular cases, but the problem will eventually have to be faced.

Coverage

Coverage of the MAP plan could exclude a significant part of the economy without losing much if any of its effectiveness as an anti-inflationary weapon. Accordingly the administrative burden can be substantially eased by excluding small firms up to a fairly substantial size. This could be accomplished without introducing discontinuities by providing each firm with a minimum fixed amount of nonmarketable entitlement—for instance, up to $100,000 for incorporated firms and $200,000 for unincorporated firms. The smaller amount for the incorporated firms is in recognition of the fact that they are more likely to have well-developed accounting systems in place. This would be alternative, not in addition to, an entitlement as calculated in the standard manner. Care would have to be exercised in defining the exclusion in a manner that would avoid opportunities for abuse.

It is not clear, either, to what extent one would want to exclude certain types of enterprise from the operations of the scheme. Regulated public utilities might be excluded on the ground that since their rates are regulated in any case they have little or no capability to respond to the incentives provided by the program. Similarly nonprofit entities, cooperatives, and mutual companies might be considered to be properly exempt, especially if sales of commodities or services constitute a small part of their activity, though in some cases there would be an outcry from competing stock companies that they would be subject to unfair competition. Banks, financial intermediaries, and insurance companies might be granted exemption on the ground that the services they supply are defined in monetary terms and thus stand somewhat to one side of the main concern with inflation of commodity or service prices. Interest rates as the price of money can be considered to be the special preserve of the Fed. Difficulties would arise with conglomerates whose operations span the exempt and the nonexempt areas, and this may argue in favor of a more comprehensive approach.

International Transactions

There is little special difficulty with the ordinary company buying from or selling to foreign trading partners on the assumption that the transactions are at arm's-length. Problems arise, however, where multinational corporations trade with related foreign companies in circumstances under which the assumption of arm's-length trading cannot be relied on. The problem is comparable to that encountered under the income tax, where the determination of where income shall be deemed to arise requires the establishment of appropriate "transfer prices" for international transactions within and among related companies.

Here again the simplest solution would probably be one of accepting the transfer prices established for income tax purposes. Yet it must be recognized that these transfer prices are themselves far from satisfactory, involving as they do attempts to apply a number of ad hoc solutions, such as the use of arm's-length prices for comparable goods, the use of a mark-up over a "fully allocated" cost concocted by accountants using arbitrary rules for the apportionment of joint costs, or a discount from final sale price, the tracing of transactions through a whole sequence of subsidiaries located in various countries, and in many cases litigation stretching over many years.

In the comparable problem of allocating income among the states for state income tax purposes, most states have decided to cut the Gordian knot by the use of somewhat arbitrary formulas, a typical one being the so-called Massachusetts formula:

$$B_{ij} = [(S_{ij}/S_i) + (K_{ij}/K_i) + (W_{ij}/W_i)] [B_i/3]$$

where i refers to the firm, j to the jurisdiction, B is the tax base, S is sales, K is property, and W is payrolls. This formula is seriously defective, however, for it fails to give due weight to the relative importance of the three factors in the determination of the income of any given company. For example, if a consulting firm located in New York and renting its premises and equipment, so that it has very little capital, should want to get nearly a third of its income allocated to Vermont, all it would have to do would be to buy a small summer camp as a vacation spot for its employees and presto! the formula puts a third of the firm's income in Vermont and only two-thirds in New York. A better formula would be

$$B_{ij} = B_i [aS_{ij} + bK_{ij} + cW_{ij}] / [aS_i + bK_i + cW_i]$$

where the coefficients a, b, and c are derived from a regression of total tax base on total factors for a suitably chosen set of firms (which might include all firms doing business in a given jurisdiction):

$$B_i = aS_i + b K_i + cW_i + u_i$$

It may be a bit more difficult to get the data by which to apply a formula in an international case than in the interstate case, although several states are beginning to apply formulas to assess multinational corporations on a "unit rule" basis, over strong objections by the multinational corporations, but with recent approval by the Supreme Court.

Periodicity

From the standpoint of getting faster results from the introduction of a MAP, the shorter the time period on the basis of which the program is operated the better, but minimizing compliance and administration costs would call for a longer period. Probably the shortest period for which accounts are drawn up with any generality is the quarter, while many firms will compile their accounts only annually. It might be possible to work on a quarterly basis for the larger firms and an annual basis for the smaller firms. No final judgment here is possible without more data than is readily at hand.

FULL EMPLOYMENT POLICY WITH MAP

Once MAP has provided assurance that inflation will be brought under control, fiscal and monetary policy can be applied unstintingly to provide a level of full employment at which a balance will be struck between full utilization of resources and flexibility. This could be in the range of 1 to 3 percent rather than the much higher levels often talked of as the best that could hope to be achieved in the absence of a program such as MAP. Fiscal policy would be fully effective, since it would no longer be frustrated by monetary contraction motivated by fears of excessive inflation. And monetary expansion would be effective in lowering interest rates to the extent needed to stimulate the desired level of investment, assuming that the financial markets could be persuaded of the effectiveness of MAP so that they would no longer be anticipating that higher interest rates would eventually have to return.

In this atmosphere it would be possible to choose deliberately how much of the full-employment national income would go to current consumption and how much to investment to provide for economic growth and enhancement of the heritage to be left to future generations. A larger fiscal deficit coupled with high interest rates would produce higher disposable incomes and consumption on the one hand and less investment and growth on the other, while a lower deficit or even a surplus with low interest rates would result in restricted consumption and the devotion of a larger portion of available resources to investment stimulated by the lower interest rates.

OPTIMUM PRICE TRENDS

Equity to Debtors

In addition to permitting a choice to be made between alternative growth rates, a MAP program will allow a choice as to the rate of inflation to be allowed in the future, by suitably adjusting the way entitlements to gross mark-ups are calculated. While the conventional wisdom has it that an anti-inflation policy should aim for a stable price policy involving a zero rate of inflation to be achieved as rapidly as possible, it is not at all clear that this is indeed the optimum policy. From an equity standpoint, indeed, it might well be considered best to aim for something closer to the average level of prices expected at the time outstanding contracts were entered into. To go immediately to a zero rate of inflation would impose windfall losses on debtors who have entered into long-term contracts on the assumption that prices would rise significantly above their current levels.

Impact on Developing Countries

The equity aspect may be especially acute with respect to the indebtedness of Third World countries. In many cases these countries borrowed heavily with the expectation that the debt could be serviced from continued sales of exports at rising prices to developed countries. Abatement of inflation and economic recession have caused the dollar value of exports out of which debt service must eventually be financed to fall way below earlier expectations and have produced a financial crisis in many of these countries. A further rapid reduction of the inflation rate to zero would further exacerbate this problem. While the return of full-employment prosperity that could be expected with a MAP program would alleviate the problem somewhat by offering enlarged markets for exports from developing countries, as would also the availability of funds at low real interest rates for refinancing, especially if a high-growth low-interest-rate policy is adopted, considerable alleviation of the burden of the outstanding debt would result from a policy of retaining a moderate rate of inflation, at least for an interim period.

Widening the Range of Growth Policy Options

On another front there is a case to be made for a mild rate of inflation to be continued into the indefinite future as a means of widening the range of options available with respect to the growth rate. Monetary policy cannot in general push money interest rates below a certain level termed by Keynesians the *liquidity trap level*. With a stable price level this imposes a limit below which real interest rates cannot be pushed and so places a limit on the amount of private investment that can be encouraged through low interest rates. And though other methods of stimulating investment are available, there may be less of a likelihood of misallocation if it is mediated through a uniform market rate of interest. A mild rate of inflation would make it possible for the monetary authority to push real rates of interest to a lower level than would be possible without the inflationary trend. Whatever course is chosen, it is appropriate that the policy be announced as far in advance as possible and adhered to, in the absence of major unforeseen developments.

11 TAX-BASED INCOMES POLICIES
Some Skeptical Remarks

R. Robert Russell

One of the enduring paradoxes of economic policymaking in the United States is the continued appeal of wage/price controls and "voluntary" guidelines despite the widespread dismissals of earlier (peacetime) programs as failures. This apparent inconsistency might be explained by the belief that earlier programs suffered from serious design flaws that thwarted their effectiveness: that the Kennedy/ Johnson guidepost program was too informal and limited in application (concentrating primarily on presettlement jawboning of major collective-bargaining settlements); that the Nixon administration's Economic Stabilization Program (ESP) of mandatory controls was too rigid and inflexible, creating onerous and intolerable market distortions and a postcontrols price surge; and that the Carter administration's Pay and Price Standards Program, while ambitious in design and coverage, lacked an enforcement mechanism and incentives for compliance. It is these assessments that lead many to advocate an incomes policy backed by tax incentives ("penalties" for noncompliance and/or subsidies for compliance).

The arguments advanced in favor of a tax-based incomes policy (TIP) are both conceptual (or theoretical) and practical (or administrative).[1] The principal conceptual appeal of a TIP is that it could provide a powerful incentive for wage/price restraint while avoiding the distortional effects of rigid (mandatory) wage/price controls. Indeed, TIP advocates often eschew use of the word *penalty* to describe the tax incentive, arguing that no stigma should be attached to price or wage increases above the standard; firms simply must pay the government "tax" on such increases. Rather than attempting to impede or undermine the working of the price system, as do conventional controls, a TIP *uses* the price system to induce anti-inflation restraint. In this sense, a TIP would be designed to internalize an inflation externality, thus enhancing economic efficiency, just as an effluent tax can be used to internalize a pollution externality. It is argued that a TIP has the same advantages over rigid controls that a pollution tax has over direct pollution controls.

One administrative argument advanced on behalf of a TIP is that it would use the existing Internal Revenue Service to implement and monitor the plan; there would be no need for the creation of a separate bureaucracy. More important is the argument that the procedural apparatus would be much less cumbersome— that there would be little or no need for elaborate exceptions and adjudication procedures, primarily because wage or price increases above the standard would be allowed (without stigmatization) so long as the tax was paid.

TIP advocates also place a great deal of emphasis on the control variable. The early TIP proposals (such as those of Wallich and Weintraub 1971 and Okun 1977) emphasized wages, primarily because wages are thought to be more homogeneous than prices and fraught with fewer measurement problems. Another possible advantage of wages as the instrument of control is the belief that labor markets are much less competitive than product markets. This view has gained credibility as burgeoning international trade has increased competitive pressures in domestic markets. Thus, wage restraint and downward pressures on labor costs are likely to be passed through in the form of commensurate price restraint.

In part because of the political reality that it would probably be impossible to enact an incomes policy that focused only on wages, leaving other forms of income obstensibly untouched, and in part because of efficiency considerations, TIP advocates more recently have proposed value-added per unit of capital and labor input as the instrument of control. The advantage of a value-added control concept is that it encompasses payments to all labor and capital inputs. Consequently, it has the appearance of fairness[2] and in addition has the efficiency property that it does not provide perverse incentives for substituting one type of capital or labor input for another. Of course, value added excludes material costs, but the argument is that restraint in the pricing of material inputs is engendered at earlier stages of production.

Another argument on behalf of value added per unit of input as a control concept is that it would entail fewer measurement problems than do prices, in part because the value-added concept is very close conceptually to the accounting concept of "revenue less cost of goods sold."

The third argument in support of a value-added TIP is that, unlike profit and cost-passthrough limitations, it does not inhibit investment incentives and productivity growth. The argument is that, at least to the extent that productivity improvements are attributable to capital investment, controls on value added per unit of input allow value added to grow with increases in capital inputs.

Drawing on his experience in administering the price standard in the Carter administration's program, Triplett (Chapter 12) has questioned the administrative feasibility of a TIP. He also argues, on the basis of the experience in that program with the gross margin standard, that a value-added standard is no easier to administer than a price standard and has the perverse property of encouraging the substitution of material inputs for labor and capital.

In my evaluation of TIPs, I avoid duplication of the remarks of Triplett, with which I am in substantial agreement. Rather, I attempt to answer some questions that are not fully explored by Triplett. There are two fundamental questions to be asked about the potential effectiveness of a TIP:

1. Is a TIP administratively feasible?
2. Assuming that a TIP is administratively feasible, is it worth doing—that is, are the benefits likely to exceed the costs?

ADMINISTRATIVE FEASIBILITY

Triplett's skepticism about the administrative feasibility of a TIP emanates from two pervasive problems with the Carter administration's price standard: (1) the impracticality of uniform rules for all companies, because of diversity of firms' cost experiences, business practices, accounting records, and so forth, resulting in a proliferation of special standards and widespread use of the "uncontrollable costs" exception; and (2) difficulties of formulating understandable and unambiguous rules for measuring price changes—aggregation (index-number) problems, data inadequacies, and the treatment of quality change and new and custom products. Two questions are raised by Triplett's analysis: (1) Are these problems as applicable to a value-added standard of the type recommended by Colander (1979c) and Lerner and Colander (1980)? (2) Are the problems equally vexing for a wage standard?

Value-Added Standards versus Price Standards

The contention that a TIP (or other incomes policy) that controls value added would be relatively easy to implement using standard accounting frameworks is dubious. For obvious efficiency reasons, a value-added standard should not penalize firms for increases in quantity. Thus, it is necessary to distinguish between changes in value added attributable to price changes and those attributable to quantity changes. This approach, however, *requires* construction of a measure of quantity. But quantity aggregates are no easier to construct than price aggregates. Indeed, price and quantity indices are dual to one another: one is obtained from the other by division into (that is, deflation of) revenue or cost.[3]

The argument that the *input* quantity indices needed for a value-added standard entail fewer measurement problems is unconvincing. Even if we were to grant the point that measuring aggregate labor-input quantity is easier than measuring aggregate output quantity, since labor inputs are not as heterogeneous as outputs,[4] we would be left with the problem that measuring aggregate capital input is a much-studied and eminently difficult task. Most noteworthy, of course, are the problems of measuring depreciation. Moreover, casual observation suggests that the problems posed by quality change and new and custom products are, if anything, more difficult for capital goods than for consumer goods.[5]

The argument that a value-added standard is preferable on grounds of efficiency and incentives is more difficult to assess. As Triplett points out, the most encompassing standard—that is, a price standard—is the most attractive, in principle, because it covers all forms of cost and therefore does not provide perverse incentives to substitute inputs not covered by the standard for those so covered. More generally, a price standard does not inhibit incentives to lower costs because all cost savings can be retained by the firm, under the standard, so long as the price limitation is not violated. (Of course, competition typically prevents firms from capturing all cost savings in the form of higher profits.)

A price standard, however, that essentially "allows" firms to retain all profit increases attributable to productivity improvements generates serious inequities and inefficiencies of another sort. The problem is that in some sectors of the economy there is relatively little scope for productivity improvement, whereas in others there is tremendous scope for (and indeed the market necessity of) productivity improvement. Moreover, competition forces most of these ongoing increases in productivity to be passed on to consumers in the form of lower prices (or price increases below what they otherwise would be).

Because of this problem, the CWPS[6] price limitation was not identical for all firms. The price-deceleration standard established firm-specific price limitations based on the annual rate of price increase over the previous two years for each firm. The idea behind this approach was that the distribution of two-year price changes would reflect, approximately, the distribution of productivity growth trends. The two previous years—roughly, the fourth quarter of 1975 to the fourth quarter of 1977—were periods of neither recession nor rapid expansion, and the unemployment rate was fairly constant. The pay standard, the price standard, and the overall target inflation rate were constructed to be consistent with one another and with constant factor shares.

The principal problem with this approach was that, for many firms, the base period was unrepresentative of the firm's trends in productivity growth and in input costs not controlled by the firm (most notably, certain material input costs). Moreover, over time, base-period experiences become less and less representative. As a result CWPS allowed companies to employ an alternative profit-margin limitation so long as they could show that "uncontrollable cost increases" made it "impossible" for them to comply with the price-deceleration standard.

When the international oil crisis initiated a rapid acceleration of prices in 1979, more and more companies left the basic price-deceleration standard to comply with the cost-passthrough provisions of the profit-margin limitation. By the end of the first program year, only one-third of the companies directly monitored by the CWPS (those with base-year revenues of $250 million or more) remained on the basic price limitation; the others were on gross-margin or profit-margin limitations. This was unfortunate, as a cost-passthrough-type standard is perhaps the worst among the various types of guidelines in terms of inhibiting incentives to cut costs. Consequently, the economic rationale of the general price standard was gradually undermined as an increasing number of companies was unable to comply with its salient component—the price-deceleration standard. Of course, the principal reason for this was an international run-up of materials costs that was largely unrelated to domestic economic policies; nevertheless, an incomes policy must be judged, in part, on its resilience in the face of extraneous shocks such as those that occurred in 1979.

As noted above, the value-added standard, while inhibiting incentives to reduce materials cost, retains incentives for capital investment because of the adjustment for expansions of input quantities. There is, of course, much truth to this, but it is not the end of the story. First, we have to reemphasize the extremely difficult problem of dealing with quality changes in capital equipment. A good deal of technological progress takes the form of quality improvement of capital goods. This is reflected in part in the sustained growth of total-factor productivity—productivity of labor *and* capital. Moreover, the growth in total-factor productivity also varies considerably across industries (and across firms within an industry), so that the problem of diversity of productivity trends across firms pertains to the value-added-per-unit-of-input standard as well to the price limitation.[7]

In sum, the net outcome of an assessment of the relative advantages and disadvantages of the value-added and price standards is unclear. What is clear is that both have serious problems and these problems are likely to grow in severity over the course of the program.

Wage Standards versus Price Standards

On the surface, administrative problems would appear to be more serious for a price standard than for a wage standard because of the extreme heterogeneity of products as compared to labor inputs. I would argue, however, that there are wage-standard analogues to the two classes of price-standard problems identified by Triplett: (1) heterogeneity across firms and the need for multiple standards and (2) measurement problems (aggregation and new and custom products). The pay-standard analogues are (1) the wide variety of pay practices and structures and the varying market situations of firms and (2) difficulties of measuring compensation components other than straight-time wages and salaries (incentive pay, cost-of-living adjustments, and fringe benefits). Because of the heterogeneity of pay practices, any chosen method of aggregation and measurement will limit the compensation increases of different firms and different employees in vastly different ways.

Diversity of Pay Structures and the Index-Number Problem.   As with the formulation of the price standard (chronicled in Triplett's paper), the pay standard in the Carter administration's program started out to be quite simple. Multiyear collective-bargaining agreements were evaluated prospectively by a fixed-weight index-number calculation, essentially measuring the (weighted) average increase in the pay rate for a job. This method, also called the "ice-cube method" because it freezes the work-force composition at a base-period level, is singularly appropriate for collective-bargaining agreements because they are typically characterized by highly structured job classification schemes with formal entry-level-to-job-rate progressions.

Initially, compensation increases of nonunion employee units were to be calculated using the so-called double-snapshot method—essentially a unit-value construction. This involves a comparison of average compensation rates (total compensation divided by total hours worked) for active employees at the beginning and end of the measurement period. This method was adopted because of its simplicity and lack of ambiguity. It quickly encountered a great deal of opposition from compensation experts throughout the business community, however, because it can be significantly affected by changes in the functional composition of the work force and, as a result, treats different work forces and firms quite disparately. In any company with salary ranges and a possibility of promotion from within—the most common compensation structure for nonunion work forces—the double-snapshot method tends to understate the average increase granted to continuing employees and the weighted-average salary-range adjustment. This is because employees who quit or retire tend to be earning salaries at the tops of their salary ranges, whereas replacements are hired in at the bottom of their salary ranges. Consequently, if a firm gave, say, no salary increases, average compensation calculated according to the unit-value construction would show a decrease. The tendency for the turnover in promotion processes to reduce measured average changes is called "slippage" by compensation administrators, and slippage values of from 1 to 3 percent are quite common. Employee groups with wide salary ranges and high turnover tend to experience the greatest slippage, whereas slippage is relatively small for employee groups with flat rates and little turnover.

The downward bias of the double-snapshot technique is even more pronounced for growing firms, since new employees in lower ends of salary brackets will further reduce unit-value changes. On the other hand, work-force reductions, which tend to be concentrated among low-tenure low-paid workers in each range, work in the opposite direction.

In an expanding economy, the double-snapshot calculation method tends to understate hourly compensation increases for most employee units. One of the principal problems was that the degree of slippage varied considerably among firms, thus giving some firms much more flexibility than others in adjusting non-union wages. Moreover, many firms were in a declining position, so that their allowable pay increases were actually *below* the pay standard. Because of the apparent inequity of the double-snapshot approach to calculating wage changes, CWPS agreed to allow a firm to adjust changes in the compensation of its labor force using a fixed-weight index of wage changes. Firms obviously chose the method that was more to their advantage.

This, however, was not the end of the complications. Many smaller firms for whom the ice-cube method would have been the more desirable way to calculate wage changes contended that they were unable to make such sophisticated calculations. Consequently, CWPS adopted yet another option for calculating average wage increases: the "continuing employee" or "melting ice cube" method. This entailed a computation of average salary changes for those employees who were in the work force throughout the measurement period; new entrants and terminated employees did not enter this computation. Thus, this is a unit-value technique applied to continuing employees only. It also eliminates the effect of mix changes and turnovers. To make this method comparable with the other methods, it was necessary to exclude those portions of compensation-rate changes attributable to legitimate promotion and qualification changes. The problem of distinguishing between merit increases and longevity increases turned out to be a major headache for CWPS. A lengthy and controversial dispute over the issue with the unions representing public-school teachers was never fully resolved.

The point of this discussion of aggregation across various types of employees is that, although CWPS started out with the intention of having a very simple rule to be applied to all (nonunion) companies, the diversity of company pay structures and pay situations and the inability of some firms to calculate index numbers forced CWPS to adopt alternative methods of calculation. The availability of a choice of methods undoubtedly led to a great deal of slack in the standards.

Measurement Problems: Nonwage Compensation and COLAs. The existence (and increasing relative size) of many types of labor compensation other than fixed hourly pay raises significant problems for the administration of a limitation on the hourly compensation of workers. Because the share of labor compensation accounted for by straight hourly pay varies considerably among different types of employment, controlling straight-time hourly pay alone would be highly inequitable. Moreover, it would result, to the extent that the limitation were binding, in a shift of compensation away from wages and salaries to other types of compensation. This would be distortional and would undermine the effectiveness of the incomes policy. For this reason, pay limitations have tended to be as encompassing as possible. This, however, raises significant measurement issues. I will briefly outline a few of them.[8]

Incentive pay. The treatment of incentive pay—piece-work pay, commission plans, group production incentive plans, profit-sharing bonus plans, and discretionary bonuses—poses special problems for wage/price programs. In addition to the danger that controls will interfere with the salutary incentive effects of such programs, there is also the problem that employer costs of these programs cannot be determined in advance. The ideal approach would be to require that firms design incentive compensation packages with an expected pay-out that satisfies the wage standard, but this approach would require quantification of the concept of performance, an extraordinarily difficult measurement problem for all but the most basic incentive programs.

Future-value compensation. The salient characteristic of future-value compensation is that its value will not be known until some future time. The problem posed for a controls program, therefore, is that of evaluating its cost. The most common type of future-value compensation is a stock-option plan, providing an option to buy a certain number of shares at a given price at any time over some specified period. Until the option is exercised, the cost to the employer is unrealized and unknown. The ideal approach would be to assign a market value to such awards when they are granted, but such an assignment is difficult if not impossible because of the absence of markets (stock options are actively traded for only a handful of major stocks, and the exercise periods of marketable options normally do not exceed one year).

Fringe benefits. Excluding fringe benefits from the calculation of labor compensation in an incomes policy would result in serious inequities and would exacerbate existing distortions that encourage payment in the form of fringe benefits. The problem posed by their inclusion is whether these fringe benefits should be measured in terms of the value of the benefits received by the employees or by the cost to the employer. While benefits and costs coincide in the case of wages and salaries, they can diverge markedly for many types of fringe benefits. Thus, the cost of employer-provided health insurance can increase either because of improvement in coverage or because of medical-cost inflation. The first factor is controlled by firms, but the latter is not. Also, the timing and magnitude of employer cost increases for medical insurance plans vary across plans and insurance providers, depending on plan experience and other factors. Similarly, the employer cost of defined-benefit pension plans can be significantly affected by actuarial computations based on planning assumptions about retirement ages, longevity after retirement, earnings growth rates, and rates of return. Thus, as with health insurance costs, the linkage between changes in employer costs and changes in employee benefits is broken.

Cost-of-living adjustments. About half of the union workers in the United States are covered by cost-of-living adjustments (COLAs). Evaluating COLAs in assessing collective-bargaining agreements poses special problems because the payouts depend on future inflation and are therefore unknown at the time a collective-bargaining agreement is signed. Should COLAs be treated like any other form of wage payment? To do so could result in noncompliance by firms because of increases in inflation that are totally beyond their control or, alternatively, in the virtual abrogation of COLAs in union contracts. Should COLAs alternatively be evaluated prospectively on the basis of a government-dictated inflation assumption? This was the approach in the Carter administration program, and, more than any phenomenon other than the international oil crisis, it ultimately undermined the credibility and effectiveness of the program: As inflation heated up as a result of the oil crisis, the inflation rate substantially exceeded the rates stipulated in the rules for evaluating COLAs, resulting in wage increases for COLA-protected workers that were far above the standard (1½ to 1¾ percentage points on average) but still in compliance.

Concluding Remarks on Administrative Costs. The point of the foregoing discussion is *not* that the many questions raised by wage-measurement problems do not have answers. On the contrary, both the Pay Board in the Nixon program and CWPS in the Carter program confronted these and many other questions and arrived at resolutions of the quandaries. Rather, the points are the following. First, there was a degree of arbitrariness in all these decisions. As a result, they remained controversial and problematical, since any decisions worked to the advantage of some and the disadvantage of others.

Second, what I have described is merely the tip of the iceberg. Firms and unions that wanted to get around the guidelines usually had enough ingenuity to do so. One example from the Carter program is the use of "trigger COLAs," calibrated to begin COLA payments if and only if the inflation rate exceeded that stipulated by CWPS for evaluating COLA clauses (7 percent). According to CWPS rules, this COLA clause had to be evaluated at zero. yet, it clearly had an expected cost above zero, even if the expected inflation rate had remained equal to 7 percent, because of the asymmetry of the COLA clause.

Another example is one that helped to shoehorn the Teamsters contract into compliance (which, incidentally, did as much to undermine the credibility of the program as any other Carter administration decision). The Teamsters contract called for increased retirement benefits for retired as well as active employees. Under CWPS rules, strictly interpreted, these improved benefits for retirees were not counted as part of the compensation, since they were not "employees."

A perusal of CWPS files would drum up a long list of similar complications that were not foreseen when CWPS attempted to formulate simple rules for wage restraint. In addition, I have not mentioned the many exceptions to the pay standard in the Carter administration's program, which required formal descriptions of phenomena like "tandem pay increases," "acute labor shortages," and "gross inequity."

The need to deal with unforeseen circumstances, revelations of ambiguities in the rules, and discoveries of loopholes results in a rapidly growing body of regulations and case law. Initially, the regulations may be motivated primarily by economic considerations, but eventually, as case law develops and rulings proliferate, the lawyers take command, and the process loses many of its economic underpinnings.

True, the same thing has happened to the tax code in the United States—an ever-growing and increasingly complicated body of law. There are, however, two factors that make the codification of a tax-based incomes policy more problematical. First, the incomes policy faces most of the measurement problems of the usual tax law—essentially measuring revenues, costs, and so forth—but, in addition, introduces the problem of coping with aggregation across labor inputs, outputs, and so forth. This is an entirely new endeavor with which the IRS, companies, and accountants are ill-equipped to deal. Therefore, the tax-based incomes policy is likely, in principle, to be administratively more onerous than the existing body of tax law. More important, while taxpayers evince impatience with the more arcane and murky aspects of tax law, there is fairly widespread agreement that tax collection is an essential function of the federal government. By contrast, there is a great deal of disagreement and controversy about whether a program of wage/price restraint is properly in the domain of government policy. Consequently, there would be much less willingness to tolerate the administrative burdens of a tax-based incomes policy.

In short, the administrative problems in implementing a TIP, while not insuperable, would add a large burden to the unenviable task of running the country's income-tax program and, in my view, would submerge the tax system in a sea of controversy over the details of an increasingly unpopular program.

ARE THE BENEFITS WORTH THE COST?

Given that a TIP is administratively workable (an issue that we've seen does not admit of a simple yes or no answer), there remains the question of whether such a program is worth implementing—whether the benefits are likely to exceed the costs. This issue can be addressed sequentially: (1) Is an incomes policy of any type likely to be worth the costs? (2) Is a TIP cost effective—that is, does a TIP have significant advantages over other types of formal or informal incomes policies?

Costs and Benefits of Incomes Policies

The issue of whether an incomes policy can ever be worth the cost is one that will probably never be resolved by the profession, in part because of the difficulty of measuring both costs and benefits of such programs and in part because of the heavy load of ideological baggage that many economists bring to the study of this question. The costs of an incomes policy include the social cost of the induced inefficiencies (through the distortion of relative prices) and the direct administrative costs (the administrative burdens placed on companies as well as the social costs of the "bureaucratic army" required to enforce the guidelines).

These costs certainly depend significantly on the design features of the program. The three programs adopted in the United States in the last two decades differed considerably in terms of induced inefficiencies. The Nixon program is fraught with horror stories about market disruptions, distortion, and shortages. (See, for example, Eads 1976 and Schultze 1980.) Because domestic prices of many raw materials were held below world prices, there was a surge in exports from the United States and consequent domestic shortages. Indeed, since neither import nor export prices were controlled, some products were shipped to Canada and then reimported. The extra transportation costs added further to inflation. Perhaps the most important distortion was the squeezing of profit margins in the early phases of the program because price inflation was checked without any effect on labor costs. These margins bounced back after the controls were lifted.

There is much less evidence of induced distortions in either the Kennedy/Johnson guideposts program or the Carter Pay and Price Standards program. To a certain extent, this reflects differences in design features. (These programs were more flexible than the Nixon program.) But the principal difference is probably that the Nixon program was mandatory, whereas the guideposts and standards programs were essentially voluntary (the former more so than the latter). The Nixon program entailed two mandatory price freezes and, during the critical Phase II, required prenotification of price increases by larger companies, which were not allowed to implement them until approval was obtained. The Kennedy/Johnson guidelines were voluntary, although there were some notorious cases of presidential jawboning during the Johnson years. The Carter program embodied a procurement sanction (a threat to bar noncompliers from bidding on large government contracts), but this sanction became less credible as the program proceeded. Essentially a voluntary program, it relied primarily on the willingness (if not eagerness) of employers to use the pay standard to hold down wage increases.

Typically, when a market becomes very tight, there is an opportunity for companies in that industry to make large profits. Because compliance with the Carter administration's standards was voluntary, companies could choose, without fear of penalty of law, not to adhere to the standards if it meant substantial losses in profit. For example, six producers of cement and other building materials were formally listed as noncompliers because they refused to comply with the program when the market was tight. Had the program not been voluntary, there might well have been a shortage of cement.

While the records of the guideposts and standards programs are not replete with horror stories of market shortages, there is evidence of broader types of induced distortions. By concentrating on major collective-bargaining situations, the Kennedy/Johnson program appears to have affected wages more than prices. This may explain the rash of big settlements after the guideposts were abandoned in the late 1960s. As noted above, in the Carter program, complying employee groups covered by multiyear contracts that included formal cost-of-living adjustment clauses (COLAs) received much larger pay increases than did complying workers without such protection.

The three programs also differed significantly in terms of administrative costs: The guideposts program was administered by one or two members of the professional staff of the Council of Economic Advisors; the Nixon controls program required a veritable army of enforcers (including 17,000 IRS agents); the Carter program was administered by a staff of about 200.

Reliable estimates of either the induced-inefficiency or administrative costs do not exist for any program. As CWPS was going out of business, it surveyed companies that it monitored to ascertain their administrative costs of complying with the program. The resulting estimate, which is, of course, subject to the usual response-error biases, was on the order of $300 million for the two-year program. The government administrative costs were comparatively small—less than $10 million. The cost of the Nixon program has been estimated by one of its critics (Darby 1976a, b) at no more than $2 billion—$1 billion for administrative costs and $1 billion for induced inefficiencies.

The social benefits of a reduction in the inflation rate cannot be measured directly. If, however, we are willing to take as given the social commitment to lower the inflation rate, then we can measure the benefits of the program by referring to the social costs of reducing the inflation rate by alternative methods—fiscal and monetary restraint. Estimates of the output costs of lowering the inflation rate by one percentage point through fiscal and monetary restraint are on the order of $200 billion. Thus, if an incomes policy were to shave even a fraction of a percentage point off the inflation rate, it would be highly cost effective. Although the evidence on the effectiveness and potential effectiveness of incomes policies in reducing inflation is mixed, my own view, buttressed by some research (Hagens and Russell 1985), is that these policies, if intelligently designed and administered, can have a nonnegligible effect on the inflation rate.[9]

Is a TIP Cost Effective?

If we were to grant my conclusion that the benefits of an incomes policy can indeed exceed the cost, we are then left with the issue of what type of incomes policy is best. In particular, is a TIP likely to be more effective than the other types of incomes policies that have been adopted in this country? Recall from my introductory remarks that the conceptual argument in favor of a TIP is that it would provide powerful incentives for compliance without seriously distorting relative prices and resource allocation. I find this argument less than compelling.

In my opinion, the need for teeth behind an incomes policy to provide strong incentives for compliance is overdrawn. First of all, unless a program is so simple as to result in serious inequities and distortions, it is relatively easy for a company to devise ways to circumvent the intent of a guidepost program. Consequently, even a mandatory program must rely extensively on the willingness of companies—at least major companies—to comply voluntarily. The particular successes of the Kennedy/Johnson guideposts program were attributable less to levers that the government could pull to force compliance than to the overwhelming influence of personal intervention by President Johnson. It was his personal appeal to particular companies and unions on behalf of the national interest (and no doubt fear of incurring his wrath) that made President Johnson successful in engineering several 3.2 percent collective-bargaining settlements during the mid-1960s heyday of the guidepost program. The Nixon administration's Economic Stabilization Program had considerable success in inducing restraint on the price side (though virtually no success on the labor side) primarily because it is relatively easy to determine whether a firm is complying with a freeze or prenotification requirements. The primary way that price increases were slowed down during Phase II of the ESP was by long delays in the granting of requests for price increases. On the other hand, finding a company out of compliance, after the fact, when the rule is more complicated than a freeze, is much more difficult. Inevitably, the many ambiguities and possibilities of different (and strategic) interpretations make it easy for a company to stretch the rules. These efforts ultimately can be thwarted only by extensive monitoring and adjudication of disputed interpretations of the rules. The required staff for such an endeavor is immense. Given the administrative problems discussed above, an extensive audit and technical capability is required.

The Carter administration's threat to deny procurement contracts above $5 million to noncomplying firms received a great deal of attention (including a legal challenge by the AFL-CIO). There is evidence that this sanction had significant deterrent effects on many small companies that relied extensively on government business for their survival. (During the early phases of the program, CWPS received many calls from unknown and little-known businesses requesting interpretations of the regulations to assure that they were in compliance, stating that they could not risk disqualification from bidding on government contracts.) But the procurement sanction turned out to be ineffective vis-à-vis the large companies that were the principal targets of the program. There were opportunities to invoke the sanctions against large companies, but in each case other considerations (most notably, "national security") dominated the objectives of the standards program and the procurement sanction ultimately was waived, typically with a strained interpretation of the standards or an agreement to close-to-meaningless "corrective action" to extricate the government (much more than the firm) from an embarrassing predicament.

The reason that the Carter program was taken seriously, at least initially, by major corporations was the implementation of an idea (of Barry Bosworth's) that President Carter write the CEOs of the largest 500 corporations in the United States asking for their commitments to comply with the program. Some 450 of the CEOs replied affirmatively (although it must be noted that many of the letters were couched in cautious and legalistic wording that provided a potential escape hatch). More convincing evidence of the effectiveness of this strategy was the attitudes that we encountered when dealing with lower-level corporate executives—especially those placed in charge of administering the standards program within their company. Many said to us that their chairman had pledged to cooperate with the program and it was their job to make sure that the chairman's word was good. (I might note parenthetically that corporations—especially those with decentralized planning mechanisms—have an incentive and coordination problem not dissimilar to that of the federal government in assuring compliance with an incomes policy.) It seems that most of the large corporations felt that a commitment made to the president of the United States was more important than the threat of debarrment from bidding on federal contracts, even for those companies that dealt rather extensively with the government.

Finally, I might note that the need for a willingness to comply voluntarily with the program even extends to the income tax program itself. Our country, while not unique, is unusual in the degree of voluntary compliance with the stipulations of the tax law. There has in recent years been some diminution in the feeling of the social obligation to pay taxes (perhaps in part because of the antigovernment proclamations of some politicians), but it is still the case that corporations and individuals for the most part voluntarily comply with the tax laws, even though avoiding (and evading) taxes has a high expected return.

To summarize, I believe that, especially in countries where national business and labor organizations do not exist, it is necessary to generate a spirit of cooperation with an incomes policy in order for it to be successful. The problem is that the public tends to support, in principle, the need for an income tax, whereas there is no such general support for an incomes policy. Consequently, it is much more difficult to elicit cooperation for an incomes policy than for the tax system.

The argument that a TIP is less distortional than a traditional incomes policy because it attempts to work through the price system in internalizing the inflation externality is superficially appealing, but, I fear, ultimately a flawed notion. In the first place, a voluntary incomes policy (without tax incentives) has much of the same flexibility and, as I argue above, can be effective without strong legalistic provisions providing incentives to comply. As noted in my discussion of the cement producers, the advantage of a voluntary program is that, if a situation of excess demand occurs, firms are likely to abandon their commitment to the program and raise their prices. A voluntary guidelines program is likely to work only at the margin and only in those sectors of the economy where there is some market power.

More fundamentally, I believe that the analogy of a TIP to an effluent tax is inappropriate. The reason is that a pollution tax or an artificial market in pollution rights is designed to rectify a system of distorted *relative* prices. A TIP, on the other hand, designed to rectify an inflation externality, undoubtedly *distorts* relative prices. Consequently, a TIP does not avoid the tradeoff between the costs and benefits of an incomes policy. This point is elucidated most dramatically by considering the case of a noninflationary environment. In this case, there is no inflation externality and a TIP would be strictly distortional.[10]

These considerations suggest that the cost/benefit ratio of an incomes policy becomes greater as we approach a stable-price equilibrium and that the ratio is larger the more elaborate and formal the policy. A highly informal (educational) incomes policy, like the early-1960s guideposts, may make sense in a noninflationary, or low-inflation, situation, but a formal program would make economic sense only during a disinflation era. If this is correct, do we want to embed an incomes policy in our tax system?

CONCLUDING REMARKS

As I read the record of incomes policies, I believe that they can be effective instruments of anti-inflation policies for a short period of time. If intelligently designed and prudently administered, they can lower the costs of restrictive macroeconomic policies. It is, however, a mistake to perceive them as long-term anti-inflation policies. The longer such policies are in effect, the more complicated and legalistic they become. Distortions and market disruptions, which may initially be of minimal proportions, gradually accumulate until the induced inefficiency costs of the program become onerous. In addition, the program inevitably becomes entangled in controversy over issues of equity. Important and powerful political/economic groups have selfishly different views of what constitutes equity in the design and implementation of the incomes policies. Moreover, incomes policies are vulnerable to extraneous shocks (such as the world oil price explosion in 1979). Finally, the political temptation to relax fiscal and monetary policies, under the delusion that the incomes policies can keep the lid on inflation, can generate inflationary pressures that torpedo the incomes policies.

Perhaps Okun (1981: 345) said it best:

In attempting to offer an overall appraisal of informal programs of wage restraint, I am reminded of P.T. Barnum's statement that a lamb can be kept in a lion's cage if one has an adequate supply of lambs. I believe these programs can make a noticeable contribution for a substantial period of time, but they are ultimately doomed by various types of lions—excess demand, people determined to be noncooperative, or unrelated cost disturbances.

Okun, in this quotation, refers to "informal" programs of wage restraint, but I think the comment is just as applicable to formal programs. The effective portion of the highly formal mandatory controls program of the Nixon administration lasted not much longer than a year (Phase I and II). Phases III and IV were periods of decontrol as the government attempted to extricate itself from the system of inflexible wage/price controls.

It is my belief that a TIP would disintegrate over time for precisely the same reasons that a less formal incomes policy or a mandatory controls program disintegrates over time. The forces leading to deterioration of support for the program would not be altered by the existence of tax incentives for compliance or by the absence of stigmatization for increases above the standard. The question this leads me to ask is whether we want to burden the tax system with a program that is likely to be short-lived. The tax system is already burdened with myriad well-intentioned but often cumbersome and even counterproductive measures designed to promote social and economic objectives quite unrelated to the original purpose of the income tax. Do we want to burden the tax system with a program perhaps more far-reaching than the other types of amendments, thrusting the IRS into uncharted waters—especially since, within a short period of time, there likely will be efforts to abrogate the legislation setting up the incomes policy? I think not. An incomes policy can be a modestly effective short-run anti-inflation instrument, when complemented with fiscal and monetary restraint. But let's leave the tax system out of it.

NOTES TO CHAPTER 11

1. In characterizing the positions and arguments of TIP advocates throughout this chapter, I, of course, do not mean to imply that all proponents subscribe to all of the arguments—especially my particular characterizations.
2. I do not mean to imply that this appearance is illusory. Rather, in comparing the reality with the appearance of fairness, I agree with Lerner and Colander (1980: 35) that the criterion that a plan "be *seen to be fair* . . . is the more fundamental proposition" (italics in the original).
3. The assertion is not precise: In theory, if not in practice, it requires homotheticity (see Blackorby, Primont, and Russell 1978: 206–08).
4. See, however, the discussion of labor-input measurement below.
5. Lerner and Colander (1980) advocate use of a financial measure of the flow of capital services. This approach is not, of course, without its problems, as acknowledged by Lerner and Colander (1980: 56–57).
6. Following Triplett, I frequently refer to the Carter administration's Pay and Price Standards Program, and various aspects of it, with *CWPS* as the modifier, but this certainly gives too much credit (and blame) to the Coun-

cil on Wage and Price Stability, since many decisions were made by high-level administrative officials outside CWPS.

7. These problems are not avoided by using the financial measure of capital inputs proposed by Lerner and Colander (1980); firms receive an increased value-added allowance equal to the (initial) interest costs (at "the" market rate) of the investment, although this investment would typically allow the firms to produce the same output with less labor. The scope for such productivity improvements varies across industries.

8. For a more complete discussion of these measurement issues, see McMenamin and Russell (1983).

9. The most common "design failure," in my opinion, is the failure to complement the incomes policy with disinflationary fiscal and monetary policy. The Kennedy/Johnson guideposts were explicitly designed to prevent a round of cost-push inflation while the Kennedy administration "got the economy moving again." Initially, because of the existence of substantial unemployment and idle plant capacity, such policies were not deemed to be inflationary. Eventually, however, as Vietnam War expenditures overheated the economy and President Johnson repeatedly resisted the entreaties of his economic advisors to raise taxes, the guideposts came to be seen as a substitute for fiscal and monetary restraint. It is also widely believed that the Nixon administration used the mandatory controls program to keep the lid on prices while it pumped up the economy in preparation for the 1972 election. Finally, the Carter administration stressed the complementary roles of the Pay and Price Standards Program and restrictive fiscal and monetary policies, but the latter proved to be inadequate to the task until the credit crunch of early 1980 — long after the standards program had begun to disintegrate.

10. Insofar as a TIP can lower the NAIRU, it is not strictly distortional in a noninflationary environment (see Seidman 1979). Even in this case, however; a tradeoff between lowering the NAIRU and distorting relative prices exists. Moreover, I believe that carefully targeted employment subsidies would be more effective than a TIP in lowering the NAIRU. This is an issue that merits study.

12

CAN TIP-MIP-MAP PROPOSALS WORK?
Lessons from the Council on Wage and Price Stability

*Jack E. Triplett**

Some tax-based or market-incentive incomes policies (TIP or MIP) operate on wages. Others are directed toward control of prices (see the review in Colander 1981: 49–56). Yet others (primarily the Lerner/Colander MAP) substitute a control on value added. For both "wage" and "price" TIP-MIP proposals, the Pay and Price Standards of the Council on Wage and Price Stability (CWPS— generally pronounced "Cowps") offer direct lessons about program design and the problems that are likely to emerge if any of these proposals are put into effect. For the MAP proposal, the experience is not quite so exact, yet some portions of the CWPS Price Standards offer instructive suggestions. Experience with the Pay Standard is discussed in McMenamin and Russell (1983), Nichols (1983), and Russell (Chapter 11, this volume). The present chapter deals with the Price Standards.

In two respects, the CWPS experience provides a test for administrative problems and feasibility of incentive anti-inflation proposals. First, like most incentive anti-inflation proposals, the leverage of the CWPS standard was applied to economic decision making units—firms, or portions of firms that operated as entities for accounting, financial, marketing, and other decision-making purposes. This differs from, for example, the Nixon-era controls program, which limited individual product prices.

Second, economic principles were applied in the design of the CWPS program. CWPS was probably as close as one is likely to come to a program that is

---

*The author was assistant director for Price Monitoring, Council on Wage and Price Stability, from January to September 1979. This chapter represents solely views of the author and is not an official position of the Bureau of Labor Statistics.

designed by economists to pursue economic objectives. Not surprisingly, CWPS regulations and data collected under the standards have content similar to many proposals in the incentive anti-inflation literature.

Set against these two advantages, some features of the CWPS program limit its applicability as an incentive anti-inflation plan experiment. First, it was a voluntary program. Rule enforcement, and responses of subject firms, differed substantially from what one would expect had the standards been entered into tax law, or administered by formal regulatory machinery, such as that envisioned for TIP–MIP–MAP proposals. This chapter documents some of these situations.

Additionally, the CWPS standard was conceived as only one part of a three-pronged anti-inflation program, and it was explicitly short run in nature. Any permanent program would have provoked somewhat modified behavior by firms that were under the standards and undoubtedly would have set in motion a different constellation of political and regulatory pressures and responses. I believe that permanent or long-term TIP–MIP–MAP proposals will therefore confront more difficult obstacles than CWPS faced; this chapter discusses the more serious of those expected problems.

The following two sections outline the CWPS price standard in the context of the Carter administration anti-inflation program. The third discusses those administrative details so often overlooked in discussing incomes policies in the abstract, yet that make so much difference to the feasibility and effectiveness of policy proposals, and emphasizes the lessons CWPS experience provides for incentive anti-inflation plans. The final two sections contain reflections on the lessons the CWPS experience suggests for these proposals.

THE ROLE OF THE STANDARDS IN
THE ANTI-INFLATION PROGRAM

On October 24, 1978, then President Carter announced a three-part anti-inflation program (see the "White House Fact Sheet" in Carter 1978: 1845):

1. First, fiscal restraint was to reduce the federal share of GNP to 21 percent and lower the federal government deficit, then estimated at $40 billion, to around $30 billion. This action, with complementary monetary policy, reversed the mildly expansionist policy followed in the first year and a half of the Carter administration. Slowing the economy was intended as the major inflation-fighting weapon.[1]

2. Second, the administration promised to reduce growth in cost-increasing regulatory and other government programs. It was widely perceived that the sheer number of new environmental and social initiatives as well as traditional agricultural price supports and other direct and indirect subsidies had increased production costs across a broad spectrum of the U.S. economy. As events turned out, this part of the anti-inflation effort was almost entirely ignored by the

White House Domestic Policy Staff, which invariably found reasons to put supposed (one is tempted, from the nature of some of these arguments, to say "imaginary") political expediencies ahead of an anti-inflation effort that had publicly been described as the president's "number one domestic policy" priority (see the Epilogue, below).

3. The third element of the anti-inflation program consisted of the Pay and Price Standards promulgated by the Council on Wage and Price Stability. The Pay Standard parallels the earliest of the TIP proposals, those that focused on holding down labor costs. The price standard had several alternative parts, which are discussed in the next section.

Various parts of the administration formed different conceptions of the role to be played by the Pay and Price Standards in the anti-inflation effort. My personal view, one that motivated (perhaps *rationalized* is a better word) my taking on the administration of the Price Standards, interpreted the standards as tools to work on inflationary expectations during the transition stage from a mildly inflationary to a mildly deflationary fiscal-monetary stimulus. I am not suggesting they were necessarily the only or the best tools for influencing expectations, only that they were available and that was their purpose. I never regarded the standards as feasible devices for creating a permanent shift in the inflation-unemployment tradeoff (the role that is sometimes proposed for TIP–MIP–MAP) and doubt if I would have taken on the job if I thought we were trying to accomplish that task.

Viewing the standards as mechanisms for influencing inflationary expectations is consistent with the original intention that the standards run for only a single year. When I arrived at CWPS at the beginning of January 1979, there was no thought of a second year of the program because the administration expected fiscal constraint to have taken hold by the summer or fall of 1979. The price expectations reasoning was also used by most of us in describing the Price Standards to business groups, trade associations, and individual firms, and I am convinced that this justification contributed greatly to the high degree of cooperation the program received from large U.S. corporations during the first three quarters of 1979.

One should not infer, however, that this was the only or even the dominant view, even within CWPS. Russell (this volume), for example, suggests a somewhat broader role (or more optimistic view) for the standards, though his position differs only in degrees from my own.

Others within the administration, however, regarded the Pay and Price Standards as controls, pure and simple (or even as meaningless window dressing to cover a wage-control program). The "voluntary" part of the standards meant, in this view, that procurement sanctions, appeals to public opinion, "jawboning," and other informal, ambiguous, and flexible sanctions were substituted for the legal and rigid ones of the Nixon-era program of formal price controls, but that the objective, functioning, and impact of the two programs were closely similar. Put another way, the price standards would put a cap on inflationary pressures, permitting more freedom to pursue other objectives without concern for their inflationary consequences. This point is elaborated in the Epilogue section of this chapter.

THE CWPS PRICE STANDARD

The CWPS Price Standard was a rather complex one because it tried to achieve two objectives that had, its designers felt, too often been ignored in the implementation of previous incomes policies and price controls programs. First, there was not one "price standard" but a number of them, in order to provide alternatives that took account of the economics of various industries, and of financial, accounting, and marketing practices and conventions.

Secondly, all the price standards were made as economically meaningful as possible, and interpretation avoided the formalistic analogies inherent in legal and regulatory activities. Whatever one might conclude about the adequacy of the economists' analysis, one cannot in the CWPS program hide behind the excuse that legal, political, or administrative interventions prevented the economists from designing the program their analysis suggested should be put in place.[2]

Among the alternative price standards, two are relevant for present purposes.

The Price Deceleration Standard (Title 6, section 705A-2, *Federal Register*, Dec. 28, 1978) was the basic CWPS price standard, the one to which it was originally anticipated that most firms would adhere. This standard called for computing two fixed-weight Laspeyres formula price indices. The first index (the base-period rate of price change) measured price changes put into effect for a company's products from the fourth quarter of 1975 through the fourth quarter of 1977. The second fixed-weight index (the program-year rate of price change) was applied to price changes during the CWPS program. In the first year (1978–79) price increases measured by the latter index number were supposed to fall 0.5 percentage points under the company's calculated base-period rate of price change. For example, if a firm or its "compliance unit"[3] had increased prices at a 7 percent (weighted) average rate over the two-year 1976–77 period, compliance with the program required a 6½ percent, maximum, weighted average rate of price change after the third quarter of 1978. A six-month check (one-half of the allowable yearly increase) and subsequently a nine-month check (three-quarters of the allowable yearly increase) were monitoring targets. The system was kept in force for the second year of the CWPS price standard, with two-year allowable price increases computed as an extension of the one-year method.

There were elements of arbitrariness in choice of the base period, the target reduction of 0.5 percentage points, and other details. Use of the company's own base period rate of price change was intended to capture to an extent trend deviations in productivity, input materials costs, and so forth across different markets, but it is questionable if it did so effectively. In any event, arbitrariness is present in all comparable programs, including TIP–MIP–MAP.

The use of an average rate of change across all of the products a company sold, rather than the imposition of some maximum rate of change on prices for each individual product (as was done in previous "control" programs), was intended to introduce flexibility into the standard. There was in principle no limit to the allowable increase in a particular product's price, so long as the sellers of it offset increases with slower rates of increase, or decreases, elsewhere. The combination of the flexibility inherent in a companywide average, as well as operation of the CWPS exception process, avoided the differential incentives across product lines that created specific shortages experienced during earlier episodes of direct controls. No shortages attributable to the CWPS program are known to have developed during the period of its existence.

A minor feature of the specific index number approach that was implemented lies in the theoretical property of the Laspeyres index as a *lower* bound on the "true" price index for outputs (see Fisher and Shell 1972: essay 2 for the proof of this proposition). The implications of this were not lost on the companies, who tried to pass a variety of alternative price index number forms past the Council's staff during compliance reviews.

For a number of industries for which CWPS determined that the Price Deceleration Standard was "inappropriate," the Margin Standards (section 705C-2) were introduced. For firms engaged in food manufacturing or food processing, and for petroleum refineries, the Margin Standards required that the gross margin per unit of output grow not more than 6.5 percent per year, with a volume adjustment that gave a slightly lower rate of unit margins in cases of increasing sales and rising margins when volume decreased. The gross margin concept was closely allied to the computation of value added by individual firms. Wholesaling and retailing firms, or the wholesaling or retailing arms of manufacturing firms, were to limit the rate of growth of unit percentage margins. Firms in all these industries had the option of applying the basic Price Deceleration Standard rather than the Margin Standards, and a few of them did so.

A third standard, the Profit Margin Limitation, was used as an "exception." This standard eventually (after some false starts) amounted to a strict cost pass-through rule. The way the profit standard was supposed to work, firms would be on it only if specific circumstances arose under either the Price Deceleration or Gross Margin Standards, so in this chapter I will discuss the Profit Margin Limitation only in conjunction with the problems that arose out of the other two.

One other piece of institutional information is necessary as background. Most "controls" programs have found it necessary to have an "exceptions" process, by which firms can apply for exemption or relief from one or more of the rules and regulations. Lanzillotti, Hamilton, and Roberts (1975) mention the existence of an entire Exceptions Division created within the Nixon-era Price Commission, though they do not describe its operation. The need for a substantial exceptions machinery reflects the fact that real-world situations are complex: "Business can live with a set of internally consistent regulations that are respected by its administrators [yet] the regulations need to be flexible to meet changing economic conditions and should be applicable to conditions in particular markets without an excessive amount of interpretation. . . . [T]hey should not be arbitrary and should not be used arbitrarily" (Lanzillotti, Hamilton, and Roberts, 1975: 200–01). It is really the perception of arbitrariness that matters, and there is a conflict between the need for a simple set of rules that are perceived as applying to everyone and a set of rules flexible enough to encompass the peculiarities of individual market situations. The need for an exceptions process will present itself in any TIP–MIP–MAP proposal, as it did in the CWPS program and in earlier periods of controls. Exceptions are, however, by their very nature, potential loopholes. The administrative staff they require grows in proportion to the length of time a program is in place and to the degree it adopts formalistic or legalistic procedures.

ADMINISTRATIVE PROBLEMS WITH THE CWPS STANDARD, AND IMPLICATIONS FOR TIP–MIP–MAP

The Price Deceleration Standard: Lessons for Incentive Anti-Inflation Plans

As noted above, this CWPS standard made the allowable company-specific price change depend on one price index number and judged compliance with the program on the basis of a second index number. Some TIP and MIP proposals involve writing the Price Deceleration Standard, or something very close to it, into tax or other portions of the legal code.

Setting up the program as a comparison of index numbers made it relatively simple, or so it appeared to CWPS economists. Laspeyres index formulas did not, however, seem simple to the public and to most executives of the firms that were expected to comply with the CWPS program. One newspaper reproduced the Laspeyres formula and implied that the formula's summation sign represented the ultimate degree of incomprehensibility in governmental regulations. Explaining the CWPS Standard and the rationale for it presented a serious problem for the program in its first few months. When I arrived at CWPS in January 1979, more than two months after the president had announced the CWPS program, roughly 90 percent of staff time was spent answering letters and telephone calls.

I once received a call from the president of a medium-size corporation (*medium-size* in CWPS terminology meant one with annual sales between $250 and $500 million). He had computed, he told me, his company's program year rate of price change in nine different ways. Under eight of them his company was in compliance with the program, but with the ninth he was not. I would not be repeating this anecdote if the ninth were not precisely the one used to judge CWPS compliance. It was not at all easy for the public to understand what seemed to the economists on the CWPS staff a straightforward calculation.

Of course, the economic system is a wonderful thing: Services find their way onto the market when a need for them arises. Major accounting firms, as well as many Washington law firms, soon began to provide commentary on the CWPS standards and guidance on computing the data the standards required. The fact that technical assistance became available to business firms, and that some of these intermediaries did a better job of explanation than did CWPS's own staff and materials, more than offset the fact that numerous interpretive errors were introduced, which themselves had to be discovered and corrected at a later date.

I dwell on the comprehension problem for two reasons. First, economists do not communicate very well with the public. One reason perhaps is that the things they want to communicate are complex. But as well, economists' training makes them think that things they have learned a long time ago are simple, when to a person without economic training the same ideas may seem quite complex, abstract, and confusing. Economic policy debates sometimes overlook as too obvious problems that the general public and program administrators find excessively complex. The fact that the CWPS program was hard for the public to understand must be considered in future designs of similar programs.

The second point to be made about the communication problem is a related one. Anyone with much experience compiling price indices knows that the formula is one of the simpler parts of the job. The really hard questions (those reviewed below) had to be discussed with business firms in a context in which those affected had considerable difficulty with the Laspeyres index number formula.

Many companies claimed they were unable to compute a price index. Some of these cases were justifiable (the CWPS standard contained a provision for exceptions for "inability to compute"). For example, some firms had no price records, particularly in large companies that gave division or establishment managers a great amount of autonomy on pricing and judged performance essentially by profit. An example was the Southland Corporation, which received an exception on showing it had some 7,000 units with no base-period price records.[4] A greeting card company had price records for each class of card, but no quantities (and only aggregate revenues) because no records were kept of cards returned by retail outlets. They were thus without the weights for the price index formula. Numerous variations on these two situations were encountered. Some other claims represented a disingenuous attempt to get around the program's compliance rules and to get onto the Profit Margin Limitation (which was the alternative standard for the "inability to compute" cases, and at least in the early months of the program was regarded by the companies as a less confining standard).

The CWPS staff dealt with inability-to-compute cases by attempting to find some method that resolved the particular problem the company had raised. This was largely an educational chore, but it became urgent because each exception granted in an inability-to-compute case generated a dozen others (the accounting firms and law firms that had begun to specialize in CWPS cases saw to that).

Many companies argued that they produced too many products to make constructing a price index practicable or that it would be burdensomely expensive. The count of the "number" of products a company produces does depend on how one chooses to define "product," but it is clear that the pricing structure of many U.S. corporations involves a very large number of different prices. Stigler and Kindahl (1970) in discussing one class of steel products (hot rolled carbon steel sheet), noted that there may be more than 135 *million* different prices for this class of product alone, not counting those for any other steel mill products.

The CWPS answer to the "too many products" plea was to suggest the company take a sample, which could then provide the basis for compliance decisions. Sampling was also a new experience for many corporations that lacked any kind of statistical expertise.[5]

Some companies argued that the expense of sampling was unduly burdensome. CWPS evolved some rules of thumb on such claims. For example, the U.S. Distribution Group of the Pittston Company received an exception on showing that the cost of sampling would amount to 0.3 percent of revenues; but the Brink's Incorporated subsidiary of the same company found that an estimated sample cost of 0.07 percent of revenue brought a denial of its exception request because it was, in the words of the decision, "an amount that, in the Council's judgment, is not onerous" (Decision of Reconsideration, February 15, 1980, in the matter of the Pittston Company on behalf of its compliance unit, Brink's Incorporated). Data from other exception decisions showed that taking a sample of prices was a fairly costly process for some large corporations, though the expense generally amounted to a small fraction of sales revenues. The CWPS evaluation document (Council on Wage and Price Stability 1981) used this and other data to estimate compliance costs. These data are relevant to the potential compliance costs of TIP–MIP proposals.

Firms also resisted sampling on grounds other than cost. One company that had selected a sample of its products argued that with the (large) sampling error on its estimate, one could not reject the hypothesis that the company was in compliance with the CWPS Price Deceleration Standard, even though its measured program year rate of price change clearly exceeded its allowable rate. This issue was resolved in an informal way, and to my knowledge it was never again raised explicitly during the course of the CWPS program.

However, other companies were clearly apprehensive, and though they presented different arguments, I believe their root concern was the possibility that they might have been found out of compliance because of type II error. For example, the Auto Carrier Division of Ryder Systems Incorporated claimed their data were not normally distributed, that their prices were not serially correlated, and that the null hypothesis being tested was a very small number, so that it would have to take at least a 25 percent sample of prices, the cost of which would be excessive. Similarly, the Sherwin-Williams Company claimed that using a sample to judge the company's price movements was "experimental." Though the council denied the relevance, factual basis, or logic behind all of these claims and insisted that smaller and less costly samples would be adequate, I suspect the real concerns of these companies lay in the well-established sphere of sampling error, had they been sophisticated enough to make the correct statistical arguments.

One presumes that the implementation of a TIP-MIP proposal might envision sampling as a method for checking compliance. At this point the difference between voluntary and mandatory programs becomes relevant. Suppose the CWPS Deceleration Standard had been written into (say) the tax law as a TIP. And suppose a company went to court with the argument that one could not reject the hypothesis that what it had done was legal, or that its tax penalty was improperly assessed. Arguing statistical methods before a court of law is not novel, but introduction of statistical arguments in tax cases is. Adding the problems of sampling theory to existing ones of jurisprudence in the tax area (tax law already has a special court structure) seems anything but a simple and uncomplicated policy proposal. It would probably take years to work out an appropriate body of legal case law.

Another vexing class of CWPS "inability to compute" cases involved "custom" products, which products were excluded from the Price Deceleration Standard (section 705A–3h). If a construction company built a bridge in the base period and an office building in the current period, it does not make much sense to ask whether the price of the office building is higher than that of the bridge, nor is there a very well-defined conceptual basis for relating the one to the other.[6] The custom products exclusion was perceived as another loophole opening to the more attractive Profit Margin Limitation. A standard joke among the council staff involved the company that claimed it made "custom" telephone poles because it carefully cut the holes exactly where the customer specified them.

CWPS staff handled the more outlandish of these "custom" claims informally. But we were administering a voluntary program. We did not have to go into a law court with legal counsel and argue the definition of a "custom" product. Any legally sanctioned, mandatory price program must deal with the custom product problem, because it (1) is a legitimate problem, and (2) will be used as a way to get out from under the controls. "Custom" and "standard" describe two extremes of a continuum that cannot neatly be divided into cases for which a CWPS-type Price Deceleration Standard is or is not appropriate.

A related class of problems concerns adjustment for quality change. This well-known difficulty in the measurement of prices needs no elaboration (see Griliches 1971; Triplett 1975 contains a survey of the empirical literature on price indices and quality change).

I have recently been asked whether there are any data that could be used to partition the economy into sectors where quality change is likely to present a problem, and those where products are standardized and quality change is not a factor. In response, it is worth citing at length the case of the Marion Brick Corporation.

Marion produced and sold exactly what its name implies—construction brick. The company was cited for noncompliance with the Price Deceleration Standard in the summer of 1979. Later, the company asked that the noncompliance decision be reconsidered, arguing that, in the words of the council's decision (see Decision of Reconsideration, November 15, 1979 in the matter of Marion Brick Corporation), "after appropriate adjustments in quality, its price increases were less than those allowed under the Price Deceleration Standard." One might wonder how brick could qualify for a quality change adjustment. The details are in the council's Reconsideration Decision (handed down, incidentally, after I left CWPS):

> First, Marion argued that a service introduced in the first program year—immediate availability of bricks—had a market value equal to a specific percentage of the base-quarter product price. This valuation was based on the observation that buyers of other construction materials who desired immediate availability generally were willing to pay a percentage premium for this service.
>
> Marion's second argument was that such an adjustment was warranted due to the incremental cost it incurred in improving the physical characteristics of its brick (color retention, heat and cold durability, tensile strength and resistance to stress), and in improving the services associated with the sale of its bricks. While there were certain offsetting adjustments that the company did not consider, the Council generally accepts this cost-justification method of assessing the value of documented changes in product characteristics. On a per-unit basis these costs provide a measure of the market value of the composite quality change.

The point of the Marion Brick case is this: Quality change, or noncomparability in the transactions for which prices are gathered, is a pervasive phenomenon. For price measurement and for price control purposes, it is simply not valid to suppose that one can find large sections of the economy for which this problem will not arise. The quality problem arose during price controls in World War II and led to assertions that the true price increase during controls was greater than what was measured. The Price Commission in the early 1970s handled it in a way comparable to CWPS. In all three cases, it was not only a problem for the efficacy of controls, in the sense that diminished quality could mask true price increases; it was also potentially the source of much controversy berween the companies and program administrators.

In the CWPS program, we told companies presenting quality change arguments that they should follow the cost-based adjustments used by the Bureau of Labor Statistics in the Producers Price Index—that is, the companies should compute the resource costs, at fixed factor prices and scales of output, of quality changes in the products they made and use these estimates to adjust their company's specific price index for the value of quality change. Obviously, that procedure uses the company's own internal data in a way that cannot be checked very effectively. Because CWPS was running a voluntary program that relied on and received a very wide degree of support, we felt such procedures could be employed without great damage to the program.

I would have much more serious reservations about the feasibility of quality adjustments based on internal cost data in a TIP–MIP program. Even within the Bureau of Labor Statistics, where the only purpose is to produce a published price index, use of cost-based data for making quality adjustments requires decisions that are sometimes subjective and sometimes arbitrary, partly because the data are not always entirely appropriate. In a price TIP–MIP program, one would inevitably have to undertake very detailed cost audits of quality change in order to measure the true price changes put into effect. From long experience with this problem, I feel that even with audits there are too many cases that could not reasonably be classified, and that the economic analysis of what economists mean by quality change is far too little developed to stand up to legal challenge.[7] In short, I believe that quality change, alone, might sink any TIP–MIP plan that uses something similar to the CWPS Price Deceleration Standard.

This listing by no means exhausts the technical issues that arose in administering the Price Deceleration Standard. There were the cases of new products, sold in the control period, but not in production in the base period. There were product mix cases: The company computed an average price for (say) widgets as one of the Ps in its price index, only to find that unexpected shifts toward (or away from) deluxe widgets put it inadvertently out of compliance, or masked its general price increases.

All these cases were not only difficult for the CWPS staff (and for the companies themselves) to resolve, they also presented opportunities for what we referred to as "gaming." The CWPS evaluation document (Council on Wage and Price Stability 1981) argued that gaming was minimal in the first year of the CWPS program, and I agree in the sense that it occurred in a very small proportion of the total number of corporations that we dealt with. But if a similar proposal were enacted into tax law in the form of a TIP, and if it were to continue as a permanent feature of business regulation, an army of lawyers and accountants would soon be determining exactly how far the law could be pushed and what kinds of loopholes could be opened in it. The CWPS record is ample evidence showing where those loopholes would occur, and how seriously they would inhibit the efficacy of comparable TIP–MIP proposals.

The largest class of exceptions from the CWPS Price Deceleration Standard involved cases of "uncontrollable costs." Uncontrollable cost cases arose because the 1979 boom in raw materials and petroleum prices[8] meant that many companies were experiencing input cost increases that could not be recovered within their allowable CWPS output price increases. Materials price inflation is likely to be a feature of other inflationary situations as well,[9] and so it may plague any TIP–MIP proposal that is similar to the CWPS Price Deceleration Standard. Though administration of the exceptions machinery, and the implementation of the profit margin limitation, absorbed a very high proportion of CWPS administrative resources, detailed discussion would take us too far afield (see Council of Wage and Price Stability 1981).

In summary, the administrative difficulties experienced under the CWPS Price Deceleration Standard can be grouped under three headings:

1. "Uncontrollable" input costs, handled by CWPS by permitting (nearly) full cost passthrough to final product price;
2. Educational, communicative, and data deficiency problems, which required working with complying firms to explain unfamiliar economic and statistical concepts, and to determine relatively inexpensive methods for accumulating the data for CWPS compliance checks where the normal accounting records did not contain it;
3. Measurement problems that are well known in the literature of economics— quality change, custom products (such as construction), new products or new product varieties, and so forth.

Any TIP or MIP that parallels the CWPS Price Deceleration Standard must evolve administrative machinery for dealing with each of these classes of problems. In some of them (the measurement issues are the best examples), we can be sure that whatever measures are brought to bear, resolution will not be very satisfactory. Moreover, the machinery must be more elaborate, substantial, and costly than was used in CWPS because the more intractable and controversial economic and statistical questions will be subject to judicial or other legal review when the TIP or MIP is written into tax law or involves contractual relations among private parties. Thus, what was an educational or communication problem under the voluntary CWPS standards would become a legal issue under TIP– MIP, with consequent escalation of costs of administration and of compliance.

THE MARGIN STANDARDS: LESSONS FOR MAP

As mentioned above, special CWPS standards were developed for certain industries, which were called on to limit their gross margins, a concept approximating value added. Setting the control on value added is a feature of some forms of TIP–MIP–MAP, particularly the MAP proposal of Lerner-Colander (see Colander 1981), though their proposal differs from the CWPS Margin Standards in ways discussed below.

For food processing and petroleum refining industries, the margin was defined as revenue less purchased food and petroleum, respectively. In wholesale and retail trade industries, the margin amounted to revenue less the cost of goods purchased for resale. In three of the four cases the gross margin thus approximated value added plus purchased energy and a few other components such as packaging and containers.[10] In the following we use *margin* and *value added* interchangeably, unless otherwise noted.

In the CWPS program, use of margin standards was confined to cases where the computation of a price index was thought to be impractical because of accounting and record keeping conventions (wholesale and retail trade) or for cases for which projected high increases in raw materials or purchased inputs were expected to drive whole industries off the Price Deceleration Standard (this reasoning applied to food processors, which were subject to volatile swings from uncontrolled agricultural prices, and to petroleum refineries because it was already clear in 1978 that crude petroleum prices would increase sharply). So far as I can determine, there was never any thought that it was *preferable* to control the margin or value added rather than the output prices themselves.

Problems that developed with the margin standards can be grouped under three headings: (1) measurement issues comparable to (but different from) those that interfered with administration of the price deceleration standard; (2) input and output "mix" adjustments and other factors that necessitated a detailed industry-by-industry view of special circumstances (parallel to the exceptions machinery that was required under the Price Deceleration Standard); and (3) distortion of input proportions and inhibition of input substitution—a serious economic problem that had no counterpart under the CWPS Price Deceleration Standard but that does have parallels in the artificial shortages and distortions that accompanied earlier "controls" programs.

It is convenient to consider first the third of these problems—economic distortion caused by a value added standard.

Value added is a problematical economical concept. In a competitive economy, value added consists of payments to labor and capital inputs, excluding materials and other inputs. It has been observed (Sims 1969; Sato 1977) that value added is therefore a meaningful economic concept only when the production function is separable on its capital and labor inputs. This result is a special application of standard theorems of production and aggregation theory (see, for example, Blackorby, Primont, and Russell 1978).

The major economic problem with controlling value added, then, lies in its arbitrary separation among inputs to the production process. Whenever limits, taxes, or controls are placed on value added, it inhibits substitution of (say) capital for materials, but encourages substitution of materials for capital. This problem was recognized in the administration of the CWPS standard, but it was thought (the standards having, originally, a one-year time horizon) that the period involved was too short to influence corporate planning for input substitution.

By the end of the first year of the program, however, we were receiving complaints about the Margin Standards' interference with input substitution. For example, a delegation from a wholesaling-distribution trade association presented us with an elaborate set of charts showing historical trends of input costs (wages and fuel) in their industry. They claimed that on the basis of historical labor/energy price trends, distributive firms had deliberately centralized operations in order to reap scale economies associated with labor saving in larger warehouses, accepting in the process increased fuel usage from longer hauls. The rapid run-up in energy costs in 1978–79 required, they maintained, that much recent capital investment be undone; but the CWPS margin standard prevented this because energy-saving shifts required increased capital and labor (and therefore growth in value added). The longer-term movement of energy prices now roughly approximates the average inflation rate, so it is not clear from the present perspective that the argument was valid in this particular case. But this example shows that controlling value added distorts investment planning and produces potential effects on productivity.

The MAP proposal concerns value added per unit of input; CWPS operated on value added per unit of output. This does not change the argument. Distortion occurs because a control or rule placed on value added encompasses capital and labor inputs and excludes others. The distortion is independent of whether value added is divided by measured output or by measured inputs.

A second class of problems were administrative: Value added may rise or fall because of shifts in the mixes of inputs or outputs that have no implications for inflation or because of factors that are out of control of the firm's management. Accordingly, in any program operating on value added, mechanisms must be put in place to review or adjust for these special situations. Because some of them will be specific to particular industries, this requires an administrative staff of considerable size and expertise.

An excellent example from the CWPS experience concerns petroleum refineries. Crude oil is not a homogeneous commodity. It varies along a number of dimensions. One can produce a mix of, for instance, gasoline, heating oil, and petrochemical feed stocks from any variety of crude, but some types of crude oil require more refinery operations (and hence greater value added per barrel of input) than others. If the refinery switches from one kind of crude to another, it may alter its value added in a direction that has little to do with product price movements. In fact, conservation of scarce natural resources generally implies increases in value added.

Comparably, changes in the mix of outputs also affect value added. For example, higher-octane (lead-free) gasoline requires more refinery operations, for any given type of crude input, than does lower-octane gasoline. Accordingly, the high octane product has higher value, other things equal. A shift in the automotive stock toward more "performance" oriented engines, or in federal law as to lead-free gasoline, will thus imply differential demand growth for gasoline types and change refinery value added, again in a way that has little to do with product price movements.

For these reasons CWPS permitted input and output mix adjustments in administering its margin standards. Though it is feasible to monitor adjustments for mix effects, they are not easy to check and require a great amount of staff time with highly specialized expertise. We were fortunate in CWPS that we had the required expertise in the energy area (though not necessarily a sufficient number of staff). A TIP–MIP–MAP proposal must assemble it for every industry in the economy.

Retailers and their trade associations claimed that a firm might have a margin *target*, but that the margin *realized* was the outcome of corporate planning interacting with elements that were outside their control. It is probably true that realized prices also have an element that is beyond the control of the corporate planner, but this problem is clearly more severe when margins or value added are the controlled variables (because x percent "inadvertent" realized prices over target will push up margins by $x \cdot y$ percent, where y is the inverse of the average percentage margin).

On this matter, it is worth quoting in full "Special Sectors Question and Answer #9" (*Federal Register*, vol. 44, January 25, 1979, p. 5364):

Q. Because of changes in the mix of product sales, and improvement in loss experience ("shrinkage"), or changes in the rates of movement of merchandise at initial markups vs. marked-down prices, a retailer might fail to satisfy the percentage-margin standard for reasons beyond its control. Will the company be judged to be out of compliance?

A. No. As long as a company makes a good-faith effort to comply with the standard, an inadvertent overshooting of the margin target will not result in a determination of noncompliance. A good-faith effort requires that retailers adopt a markup (and mark-down) policy that can be expected to generate percentage margins that comply with the standard. If there is no change in policy regarding mark-downs, shrinkage, etc., the retailer can simply project past experience regarding these factors. However, a change in policy or practice regarding any of these factors should be reflected in the mark-up policy. Finally, if a company overshoots the margin target, it will be expected to adjust its markup policy in the next year to compensate for the excessive margin during the first program year.

Note the language "good faith effort to comply" in the CWPS "answer," along with the provision that an inadvertent breaking of the standard could be compensated by an offsetting reduction later on. This was characteristic of CWPS "remedies" because it was a voluntary program. A mandatory program would have to have a well-defined set of rules for dealing with such situations or be in conflict with due process procedures.

The computation of gross margins (and also value added) is affected by accounting conventions. For example, changing from FIFO to LIFO for inventory valuation will change the margin and also may change value added. This implies that imposing a MAP involves at least as much effort in regulating accounting practices as is now put into relevant aspects of tax law.

For all these reasons, I do not regard a gross margin standard, or a value-added "rule" under a MAP, particularly easy to administer. We at CWPS felt the Price Deceleration Standard, with all its problems, was simpler than the Margin Standards—easier to explain, easier to administer, involved fewer arbitrary rulings arising out of special cases, presented fewer opportunities for "gaming" and evasion, and, above all, caused less distortion. My judgment, moreover, is that this administrative case would move even more strongly against the value-added standard the longer the program remained in place and the more it moved away from a voluntary, toward a legalistic, approach.

Discussion of measurement issues completes the three categories listed above. In the section on the CWPS Price Deceleration Standard, I remarked that a large proportion of the administrative problems encountered with that standard were simply manifestations of problems that were familiar and well documented in the price measurement literature. Since the conceptual difficulties in measuring prices are so well understood by economists (though of course price indices are computed regularly and even found to be useful, despite their conceptual and empirical shortcomings), the argument that price "controls" programs are limited by these problems falls, as it were, on fertile soil. There is little empirical or conceptual literature on the measurement of value added, but that does not mean that—by default—it poses less serious problems.

The CWPS standard applied (approximately) to value added per unit of output. There was available a "volume adjustment" that permitted firms to adjust margins, as they moved up or down their short-run cost curves, which adjustment involved computation of output measures. We pass over this matter with the observation that if one knows how to measure the output, one knows how to measure the price, the measurement problems being exactly equivalent (one is tempted to borrow terminology from the production and cost function literature and say that they are "dual").

A MAP applies to value added per unit of input. The most nearly relevant measurement literature is thus that on measuring productivity, for in the versions that compute productivity ratios on value added (or GNP or NNP originating), MAP's value added per unit of input can be written as[11]

$$\pi \cdot P = \frac{(VA/P) \cdot P}{f(K, L)}$$

where π is the rate of multi-factor productivity change and all other variables are to be understood as index numbers or measures of change.

Thus, MAP's value added per unit of output does evade all the problems of measuring prices and quantities of outputs, since they cancel out of the numerators, but does so by incurring the problems of measuring prices and quantities of inputs. Is this a net gain? I do not think so.

Forming an index or other measures of capital inputs (or of their prices) involves conceptual and empirical problems that are as well documented in economics as those of output price measurement, and at least as formidable. It is unnecessary to summarize these issues (for a recent statement that only culminates a lengthy and contentious literature, see Usher 1980). It is probably the professional consensus that capital measurement is more difficult than other forms of price and output measurement, largely because of the durability and vintage issues.[12] In any event, there is clearly little net gain in moving the measurement focus from output to capital inputs.

Measuring labor inputs and factor prices is often regarded by the profession as a simpler problem. As one participant in the Middlebury conference put it: "Average hourly earnings is good enough."

Recent advances in the analysis of labor markets, however, have elaborated the theory so that it encompasses empirical regularities that have long been observed, but on which traditional neoclassical labor market theory had been inchoate. An important implication of this modern, richer theoretical view of the labor market, with its greater integration with empirical research, is that labor market measurement can be seen to involve most of the conceptual difficulties that plague the measurement of capital, plus a few unique and intractable ones of its own (Triplett 1983: 25-26, 49-50):

> The human capital innovation in labor economics . . . applied to decision making by the worker. It left largely intact the traditional analysis of the employer. Though the human capital view emphasized that employers were hiring a labor input that was not homogenous, employment decisions were still treated as functions of current period prices. The most recent revolution in labor economics completes the circle: The employment of labor (as has long been understood for the capital input) requires a multiperiod optimization model on the demand side, as does the worker-training decision on the supply side. Both supply of and demand for human skills are now seen as problems that have a strong capital theoretic component.
>
> What makes the labor input uniquely difficult is that the seller of labor cares not just about the wage but also about employment conditions and other characteristics of the buyer. Because there is so much employer heterogeneity, the variety in compensation packages will be great. And variation in elements of the compensation package leads to variation in the quantities of other inputs, especially capital. This dependence between quantities of one input and "prices" paid for another poses special and very difficult problems for measurement of labor cost.

I have developed this position more fully in the source quoted above, and space precludes a more extended summary here. The paper by Russell (this volume) well documents the labor-side measurement problems encountered in administering the CWPS Pay Standard. Both the labor economics literature and CWPS experience thus show that measuring labor inputs (and labor factor prices) poses difficult conceptual and practical problems. Moving (as the value added per unit of input idea does) from the output measurement sphere over to the labor input side hardly implies that less difficult problems will be encountered by MAP than were experienced by CWPS in administering its Margin Standards. If anything is true, the problems will be more difficult ones.

In summary, a margin or value added standard potentially creates serious economic distortions. It limits, unless specific exceptions are arranged, input substitution across the boundaries of the value added or margin definition. Moreover, it encourages (or discourages) changing the mix of outputs, or substituting among the detailed inputs that are included in value added or the margin definition. One can deal with the adverse economic consequences of such incentives, to be sure. But it will require a large staff with specific knowledge of the industries being regulated, and a great amount of auditing and record keeping burden. And the difficulties that are posed by measurement problems are formidable.

All of these comments apply to a world in which "rights" to raise or lower value added are sold on a market. The Colander/Lerner MAP will require a regulatory agency to determine whether a value added "right" has been used correctly. The fact that a "market" exists to determine the "price" for the privilege of changing one's price does not preclude a regulatory and enforcement bureaucracy.

CONCLUSION: THE CWPS PRICE STANDARDS AND TIP–MIP–MAP

Except for the uncontrollable cost case, the major problems with the CWPS Price Deceleration Standards and its controls mechanism have one thing in common: They are largely measurement issues, most of them exactly parallel to technical difficulties that arise in the production of price indices, productivity ratios, and so forth. Some of them (the quality problem, for example) are subjects of substantial professional literatures. A standard on margins or value added suffers from parallel problems, except that in this case the measurement problems interact with the possibility of introducing economic distortions.

All past programs have confronted measurement problems. In the CWPS program they were resolved at the staff level, for the most part, primarily as the outcome of a collegial exchange. The Nixon-era Price Commission resolved them by administrative fiat, in principle subject to judicial review. TIP–MIP–MAP programs that are directed at any price, price aggregate, margin, or value added computation must also deal with them. Moreover, any *mandatory* TIP–MIP–MAP program must incorporate due process rules comparable to those now in force for appeal of tax rulings. Due process rules will mean that decisions on measurement issues will be legally contested. Because we have no precedent from the Price Commission experience, we cannot be sure what would transpire in a judical proceeding on a measurement issue, but my presumption is for a massive process on any issue where a sufficiently large amount of money rides on the outcome (an automobile price increase involving deduction of the cost of mandatory pollution devices, for example).

As I understand them, simplicity is a major argument of the proponents of TIP-MIP-MAP. But arguing before a court methods for adjusting for quality change, allowing for new and custom products, methods of measuring capital inputs, and statistical hypothesis testing for compliance with the law, are not simple matters at all. The lesson to be drawn from the CWPS experience for TIP-MIP-MAP is this: These proposals look simple until one examines them closely. The more one looks, the more complicated they get.

I do not want to be misunderstood as espousing some sort of "impossibility theorem." All the problems I have been discussing can be addressed, given sufficient staff resources; and all can probably, with enough ingenuity and effort, be reduced to sufficiently manageable proportions that a controls program can operate at some acceptable level of proficiency. What I am contending is that such a program will be costly to administer, both for the government and for the companies that are subject to it. The size of the CWPS staff is nowhere near the staff size that will be required to administer a mandatory TIP or MIP program, because a mandatory program brings out more attempts at evasion, and because formal regulatory machinery and processes are always *very* expensive. Compliance cost estimates for CWPS are undoubtedly an understatement of the burden that the program put on complying corporations, but the true compliance costs of CWPS are also a considerable understatement of the compliance costs of a TIP-MIP-MAP, if the latter were built into the tax code, or involved other legal sanctions, or required recourse to principles of contract law and torts.

Just because the costs are high does not mean an economic policy must be rejected. But it is a considerable step forward to recognize what the costs are. Our experience with CWPS and other controls programs tells us that traditional and intractable issues of economic measurement ultimately provide the limit on program feasibility, and trying to resolve these research issues in an administrative and legalistic context accounts for a large share of the costs of compliance and administration. Though at one level TIP-MIP-MAP seem to be simple policy tools, there is nothing in them that obviates or ameliorates any of the measurement problems that have beset previous controls programs: If anything, the measurement difficulties will be worse because TIP-MIP-MAP implicitly removes economic measurement issues from the realm of economic research to the arena of legal adjudication.

Moreover, the potential for economic distortion in proposals such as MAP, that rest on measures of value added, is considerably greater than has been realized. The case for TIP–MIP–MAP has been built on the arguments of simplicity and low economic cost. The closer one looks at the administrative details that must be worked out for implementation the less compelling the simplicity and cost arguments become.

EPILOGUE: FEEDBACKS FROM CWPS, "CONTROLS," AND TIP–MIP–MAP ON THE CONDUCT OF ECONOMIC POLICY

A major argument for TIP–MIP–MAP is that it will reduce the economic cost of anti-inflation policy and give policymakers more freedom in selecting policy options. What has not been raised is in the area of political science: How is that increased freedom likely to be used? Our past experience should make us somewhat pessimistic on that score.

It has often been alleged that the Nixon administration used price and wage controls to cover an expansionary fiscal-monetary stimulus before the 1972 election. In the Carter administration CWPS, we economists maintained over and over that we were not implementing this pattern, that the administration had a three-part anti-inflation program, that the CWPS Standards were not being used as a lid on other government-generated inflationary forces but were an adjunct to conventional, complementary anti-inflation policies. Though we economists believed what we were saying, in retrospect I now think we were wrong.

One frustration at CWPS in 1979 stemmed from the fact that what I above referred to as the "second arm" of the anti-inflation effort (reduction of regulatory and other governmental cost-increasing actions) never really was implemented. Though the president's October 24, 1978, speech promised to tilt decision rules in anti-inflationary directions, as the year wore on it was difficult to point to a single decision that had come down on the anti-inflation side. Import restrictions, agricultural price supports, minimum wage increase, and on and on: In none of these policy choices did the anti-inflation commitment have a significant impact on what was approved. Even more significantly, in none of the cases that I knew about did the decision memos that went forward from the Domestic Policy Staff to the president even factor in the anti-inflation priority as an important consideration in a policy decision.

In a way, this is understandable. Policy choices do not come readily labeled with "inflation" on one side and "anti-inflation" on the other. In each of the policy decisions undertaken, the inflationary impact of that particular decision was invariably small. And set against the small inflationary impact were always a lot of other politically or socially desirable things that the administration wanted to accomplish.

For example, the administration decided to raise the domestic price of sugar (which is regulated through an import duty) in mid-1979. Almost every agency of the government, save for CWPS, urged that the price be raised, for an incredible variety of reasons, ranging from the desire to raise incomes of sugar beet farmers to greed for the revenue the duty would yield. The Domestic Policy Staff saw the issue not as inflation but as an opportunity to "do something" for a particular senator who had sugar beet farmers in his state and whose vote was being curried on a completely unrelated issue. And because an increase of a cent per pound in the wholesale price of raw sugar would by itself make but a tiny impact on the CPI, the decision memo that went to the president buried the inflation program's case so far beneath the litter of political deal-making that a bloodhound with the most exquisitely trained inflation-fighting nose could scarcely have sniffed it out.

The problem was not the sugar case in isolation but that there was an unending string of sugar cases. In each of them the inflationary consequences of the decision were small; in each of them, there were desirable (to someone) objectives on the other side. But they added up.

I now feel the CWPS Pay and Price Standards influenced policymaking *away from* an anti-inflationary stance. No administration, Democratic or Republican, wants to make those anti-inflation policy decisions anyway. There is no interest group backing anti-inflation as such, and the impact of each separate decision on all consumers is small. With the CWPS Pay and Price Standards in place, it was only too easy to say, "We can depend on the Standards to take care of the inflation problem, and approve this or that or the other inflationary policy decision, each of which has so many desirable features on the other side."

We all thought that the Domestic Policy Staff could not add, and that they did not understand that a sufficient number of small inflationary decisions added up to a big problem. I now think that was wrong. We economists were the ones who did not understand. In the Domestic Policy Staff view, the CWPS standards would take care of inflationary problems, which meant that domestic policy could be conducted free from the constraint of concern for inflation. I now believe that is what happened (though the Domestic Policy Staff would never, of course, have described it in the way I have just done). CWPS provided a convenient excuse for undertaking inflationary policy that was desired on other grounds. As the result, we no doubt had more inflationary action by the administration with the CWPS Standards in place than would have occurred without them. The Carter administration wound up, then, despite its protests to the contrary, in nearly the preelection posture of the Nixon administration before it, and indeed of the Johnson administration before that.

And this, I believe, is the most important long-run lesson that the CWPS experience brings to discussion of TIP-MIP-MAP policy proposals. Some think TIP-MIP-MAP will limit inflation, others that they will shift the inflation-unemployment tradeoff frontier. I believe they will do neither. Rather, if TIP-MIP-MAP plans are put into effect, their major impact will be to encourage even more special interest spending and protectionist regulation than would have occurred otherwise. The more successful TIP-MIP-MAP proposals are at shifting the Phillips curve to the left, the more leeway for other policy proposals that shift it back to the right.

Proponents of TIP–MIP–MAP argue that the plans will create additional freedom for economic policymaking. Our experience shows that policymakers will spend this additional freedom on publicly attractive proposals that have inflationary consequences, leaving us, perhaps, with the administrative and compliance costs of TIP–MIP–MAP *plus* inflation. TIP–MIP–MAP proposals cloak the real cost of government economic and social policy decisions and cannot but make those decisions worse ones.

This will, perhaps, be thought a pessimistic assessment. But we now have experience with two very different administrations that behaved essentially in the same way. My argument rests largely on that parallelism.

NOTES TO CHAPTER 12

1.   In retrospect, even in the absence of the oil crisis of mid-1979, the degree of fiscal restraint was probably too small to do the job, owing (in my judgment) to the run-up of inflationary expectations in the 1970s.

2.   The economists' influence over the construction of the CWPS Price Standard is in marked contrast to the Nixon-era controls program. Lanzillotti, Hamilton, and Roberts (1975) note throughout that the Price Commission was often constrained in its policies by decisions that had been made before it was formed, by changes made by the Cost of Living Council (which was above the Price Commission), and in some cases by political intervention in particular situations. They describe (p. 201) a White House meeting between the heads of automobile companies, the secretary of the treasury, and the chairman of the Cost of Living Council, at which automobile price increases approved by the Price Commission were reduced, presumably for political reasons.

The design freedom enjoyed by CWPS economists was attributable to (1) the fact that the standards made no legislative journey through Congress (as TIP–MIP–MAP proposals would have to do); and (2) a perhaps unique episode of policy-making in the Carter administration, during which the kinds of political pressures that are normally brought to bear on important economic policy initiatives failed to focus on the proposed Pay and Price Standards. I have no personal knowledge of an intervention in a CWPS Price Standards case by Carter administration officials as high as the secretary of the treasury. However, some persons having knowledge of both programs have suggested to me that the degree of attempted political intervention was probably greater in the Carter administration than in the Nixon program but that it involved a lower-level official, and most intervention was intended to permit a larger price increase than CWPS would have permitted, not a lower one. In the first year of the CWPS Price Program, it was very common for firms accused of violation of the Price Standard, or who were requesting favorable action by the council, to let it be known that they had contacts on the White House staff. A phone call from a political operative somewhere in the White House to a staff economist at CWPS requesting "information" on a proceeding involving a particular company had a chilling effect on the staff, even if the same official insisted that he had no intention of political interference in CWPS administration. With the continuing increase and sophistication of special interest political influence on government, political intervention is a factor that must weigh in the decision to adopt any future, similar, program such as TIP–MIP–MAP.

3.   Firms were permitted to structure themselves for compliance purposes into any number of "compliance units" for which usual accounting practices were followed.

4.   References to individual cases in this paper are inserted solely to permit students of the CWPS experience, or designers of TIP–MIP–MAP proposals, to locate more details and documentation of points discussed. I have chosen as examples primarily cases that arose during the first program year and that went through the CWPS "reconsideration" process. First, these are cases I had some familiarity with. Second, reconsiderations received more review and attention, so that they best represent the principles used in administering the program and are also a bit more fully documented than exceptions cases that did not proceed to reconsideration. CWPS exception cases are published in Bureau of National Affairs (1979–81).

5.   I was surprised that statistical or economic consulting firms did not provide this service in the way that the accounting and law firms had done for their specialities.

6.   Construction price indices are a notorious lacuna in the U.S. statistical system. See Creamer et al. (1977).

7.   Some of these technical matters were in principle subject to court appeal during the Price Commission control program of the early 1970s. However, administrative powers under the enabling act for this program were very broad, so that decisions were harder to challenge than they are likely to be in any future TIP or MIP (the political circumstances that led Congress to bestow so much power on the president are not likely of duplication). And the Price Commission program went through so many changes that it really amounted to four different programs, and by the time an appeal could be pursued through legal processes, a new program was in effect and the case was moot.

8.   Agricultural, fishing, forestry, and mineral products were excluded from the Price Deceleration Standard under section 705A-3.

9.   It is well established that materials prices are cyclically more volatile than those of finished goods.

10.   A value added standard was actually broached in one or two of the four cases but dropped because of industry representations that value added was too complicated and difficult to compute and did not match customary business record-keeping practices. "Cost of goods sold," in contrast, has an accepted accounting definition that made compliance with a gross margin standard administratively more feasible and less expensive.

11.   There is some element of arbitrariness in this statement. I have been unable to locate a precisely defined statement of the computation method Lerner and Colander have in mind, and take it that these are details that have been left to future working out. Thus, the following applies to one plausible formulation, but a similar argument will apply to alternatives, such as computing value added relative to an index of all inputs.

12.   My own view is that these are matters of degree, "capital theoretic" issues arising in everything from the measurement of consumer prices (see Pollak 1975) to labor inputs (Triplett 1983).

13 WHY AN INCENTIVE ANTI-INFLATION PLAN SHOULD BE IMPLEMENTED

Laurence S. Seidman

The chapters by Jack Triplett and Robert Russell make an important contribution to the analysis of incentive anti-inflation policies. In the past, Triplett and Russell have both written on the theory and practice of price measurement. At the Council of Wage and Price Stability, they accumulated practical experience implementing a price restraint policy. Their insights deserve respect.

Proponents of incentive anti-inflation policies accept Triplett's conclusion that the policy will be costly to administer. It is important to emphasize, then, at the outset, that Triplett's important conclusion—that a TIP or MAP is feasible though costly—is accepted by most advocates.

Triplett and Russell may give the impression that advocates have ignored these costs. But that is not so. In fact, the original Wallich/Weintraub TIP article (1971) emphasized the importance of trying to reduce administrative costs. For this reason, the authors proposed limiting TIP to the largest corporations. Because they judged price increases harder to measure than wage increases, they limited TIP to wage increases. Moreover, they devoted much attention to the measurement problem.

For several years, I have been convinced that the coverage of TIP or MAP must be limited to large corporations. As Triplett argues, a staff much larger than the CWPS staff would be essential, even if coverage is limited to perhaps the largest 2,000 corporations. I fully agree that a high ratio of monitoring staff to covered corporations is essential.

THE VIEW FROM THE FRONT LINE

While Triplett and Russell offer valuable insights from front-line experience implementing the Carter voluntary plan, they tend to underestimate the handicaps under which they labored. What were these handicaps?

First, theirs was a tiny staff. Second, theirs was a "start-up" experience. Almost any start-up experience entails numerous costs and problems that subside over time.

Third, theirs was a voluntary program. TIP and MAP advocates would predict frustration for those trying to implement such a program. Our economy runs on financial incentives. A voluntary program ignores this fundamental fact. When the program fails to restrain price increases, criticism mounts, and hard-working competent administrators naturally feel they have been given an impossible assignment.

At the time the Carter plan was announced, most TIP advocates predicted its failure. The plan did not give firms a strong financial motive to restrain price increases: It merely exhorted them. Its staff was highly competent but much too small. Many of us therefore opposed the program. Moreover, we feared that its inevitable failure would harm the price incentive approach because we would be told: "Price restraint has just been tried, and it failed." The outcome has been just as we feared. The failure of the Carter plan has cast a shadow over all price restraint policies.

While Triplett and Russell never expected the Carter plan to subdue inflation single-handedly, they clearly had some hope for the plan when they joined CWPS. They gave extraordinary effort to try to make it succeed. They and their small staff were highly competent and committed. At the end, they were disillusioned. As they readily acknowledge, it is an experience they prefer to forget.

We should recognize, then, that the view from the front line can contribute important insights but also has its bias. Triplett and Russell were sent out to fight a hopeless battle. They can surely tell us about certain problems that must occur in any battle. But we should also realize that they were given inadequate weapons and inadequate troops. Having suffered in the trenches, they give gloomy accounts. Who can blame them?

TWO KINDS OF NAIVETE

Triplett is properly worried that a naive listener may underestimate the administrative, compliance, and distortion costs of TIP or MAP. While I fully accept his concern, I want to argue that there is another danger as well. A naive listener, on hearing Triplett's (and Russell's) examples, may fail to recognize that other governmental policies entail similar serious problems. To emphasize this point, let's consider two examples: (1) the income tax and (2) a tax or marketable permit policy to discourage environmental pollution.

Should the United States Adopt an Income Tax?

Imagine a debate over whether the United States should adopt a personal and corporate income tax. Analysts (like Triplett and Russell) would explain the serious administrative, compliance, and distortion costs of such a tax. Our listener would not remain naive for long as examples proliferated. Analysts would ask: What is income? What should be included and excluded? How can depreciation be measured? What about capital gains that have accrued but not been realized? What about a change in the value of inventories? How can the income of the self-employed be monitored? Tax shelter strategies would be explained. Analysts would predict a large diversion of skilled labor to the "game" of tax avoidance. After weeks of testimony, our listener might well be ready to conclude that a personal and corporate income tax is simply unfeasible and undesirable.

But we know that such a conclusion would be incorrect. Despite its numerous problems and significant cost, the income tax has proved feasible. It has served its function of raising revenue to finance government expenditure. In retrospect, most citizens would conclude that the benefit of an income tax outweighs its cost, even though the cost has been large and the income tax entails serious inequities and inefficiencies.

Consider, for example, Triplett's perhaps most memorable example: the Marion Brick case. The case surely illustrates the difficulties of price measurement. But only a naive listener would be unaware that the personal and corporate income tax have generated countless Marion Brick cases involving the difficulties of income measurement.

If the proposal to adopt the income tax were currently being debated, imagine the impact, not of a short paper of examples (like Triplett's or Russell's), but a book of examples—specifically, a law school textbook of cases that might arise under the personal and corporate income tax.

Should the United States Adopt Either a Tax
or Marketable Permit Policy to Discourage
Environmental Pollution?

This is a debate that is currently in progress. Most economists would answer yes. Yet there are significant practical problems with either a tax or marketable permit policy. Can pollution from a particular firm always be satisfactorily measured and monitored? With marketable permits, what rules would govern the permit market? Would speculation occur? Would there be a futures market?

When would a firm have to possess permits? What avoidance strategies would arise, and how would the government try to counter them?

While these questions may have discouraged some economists, most remain sympathetic to this incentive approach to pollution. Even though significant practical difficulties accompany such a policy, many economists nevertheless believe that the benefit would outweigh the cost.

I have chosen this example for an obvious reason: TIP is analogous to the pollution-tax, and MAP is analogous to the pollution permit policy. TIP and MAP utilize a price incentive to discourage inflation instead of pollution. The policies share many common problems. Yet a recognition of these problems, in the case of pollution, has not significantly weakened the support of economists for the price incentive strategy.

The central point is this: It is not the cost side, in itself, that decides the issue; it is a weighing of cost against benefit. As Triplett states, a TIP or MAP can be implemented, though at significant cost. The real issue is an assessment of how the benefit compares to this significant cost.

So there are two kinds of naivete. Triplett is right: Some naive listeners may incorrectly think that a TIP or MAP would be simple and cheap to implement. But there is another kind of naivete. Some naive listeners may fail to recognize, on hearing Triplett's and Russell's examples, that many other governmental policies have similar difficulties and costs.

THE BENEFIT OF MAP

The real issue is how the benefit of MAP or TIP compares to its significant cost. For illustration, I will consider a permanent MAP that applies to the largest, perhaps 2,000, corporations and is implemented by a large staff that makes possible effective auditing. How would a "MAP economy" compare to today's "mapless" economy?

In the current economy, econometric estimation suggests that the unemployment rate must be held in the 6.5 to 7.0 percent range to keep the inflation rate constant. A lower unemployment rate, achieved by an expansion in demand, would probably cause wage inflation to rise, generating rising price inflation. Thus, demand management must avoid pushing the unemployment rate below this range.

In a MAP economy, it would be possible to run the economy at a permanently higher level of demand and a permanently lower unemployment rate. For example, in 1972, under the Nixon administration's Phase II Controls program, the unemployment rate was 5.6 percent; yet the inflation rate fell from 5.0 percent in 1971 to 4.2 percent in 1972. When the program was made voluntary in 1973, with the unemployment rate 4.9 percent, the inflation rate rose to 5.8 percent.

The crucial advantage of MAP over controls is that it permits relative prices and wages to change automatically in response to market forces. But MAP would constrain the average price level as effectively as a rigid controls program. The experience of 1972, and of World War II, is that an effective price controls program does enable the economy to be run at a lower unemployment rate without causing the inflation rate to rise. MAP should be able to do the same, while better preserving allocative efficiency.

Let's compare a MAP economy run permanently with a 5.5 percent unemployment rate, to a mapless economy run permanently at a 6.5 percent unemployment rate. Assume the inflation rate is permanently near 0 percent in both cases. A conservative Okun's Law of 2 to 1 implies that with the unemployment rate 1 percent lower in the MAP economy, real output would be 2 percent greater—roughly $80 billion greater in 1985.

The administrative and compliance cost under an effective MAP, with a large competent staff, would not exceed several billion dollars. The $80 billion gain in real output would be many times greater than this administrative and compliance cost.

While MAP would allow market forces to influence relative price and wage changes, thereby preserving significant allocative efficiency, it is likely that some inefficiency and distortion would result from MAP. No one—neither a critic nor a supporter of MAP—has provided an estimate of the cost of MAP inefficiency.

While the net impact on efficiency is therefore difficult to estimate, the impact on distribution is easier to discern. A MAP economy—run at a 5.5 percent unemployment rate—would provide greater opportunity and earnings for low-skilled persons than a mapless economy run at a 6.5 percent unemployment rate. Such persons would constitute a large share of the more than 1 percent increase in employment that accompanies a 1 percent reduction in the unemployment rate (more than 1 percent because of the increase in labor force participation that occurs when the unemployment rate falls, the vacancy rate rises, and jobs are easier to find).

Citizens who value improving opportunities and earnings for low-skilled persons willing to work might prefer a MAP economy to a mapless economy, even if the MAP economy were somewhat less efficient. For example, suppose that MAP allocative inefficiency were 3 percent of GNP, so that, combined with the 2 percent increase in output from the lower unemployment rate, the net cost of MAP were 1 percent of GNP, or national income. Citizens willing to accept a 1 percent income loss—provided others are doing the same—to achieve greater opportunity and earnings for low-skilled persons should favor switching to a MAP economy.

This example concedes the possibility of a net reduction in efficiency due to MAP and explains why a citizen might still favor a switch to a MAP economy. But I want to reemphasize that no estimates of the efficiency cost of MAP exist. All that is known is that the MAP output gain, due to the lower unemployment rate, would be many times greater than the administrative and compliance cost of MAP.

HOW WOULD THE FED RESPOND TO TIP OR MAP?

At the end of his chapter, Triplett advances the argument that a price restraint policy encourages other cost-raising policies and fiscal expansion. Those who want cost-raising policies and fiscal expansion will say that the price restraint policy will take care of inflation.

But Triplett's argument would also apply to a price restraint policy implemented by the Federal Reserve. Suppose that the Fed genuinely and publicly commits itself to keep money tight enough to hold down inflation. Advocates of cost-raising policies and fiscal expansion can say that the Fed will take care of inflation—but does this mean that the Fed should avoid such a policy?

The real issue is the effectiveness of TIP or MAP in helping the Fed restrain inflation and enabling the economy to be run permanently at a lower unemployment rate (for example, 5.5 percent instead of 6.5 percent). If TIP or MAP, and tight money, would be effective, these policies should be implemented without worrying about the excuses of cost-raisers and deficit-generators.

Moreover, it is not clear that these excuses should be taken seriously. Consider the advocates of cost-raising policies—such as import quotas, or payroll tax increases for Social Security, or safety regulations—and the advocates of tax cuts and government spending increases, and consider the politicians who support these policies. Would these advocates and politicians really change their behavior if the Fed publicly surrendered to inflation, and if TIP or MAP were not implemented? Would they really say that now we must avoid these policies because no one else is preventing inflation?

More important is whether the Fed would give up its commitment to hold down inflation and declare that now TIP or MAP will take care of the problem. If the Fed were likely to react in this way, it would be a serious objection to TIP or MAP because Fed commitment is essential, even with TIP or MAP.

But why should we expect the Fed to behave in so foolish and irresponsible a manner? In recent years, the Fed has demonstrated a determination to keep money tight enough to reduce inflation, even when this required a severe recession. An effective TIP or MAP would make it easier for the Fed to hold down inflation.

It is sometimes claimed that the 1972 episode demonstrates that the Fed will conduct an inflationary monetary expansion if price controls are implemented. It is true that the Fed implemented a monetary expansion that helped reduce the unemployment rate from 5.9 percent in 1971 to 4.9 percent in 1973. Moreover, the inflation rate rose from 4.2 percent in 1972 to 5.8 percent in 1973.

But the Fed's monetary expansion led to an increase in inflation only because the controls were removed (made voluntary) at the beginning of 1973. Perhaps the Fed should have anticipated that controls would be ended, and that with-out controls a 4.9 percent unemployment rate would cause inflation to rise. But the Fed's monetary expansion did not raise inflation in 1972, while the controls were in place. The expansion reduced unemployment without any increase in inflation.

Traditional price controls, because of the problems that result from rigidity, are likely to be terminated after a brief duration. By contrast, TIP or MAP should significantly reduce these problems and should therefore stand a better chance of permanence.

If TIP or MAP is in place, the Fed should be able to bring down the unem-ployment rate perhaps 1 percent below the current constant-inflation unemploy-ment rate of approximately 7.0 percent, without causing inflation to rise. Is it realistic to assume that the Fed would accelerate monetary expansion until TIP or MAP breaks down and inflation rises? Or is it more realistic to expect the Fed to proceed gradually and to stand ready to tighten if inflation should begin to rise, despite the presence of TIP or MAP?

IV POLITICAL FEASIBILITY

14 EUROPEAN EXPERIENCES WITH TAX-BASED INCOME POLICIES

*Sheetal K. Chand**

Europe has pioneered in the formulation and application of incomes policies of various kinds. In the immediate postwar period, policies of income restraint were applied to contain real wages in order to facilitate reconstruction. In the 1960s, with historically low unemployment levels, incomes policies were directed at inflation control. More recently, inflation and major supply shocks have led to a search for noninflationary policies that are employment-promoting. An interesting feature of such policies is their increasing recourse to tax/subsidy instruments. For the most part, however, the use of these fiscal instruments in the context of the wage bargaining process has been to grant concessions in order to induce a more favorable outcome. With the possible exception of tax indexation policies—which could have the effect of restraining "tax push" demands for higher wages—the "bribery" use of fiscal instruments does not carry the behavior modification implications of tax-based incomes policies (TIP). Only France appears to have implemented a full-fledged TIP for the purpose of discouraging inflation-promoting behavior. To a limited degree and at a highly aggregative level, Belgium has also implemented a variant.

The French and Belgian experiments were undertaken in the mid-1970s and both were discontinued after being in force for a short period. While the limited use of TIPs is in part attributable to their still being a novelty, there has also been some recent shift in sentiment away from what is regarded as excessive government intervention. In any event, TIPs need not be of active interest to all European countries, as several do operate fairly successful incomes policies,

*Views expressed in this paper are those of the author and should not be attributed to the International Monetary Fund.

notably Austria and Germany.[1] The latter countries are characterized by permanent institutional arrangements that facilitate a consensual approach to wage settlement. In some of the other countries, however, such permanent incomes policies are not to be found, and a more adversarial relationship prevails between labor and business. In these countries there is occasional recourse to limited-duration incomes policies, which may succeed in temporarily restraining wages and prices but are invariably followed by a "catch up" phase. Although permanent incomes policies of the more traditional variety have not found favor in such countries, it is possible that a permanent TIP arrangement may prove more acceptable.

The purpose here is to examine the French and Belgian experiences and to draw some lessons as to the feasibility of a TIP. Because the real-life experience with TIP is still very limited, the assessment is supplemented with a brief review of some successful applications of the more traditional incomes policy. This is undertaken in order to identify key factors accounting for their success, as they are likely to have a bearing on the success of a TIP, given that the latter is a decentralized alternative to the traditional incomes policy. Such preliminaries are dealt with in the following section, while succeeding sections present the two case studies. In the final section some broad conclusions are drawn concerning the design characteristics and preconditions that are likely to ensure the success of a TIP.

THE NEED FOR TIP: AN INTRODUCTION

Some Characteristics of Successful Incomes Policies

In a perfectly competitive textbook environment, where optimizing individuals have full information and market institutions function perfectly, the problem of persistent stagflation cannot occur. Any tendency for the inflation rate to rise (provided aggregate demand management is noninflationary) will be automatically choked by an (incipient) rise in unemployment that will convey the appropriate signal to owners of productive factors to moderate their claims for higher factor income. However, in practice transactions are constrained by imperfect information, and markets perform with varying speeds. Consequently, significant unemployment could occur before a cost-push inflationary pressure is eliminated. The position is likely to be aggravated by contractual relationships governing wages and other elements of factor income, as these introduce more sluggishness in markets, laying the potential for even higher unemployment. The surrender of individual decisionmaking powers to unions could also worsen the potential for unemployment, both because of an inflationary wage-spiral bias that unions might impart and (if the union is to be credible) from strikes. The practice of indexing wage income to inflation, usually measured in terms of a

cost of living index, can also be unemployment increasing as it prevents necessary adjustments in real wages from occurring.

Institutional innovations, such as wage/price contracts, and unions serve a
variety of purposes, including those of economizing on information and making
risk more bearable, but at the cost of an added potential for higher unemployment. A fundamental problem, however, is created when deliberate attempts are
made to control unemployment. To the extent unemployment is reduced, and
transactors widely perceive the authorities as committed to keeping unemployment low, the natural, regulatory, inflation-restraining function of unemployment is eliminated. One remedy would be to reintroduce unemployment, which
is both costly and inequitable. For the economist the challenge is posed of how
to devise a policy or institution that will check inflation, while maintaining employment at a high level. The more plausible solutions tend to emphasize various
forms of incomes restraint.

It is instructive to review briefly some European experiences with incomes
policies, in view of their long and varied applications in Europe. The approach
adopted here is to classify some of the European countries according to the type
of incomes policy that they have pursued and their success in controlling inflation while maintaining employment. Such a comparison will indicate whether or
not there is any systematic correlation between the type of incomes policy and
the outcome with regard to inflation and unemployment.

Table 14-1 shows that countries with a superior record of controlling inflation and unemployment in the 1960s and 1970s are also countries with a perma-

Table 14-1. European Experiences with Incomes Policies:
Some Stylized Facts.

	Unemployment (percentage)[a]		Inflation (percentage)[b]		Type of Incomes Policy	
	1960s	1970s	1960s	1970s	Permanent	Temporary
Austria	1.9	1.6	3.6	6.3	X	
Belgium	2.4	4.9	3.0	7.4		X
France	2.0	3.7	4.0	9.7		X
Germany	0.9	2.2	2.6	5.1	X	
Netherlands	1.1	3.6	4.3	7.6	X	
Norway	1.8	1.7	4.5	8.4	X	
Sweden	1.8	2.1	4.1	9.2	X	
United Kingdom	2.8	4.7	4.0	13.8		X

a. Computed using OECD, *Labor Force Statistics*, May 1983. Data are standardized
unemployment rates which are more comparable than unemployment rates published in
national sources. Coverage for the 1960s is for the period 1965–69.

b. Average growth rate.

Source: OECD for unemployment data and IFS for inflation rates.

nent incomes policy. The central European and Nordic countries have long operated a permanent incomes policy in the context of highly centralized and synchronized wage setting practices. While virtually all countries suffered a deterioration in the average inflation and unemployment rates between the 1960s
and the 1970s, the deterioration was more pronounced with regard to both the
unemployment rates and the rate of inflation for Belgium, France, and the
United Kingdom, none of whom had a permanent incomes policy.[2] This is illustrated in Figure 14-1.

Among those countries with a permanent incomes policy, three distinct
groups can be demarcated, with differing emphasis on the goals of full employment and inflation and with varying degrees of government intervention in the
wage negotiation process. The Nordic countries showed virtually no deterioration in the unemployment rate but had a somewhat worse inflation performance
than the central European economies of Austria and Germany, while the Netherlands underwent the most pronounced increase in unemployment.[3]

It is, perhaps, noteworthy that, unlike the Netherlands, Germany prohibits
by law the indexing of wages to inflation, while Austria pursues a similar de
facto rule. Consequently, there would be less tendency for real wages to rise
excessively in Germany or Austria and cause labor to become overpriced, which
would lead to classical unemployment. Such a phenomenon became important
in the 1970s, when supply-side shocks eroded the terms of trade of several industrial countries and led to a wedge between the price of domestic output and
the consumer price index, as the latter includes imports as well. In a context
where the real income of an economy has been reduced, indexing one source of
factor income to the consumer price index would result in reduced shares for
other factors. If profits are eroded, investment could suffer, with possibly adverse effects on the rate of growth of the economy and of employment.

The limited evidence cannot support anything more than speculation. Nevertheless, drawing on various strands, the following hypotheses can be advanced:

1. A high degree of egalitarianism tends to reduce friction between the different parties to the wage negotiation.
2. In such a context it is easier to institutionalize the wage bargaining process in
   the form of a permanent incomes policy.
3. Under a system of permanent restraint, the phenomenon of accelerated
   bursts of wage/price escalation (catch-ups) will usually be avoided.
4. A common characteristic of the institutionalized wage bargain is the tendency for wage negotiations to be undertaken in a synchronized manner—
   for example the "spring offensive" in some countries. This has the benefit
   of curbing "leapfrogging" that would otherwise result when different seg-
   ments of the labor force attempt to maintain a relative wage structure that
   they have become habituated to.
5. To the extent wage indexation is avoided, the domestic economy partici-
   pates more evenly in any externally imposed burdens and avoids potentially

Figure 14-1. Inflation and Unemployment Rates in Selected European Countries: The 1960s and the 1970s.

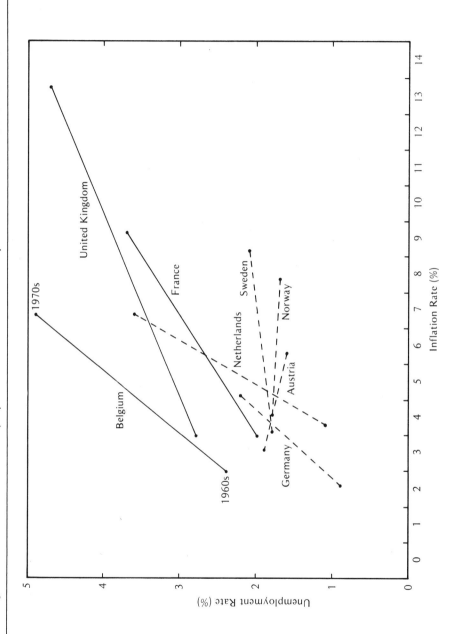

stagflationary consequences of distributional conflicts that could otherwise result. It can be conjectured that countries that exhibit some of the preceding characteristics tend to have a superior price and employment record.[4]

While it is extremely difficult to measure the relative degree of egalitarianism, it is, perhaps, no coincidence that countries purportedly exhibiting a more egalitarian distribution of wealth and income, as with the Scandinavian and central European countries, tend to have institutionalized incomes policies. A noteworthy feature of such economies is their homogeneity and a higher degree of centralization in the organization of the economy, particularly with regard to labor and employers. Consequently, for such countries a TIP may not be relevant, as successful institutions to moderate wages are already present. By the same token, their experience may not be applicable to countries that rely more on the market mechanism to regulate wages or where labor forces are more decentralized, as in France. For these economies a decentralized incomes policy, such as a TIP, could be more appropriate.

TIPs: An Introduction

The arguments in favor of a TIP, basically that a policy of relying on the tax system to discourage inflation-promoting behavior is less damaging to a market-based allocative system than are direct controls, or even other more traditional incomes policies, by now are well known.[5] Broadly, the proposals concern the internalization to the individual transactor of the social costs of inflation. The schemes vary, some bearing directly on the firm—with a view to stiffening its resistance to wage increases—while others impact on labor, in an attempt at modifying its behavior in more acceptable directions. Common to these schemes is a normative rate of inflation and the application of fiscal penalties or rewards depending on the extent of compliance with the norm.[6] At the macroeconomic level, it is assumed that these schemes are operated in the context of noninflationary aggregate demand management.

Generally, TIPs are compatible with rational, optimizing, behavior of transactors. Even though there are likely to be some dead-weight losses associated with a TIP—as it introduces some unavoidable distortions to the optimum market allocation—the costs could be substantially less than those of the feasible alternatives. As long as transactors are not assumed to have perfect information or to be fully aware of the consequences of their actions, a TIP that fits the situation can, in principle, always be found. However, the microfoundations governing the effects of TIPS remain to be developed. Essentially, an appropriate microfoundation would attempt to capture the greater elements of risk attributable to the TIP, as a consequence of its penalties and rewards, that has the effect of making transactors more restrained in their wage and price-setting behavior. While transactors are free to charge what price they believe the market will bear, they will be more cautious because of the possibility of a TIP penalty being exacted. In macroeconomic terms, a braking effect would be exerted on wage/price escalations.

Granting the microfoundations, the main issues concern the design of a TIP and its implementation. Obviously the design of a TIP will be conditioned by the prevailing fiscal environment. Thus it is no surprise that in the United States, the lack of a value-added (profits and wages) tax system (VAT) has led to the bulk of the proposed TIPs emphasizing various components of the corporate income tax, the individual income tax, or payroll taxes.[7] Objections can be raised to each of these proposals with regard to their economic side effects and administrative requirements. Regarding the economic side effects, a VATIP appears to be among the least distortionary of the TIPs that impact on firms because it focuses on the value added by the enterprise and does not discriminate between different sources of income or different forms of industrial organization.[8] Nevertheless, because profit margins are more directly under the control of the firm than are wage costs, there could be a tendency for the burden of the TIP to fall more heavily on profit margins. The outcome, however, depends on the strength of labor's resistance. If the latter is excessive, an excise duty type of TIP on labor income, as in the Belgian TIP, could be appropriate. Both forms of TIPs are examined next.

THE FRENCH VATIP

VATIP

Before considering the French experience, some broad features of a VATIP should be noted. The essence of this TIP is to discourage excessive (inflationary) increases in value added by applying a penalty tax as follows:

$$T_t \left(V_t - (1 + e) V_{t-1} \cdot \frac{Q_t}{Q_{t-1}} \right) \qquad (14.1)$$

where T_t is the penalty tax rate at time t, Q_t is the level of output at time t, e is a permissible expansion factor (allowance), and V_t is value added, defined as the difference between the value of final sales by the firm less the value of inputs consumed in production (excluding factor inputs).

Unlike the conventional value-added tax, which applies to an appropriately defined V_t, the base of the VATIP is incremental. A reference year's value added will increase according to the expansion in the firm's level of output and growth in factor productivity. The resulting "permissible" level is subtracted from the actual level in the year of concern, and the penalty tax/subsidy levied on the difference. The bulk of the information is generated through the routine application of the VAT; the only additional information required by this TIP concerns estimates of the growth rate of both the firm's output and in the productivity of its factor use. The last is usually handled by imposing an economywide productivity norm. However, the measurement of the firm's output increase is more problematic for the typical multiproduct firm. One solution that has been proposed is to use an unweighted index of labor hours worked. A drawback is that this not only provides a disincentive to investment, but also a discincentive to the employment of better paid and thus generally skilled labor. The particular solution adopted by the French authorities is described below.

The French Experience

Aside from having some of the weakest unions in Europe, which have generally been ineffective in collective bargaining, France has also had a tradition of price controls.[9] Following a particularly unsatisfactory experience with these controls in the early 1970s, a tax on excessive increases in a firm's value added was officially proposed in 1974 with the express intention of ensuring that productivity gains would be passed on to the consumer rather than dissipated in excessive wage increases.

Reactions to the proposal were unfavorable both among union leaders and firms. The latter viewed the tax as a penalty on more productive firms that would reduce incentives for innovation, raise unemployment, and impose a major administrative burden on the firms. The opposition parties were opposed to the proposal on the grounds that it would restrain justifiable wage increases.

After considerable debate, an attenuated version of the original proposal was finally ratified with effect from January 1, 1975. Broadly, the tax was on the amount by which value added in a particular year exceeded a specified norm. In computing the norm, exports were excluded from the base, while an adjustment was made for increases in production between two years. The "norm" combined both a notion of the average productivity increase in industry and the acceptable increase in the price level.[10]

A clear distinction was drawn between the notion of value added employed for the ordinary VAT and for the inflation tax. The latter employed a more economic concept of value added that took account of changes in inventory and accorded a different treatment to investment (not taxable under VAT), depreciation allowances, financial costs, and insurance costs. In addition, the inflation tax was extended to apply to financial institutions. To prevent any confusion with the tax base for VAT, the inflation tax employed the word *margin* rather than *value added* (Courthéoux 1976).

The penalty tax was assessed by computing the margin for the taxable period and for the reference period, with the difference between the two being the taxable base. Each margin is determined as the difference between final sales and purchases, with initial stocks added to total purchases and final stocks added to sales. Certain adjustments are made to the margin of the reference period, to take into account changes in production, productivity, and inflation. Mostly, those adjustments increase the margin of the reference year, thereby serving to lower the tax base. Certain expenses may be deducted from the margin for the taxable period: financial expenses, treated here as an intermediate input, thereby favoring firms that finance their operations through increased debt rather than through price increases; third-person supplies and services, thereby raising the possibility of a loophole frequently mentioned by opponents of TIP proposals (Dildine and Sunley 1978); transportation and traveling; administrative expenses; taxes and duties; increases in salaries paid to workers at the minimum wage; operating losses of the reference period; bad debts written off with respect to French customers; and certain costs associated with fluctuations in the prices of raw materials. The margin that remains following the deductions is then reduced proportionally by the ratio of exports to sales.

The justification for a production adjustment to the reference margin is that of not penalizing firms whose value added rises as a consequence of productivity increases. In order to circumvent the problem of constructing a weighted average of increases in volume for every product, an approximate method of correction was employed, whereby the weighted average change in the use of capital and labor proxied the change in production. The increase in labor was measured by the percentage change in the number of working hours, while for capital, the percentage change in the gross value of depreciable business assets was used.[11]

The adjustment for productivity gains did not differentiate between firms: A uniform adjustment would be set every year by law. Although firms with higher-than-average productivity growth would be penalized, this was not considered a problem on the grounds that it would lead to a better distribution of the productivity gains (Courthéoux 1976: 385). The adjustment for permissible inflation was also fixed by law at the beginning of each year. This was undertaken in accordance with French law that regulates the use of index clauses in contracts.

Only large firms were subject to the tax using turnover and number of staff criteria, thereby greatly simplifying compliance and administration.[12] In the first year of its operation, the tax applied to about 15,000 firms, representing up to 60 percent of the gross domestic product of industry and commerce.

The law provided for a tax of 33 1/3 percent, which was much lower than the initial proposal of a continuous rate going up to 75 percent. The tax was to be paid in four quarterly advance payments that would be fully refunded in the event the tax was abolished. Finally, the law provided for a committee to rule on requests from firms to waive the tax partially or fully, based on proof that any excess margin of the taxable period was not the result of inflationary behavior on their part.

An interesting feature of the inflation tax law was a self-destruct proviso that would be triggered whenever the price index for manufactured goods did not increase by more than 1.5 percent over a period of three consecutive months.

This occurred in the third quarter of 1975, and the tax was suspended from September 1. In the face of a deep recession, the authorities also decided to suspend the first two quarterly installments of the tax.[13] In the event, the tax finally applied only to about 150 firms that had closed their fiscal year in January or February 1975, who were in any case entitled to refunds following the suppression of the law. Although the finance law of 1976 reintroduced the tax, the new stipulation that it become effective only if the price index of privately manufactured goods rose by more than 2 percent over three consecutive months was not fulfilled. The finance law of 1977 again introduced the tax, but once again it was not enforced, and from 1977 on, it disappeared from the statute books.

This limited experience with the inflation tax facilitates neither an assessment of its efficacy in the control of inflation nor of its practicality. Nevertheless, the various provisions of the law are of interest in indicating how some of the problems that concern the application of a TIP can be resolved, at least in principle. It is noteworthy that during the period the tax was on the statute books there was a significant decline in the inflation rate. In 1974, the rate of inflation, as measured by the consumer price index, amounted to 13.7 percent. It declined to 11.9 percent in 1975, and further to around 9 percent, a level that was held for the next three years, before inflation accelerated again.

THE BELGIAN WAGE TIP

In 1976, the Belgian Parliament imposed a temporary tax on all new benefits granted to employees in new collective bargaining agreements for a period of nine months in order to moderate an explosive growth in wages, which amounted to 12.7 percent in 1975 and closely paralleled the increase in the CPI index of 12.8 percent. Of the new benefits granted to employees, the employee would receive only one-half, the other half being put into a Solidarity Fund to finance pensions. This was intended as a tax on excessive wage increases to be borne by the employee. In addition, the employer was required to pay a tax penalizing him for granting an excessive wage increase, and the amount of the tax was set equal to one-half of the new benefits accorded to employees. All wage increases resulting from existing collective agreements such as indexation and from promotion were exampted. Judging from the proceeds of the tax, which amounted to only $3 million, the deterrent effect appears to have been successful. More important, there was a marked moderation in wage growth from the previous year. Nevertheless, the scheme was in place for such a short period that it is not possible to assess its effectiveness. Essentially, this TIP functioned as an excise tax on wages. It was apparently easy to administer since, in Belgium, most wage increases are settled between employers and the unions, who represent about three-fourths of the labor force, and are then imposed on all employees including the nonunionized. An interesting feature of the scheme is its application of a double stick, which presumably rendered it more acceptable both to employers and unions.

CONCLUSION

The paucity of real-life experiences with TIP does not permit any conclusive, empirically well-founded assessment of its efficacy. In common with many other proposals that require a substantial commitment to institutional change, lead times are long. TIPs are still in their infancy, but their early baptism in Belgium, and especially in France, should help dispel some inevitable doubts at the pre-application stage.

The easiest TIP to implement seems to be the excise duty on wages TIP. When assessed on the firm, it functions essentially as a payroll tax and thus, provided aggregate demand is adequate, could be shifted forward as higher prices, which would defeat the purpose of the TIP. A more appropriate TIP—that is, however, more difficult to implement—is the VATIP. Nevertheless, contrary to the negative conclusions of Dildine and Sunley (1978) and others concerning VATIPs, the experience with the French version suggests that it is feasible in countries that possess a well-developed VAT system. For countries lacking such a system and in the absence of an enabling tax reform, the Wallich/Weintraub penalty tax on profits could be appropriate. There is, however, need for commensurate caution to be exercised.

It is instructive to recall the outcome of the relatively successful postwar attempts at stabilizing the real business cycle, which reflected the acceptance of Keynesian doctrine. The cure of one problem led to the traditional brake on inflation being largely eliminated, with well-known results. While a TIP does carry a lot of promise, in comparison to the alternatives, especially for countries with decentralized, market-based economies, it is possible that the attempt at behavioral modification through TIP could have unintended consequences. Further research is needed to establish possible side effects.

NOTES TO CHAPTER 14

1. For a detailed assessment see Flanagan, Soskice, and Ulman (1983). See also Blyth (1979).
2. For the latter countries, recourse to incomes policy has been episodic. Typically, periods during which the incomes policies were applied generally exhibited some decline in inflation rates, only to be followed by "catch-up" phases. See Flanagan, Soskice, and Ulman (1983).
3. See Skånland (1981) for a more detailed assessment of these aspects in a broader, comparative setting.
4. Among the non-European countries, Japan exhibits many of the characteristics cited.

5. See especially Wallich and Weintraub (1971), Okun (1981), Seidman (1978), Colander (1979a, c), and Lerner and Colander (1982) for rationales and for alternative TIP proposals.

6. Through a symmetric use of penalties and rewards, the TIP can potentially be designed to have zero budgetary impact.

7. Canterbery (1983), however, advocates a reform of the U.S. tax system so as to implement a VATIP, which he regards as the most suitable.

8. One important advantage vis-à-vis incomes policies that bears directly on prices is the VATIP's automatic exclusion of inflation in input prices, which tend to be decided on a case by case basis under direct controls.

9. See Flanagan, Soskice, and Ulman (1983). An interesting precursor of TIP was introduced in 1966 whereby firms were permitted to build up profit margins in exchange for guarantees not to grant wage increases beyond a certain limit. These "contrats du programme" were confidential commitments entered between firms and the authorities with no trade union participation and were regularly policed for compliance by the Ministry of Finance. The penalty for allowing wages to exceed the norm was a reimposition of price controls. By 1969 some 85 percent of French industry participated in these contracts.

10. See De Wulf (1976) for a discussion.

11. The use of gross rather than net value was justified on the grounds of discouraging firms from reducing their depreciation allowance and hence possibly investment in an effort to comply with the law.

12. Many more firms are subject to the VAT.

13. At about the same time the authorities introduced a scheme of wage subsidies to promote employment (see Kopits 1978 for an evaluation) thereby providing an avenue for restraining the growth in firms' value added through greater budgetary outlays.

15 U.S. POLITICS AND ANTI-INFLATION POLICY

Jerrold E. Schneider

The United States experienced sharp disinflation in 1979–85. Some foresee no large inflationary forces on the horizon and observe that structural changes in certain markets have removed pressures that caused or allowed inflation to accelerate in the 1970s. Resulting optimism is reinforced by a new policy regime herein labeled *quasi-monetarism*. In general, monetary policy will be tighter than prior to 1979, leaving less room for inflation to break out. In particular, the quasi-monetarist regime has the following elements: (1) The Fed will reduce money growth over the long run even while it exercises discretion in the short run, with, perhaps, nominal GNP targets being related to M1 targets; (2) monetary policy will not accommodate new inflationary surges; (3) the Fed will subordinate higher production and lower unemployment to inflation fighting far more than in the past; and (4) the Fed will accept constraints on these objectives imposed by the instability of international and U.S. financial institutions.

Is this quasi-monetarist policy regime politically sustainable? If not, is there a realistic scenario in which a political bargain (social contract) would be adopted for a less costly means of fighting inflation that included some form of incentive anti-inflation policy? Or is the alternative a resort to politically reactive policy swings? This paper explores in four sections the intertwined themes of the political sustainability of quasi-monetarism and the political conditions of a policy experiment as an alternative to quasi-monetarism. In the *first* section, the 1982 election, despite the conventional wisdom, is shown to indicate the political vulnerability of quasi-monetarism. In the *second* are arrayed elements of the potential coalition that, if mobilized, might support a high-growth/high-employment anti-inflation policy in flight from the costs of quasi-monetarism. In the *third*, conditions are given of a scenario in which political authorities would resort to an innovative anti-inflation policy. In the *fourth* it is argued that the path that anti-inflation policy takes will depend on the institutional location of the policy development process.

POLITICAL CONSTRAINTS ON QUASI-MONETARISM

The potential political demand for policy experimentation is greater than a superficial view based on the 1982 and 1984 elections suggests. That view is that the next recession will have an even lower political cost than paid in the 1982 election, which occurred two months prior to the trough of the 1981–82 recession. The reasoning is that severe inflation caused severe recession, but the next recession, reacting to mild inflation, will itself be mild. Hence, this reasoning goes, the costs of the next recession, and therefore of the present policy regime, should be politically supportable for one overriding reason: Even with a 10.6 percent unemployment rate in October 1982, the Republicans lost only twenty-six seats in the House of Representatives. However, this view is too optimistic as to the political costs and sustainability of the present regime. There are four reasons why.

First, in 1982 Republicans won many seats by razor-thin margins. The *New York Times* director of polling has noted that "adding just 48,886 Democratic votes in just the right places would have boosted the Democratic gain to 40 seats, an unquestionable landslide" (Clymer 1983: 5). Such a landslide would have produced a political shock wave and a perception in the policy community of far more severe political constraints on the monetary weapon than were inferred from the actual outcome.

Second, even after losing only twenty-six seats, the Republicans were sufficiently frightened by the election margins that they prevented President Reagan from cutting domestic spending any further. The Republicans' own polls had showed them losing at least forty-five seats a month before the election (Clymer 1983: 5). That they closed the gap to twenty-six seats was due in part, all agree, to the party's superior advantages of money and organization in 1982. However, the parties' differences in money and organization are narrowing somewhat, bringing the Democrats closer to the threshold above which the Republicans' advantage has diminishing returns.

Third, only twenty-six seats were lost in part because Reagan argued in the campaign that his program had not been given a chance to work ("stay the course"). By blaming the recession on Carter policies, Reagan deflected responsibility for recession. Such a strategy could not cut the electoral costs of a recession in a second Reagan term. Since 1952, the first midterm election after a change of party control of the presidency, such as in 1982, shows a much smaller seat loss than does the second midterm election. The 1954, 1962, and 1970 elections had an average loss of eleven seats in the House, but in the second midterm election after such a change (the 1958, 1966, and 1974 elections), the seat loss averaged forty-nine seats (Jacobson 1983: 125). Hence, the longer a party controls the White House, the weaker grows the political sustainability of such unpopular policies as tight money. Republicans fear a repeat of the 1958 election, which reflected the severe 1958 recession aimed at bringing down a 1957 inflation rate of 3.7 percent (Economic Report of the President 1984: 282). The changes wrought by Democratic congressmen elected in the "Class of '58" were felt in Congress for the next two decades. Similarly, the 1974 election, due partly to Watergate and partly to recession, greatly increased Democratic strength in Congress, pushing the ideological center of gravity in Congress ever since considerably to the left of what it otherwise would have been. Hence, even with less inflation to counteract, the next recession will be more dangerous to Republicans than recession in the 1982 election. Knowing that, they and some of the forces they represent will demand less stringent monetary policy.

The circumstances of the 1984 election do not test the political endurance of the quasi-monetarist regime. President Reagan's reelection campaign occurred with unemployment and inflation down dramatically, and a high growth rate for nearly two years prior to the election.

THE POTENTIAL COALITION FOR AN INCENTIVE ANTI-INFLATION POLICY

Beyond electoral conditions, the political vulnerability of quasi-monetarism also depends on interest groups that might be eager to escape the costs of present policies and that might support a carefully integrated mix of policies ("social contract") that included a refined incentive scheme applied to a relatively small number of large firms.

The scope of such a potential coalition is suggested by two analyses. The first (Gordon and King 1982: 241) estimates that it costs at least $1 trillion of forgone output, having a present value of 29 percent of a year's GNP, to achieve a long-run 5 percentage point reduction in the inflation rate by restrictive monetary policy. The second (Perry 1983) shows that there is no empirical basis for the view that "credible policy has speeded up the disinflation process and made it less costly."

Tucked within that $1 trillion figure is a potential coalition that would support a less costly policy. Interest-sensitive and dollar-sensitive industries and their employees have paid the heaviest price. Housing, autos, steel, consumer durables, capital goods, small businesses dependent on borrowing to finance inventories, export industries (including agriculture) and industries competing with foreign goods—all are potential supporters of an innovative anti-inflation policy. These interests are hardly political paper tigers.

Business in general would benefit if inflation could be held down without severe and prolonged recessions: Profits are procyclical. Moreover, business tolerance for the costs of recession was shown to have definite limits by the latter part of 1982, as demonstrated by a host of articles in the elite press that proclaimed the "death of monetarism" or the "monetarist mess."

Labor unions are ideologically disposed to incomes policies in general because of employment effects. But labor leaders feel strongly that the Nixon and Carter programs were little more than wage controls that provided no balancing restraint on other incomes and whose increases squeezed real labor income. To achieve labor support, labor leaders would have to be convinced that some form of balance was built into a program.

Last, politicians would have strong incentives to support such a plan. Democrats are widely viewed as in disarray because they lack a macroeconomic policy appropriate to their bases of support. Prior to the 1984 election they geared up to run on "industrial policy" before that approach was attacked so severely by some mainstream Democratic economists (Schultze 1983) that it was effectively withdrawn from the election campaign. However, that the Democrats invested so much in that planning indicates the intense need they felt for an approach to increasing employment and growth. Incumbent Republican congressmen greatly fear a recession-induced shift in the balance of power. If businesses most hurt by recession were mobilized by political entrepreneurs around a specific plan, pressure from them would increase Republican support for an innovative anti-inflation policy.

With so many potential supporters for an alternative to tight money, why then has no politician embraced an incentive plan? (Gary Hart is an exception, but he did not make his advocacy of a TIP a centerpiece of his appeal.) Opposition is based on several beliefs of elites with the greatest influence on politicians:

1. Most important is the widespread belief that past incomes policies were failures and that their design and administration could not be improved on. Allocational inefficiencies and distortions cause shortages, black markets, and proliferating "exceptions" to rules, causing the collapse of political support.

2. The belief that inflation is largely episodic, rather than a structural problem tied to non-Walrasian institutions of price and wage setting, will dissipate if inflation accelerates after the "Great Monetary Policy Experiment," after deficit reduction occurs, and when OPEC, unions, accelerated social spending, and accommodative monetary policy can no longer be blamed easily.

3. The hope attached to the credibility hypothesis in some influential quarters prior to 1982 caused some to expect that the costs of disinflation through tight money would turn out to be lower than in fact they were.

4. Another might be labeled the "Robespierre problem." Robespierre was brought to his death, having instituted the reign of terror, when it became unclear who his next victims might be. Many who in fact were not targeted but feared they might be united to bring Robespierre down. A similar situation confronts any proposal for an innovative anti-inflation policy. Anti-inflation policy proposals create widespread fear of excessive arbitrary costs and doubts about

the benefits entailed. Such reactions can be forestalled only by presenting a specific plan and mapping how it would meet various contingencies that might arise prior to trying to build political support for a policy experiment. No such plan now exists.

Any such plan must specify the structure of a political bargain because an incomes policy can be a mechanism for changing the distribution of income shares. To gain support for legislative passage in the future it may well be necessary to show beforehand how the policy formula and its administrative process will determine the distribution of income shares. Absent such a plan, some business interests will be uncomfortable opposing others, with whom congenial political relationships have been shared. The same holds true among unions. A key question is whether a wedge can be driven between business in general and those industries most responsible for inflation where supply-demand equilibration does not justify price rises. For example, if a Bosworth/Lawrence scheme (1982) for controlling commodity inflation is opposed by oil interests and agribusiness, and hospital cost containment is opposed by health industry interests (and the influence of these interests in Congress is legendary), they would have to be overwhelmed by a coalition of other businesses and labor. Economists qua policymakers must integrate systematic analyses of such "messy" political considerations with economic analyses, or a viable plan will not be constructed.

The most immediate obstacle is the first: the belief that past failures, if that is what they were, are a good guide to what we could expect in the future. This view tends to ignore several key arguments. *First*, it is possible that past efforts could be improved on because they were designed and initiated under crisis conditions with meager administrative and political resources. *Second*, in interviews with this author, some senior economists involved in past programs have asserted the proposition that many of the administrative problems, such as those involved in measuring compliance (which are also cited by opponents as the worst stumbling blocks), could be reduced to manageable proportions if larger administrative resources (presupposing greater political support) were committed to a program. That proposition ought to be a central item on the agenda of future policy research. After surveying many of the problems critics of incentive schemes emphasize, in an account that does make those problems seem overwhelming, Triplett, who is among the foremost experts on the problems usually cited, states: "All the problems I have been discussing can be addressed, given sufficient staff resources; and all can probably, with enough ingenuity and effort, be reduced to sufficiently manageable proportions that a controls program can operate at some acceptable level of proficiency." (Chapter 17.) The matter of whether agencies such as the Bureau of Labor Statistics are to be permanently given greater resources and authority to gather more data is fundamentally a political decision. *Third*, some recent research suggests that the price measurement problems that even sympathetic critics usually find most damning might be avoidable by substituting value added for price changes as the focus of the measurement of compliance (Meade 1981; Colander and Koford 1984). Whether these major claims are true also does not seem to be a question that has been fully researched. *Fourth*, an incentive scheme might become far more economically and politically feasible if the burden such a scheme must bear were reduced by being tied to other anti-inflation policies, notably the Bosworth/ Lawrence scheme for holding down commodities inflation with buffer stocks and hospital cost containment. With commodities and health industry inflation held down, expectational inflation would be less, and ensuing political support from labor and management might be far greater for an incentive scheme aimed only at the autonomous wage/price spiral. These issues belong on the research agenda, and if they can be settled positively, the probability will increase that an innovative policy will succeed.

A SCENARIO FOR A POLICY EXPERIMENT

The most likely scenario in which an incentive anti-inflation policy experiment would take place would have several key features. The first is election of a Democratic president. Every Democratic administration since 1941, and one Republican one, adopted an incomes policy. The last Carter administration *Economic Report of the President* (January 1981: 57-68, 84-88) indicates a second Carter administration would have moved beyond its real wage insurance proposal toward a wider tax-based incomes policy (TIP). It does seem unlikely, given the rightward movement of Republican activists, that a future Republican administration would construct a viable plan. But if a specific plan were developed, it is possible that some future Republican administration might accept it as a basis for a policy experiment.

A second key feature of a likely scenario is accelerating inflation. If the new quasi-monetarism does keep inflation low without severe recessions or a large gap between actual and potential output, then low political and economic costs will sustain it. Inertial or "core" inflation slowed to a very low point by the latter part of 1984. But there is pessimism about future inflation. Real long-term bond rates remain historically high, reflecting, in part, doubts about future inflation. Optimism is checked by fear of the appetites of politicians for excessive stimulation, by forecasts of U.S. budget deficits and a falling dollar, by continued slow productivity growth (Clark 1984), by doubts that structural change in wage setting has in fact occurred (Flanagan 1984) (which is not to say that wages were a significant cause of U.S. inflation in the 1970s, even if they were a transmission belt), and by the potential for an external shock down the road. Inflationary pressures may also arise from the many claimants who will use political power to increase or maintain their income shares, which only a self-conscious and well-organized countercoalition could prevent (Olson 1982). Moreover, the optimistic story about inflation ignores the central theoretical challenge to any monetarist theory—its failure to account for the sluggishness of price adjustment amid output fluctuations (Gordon 1981b).

A third feature of a scenario of policy experimentation would be political rejection of the costs of fighting accelerating inflation through further monetary tightening. In addition to election cycle constraints discussed above, tighter money will increase pressure for an alternative policy because of (1) the present instability in international and domestic U.S. financial conditions, which constrains the monetary authorities, and (2) the condition of balance sheets in a number of industries that remain weak despite recovery and that are vulnerable to higher interest rates. Although the next recession will begin with inflation at a much lower level than in 1979, requiring less severe medicine, the financial vulnerability of many economic agents will be higher than before. These agents may perceive that what was promised to be a one-time cost associated with a shift to a new policy regime is in fact to be a recurring cost. They may conclude that it is they who are to bear the brunt of the costs of continuing to hold down inflation. If so, political entrepreneurs may be able to mobilize them behind a credible anti-inflation policy alternative.

A fourth possible feature of a policy experiment scenario is slow growth. There is disagreement over how much economic growth will be sacrificed by the post-1982 monetary regime. Is tighter money politically sustainable if linked to slow growth? It is not clear from existing studies whether voters in the future would punish politicians for slow growth, despite low and steady inflation and unemployment held to a relatively narrow band between 7 and 9 percent (Tufte 1978; Kiewiet 1983; Monroe 1984). It does seem likely that President Reagan has created expectations of rising living standards through a return to higher growth rates, which, if disappointed, might produce a significant political reaction.

DEPENDENCE OF AN EXPERIMENT ON THE LOCUS OF POLICY DEVELOPMENT

Even if these conditions all obtained, a policy experiment may not be undertaken. The absence of a specific plan leaves too many doubts. Politicians are cautious and will continue to be unwilling to defend anything that sounds like rigid wage and price controls unless they can say how their plan is different. To gain support for a plan, political entrepreneurs would need to make plain to various groups and industries how their interests would be affected by a given anti-inflation program. An additional virtue of preparing a specific plan well before it is implemented is that it would be available to put in place before inflation begins to accelerate and the "catch-up" aspect of the inflationary spiral is initiated.

Under what conditions would an adequate plan—one that would serve as a basis for gathering the political support necessary for a policy experiment—be produced? Consider the following argument. Students of U.S. political institutions tend to doubt that any institution, other than the U.S. presidency, now exists that is capable of constructing such a plan. The most likely time and place in which planning would begin would be within a Democratic administration during a bout of accelerating inflation. Unfortunately, experts and former high officials are not sanguine about the quality of the planning that would occur in a presidential administration. Barry Bosworth (1981) has argued persuasively that economic policy making in the executive branch is far more fragmented and cacophonous today than in the 1960s. In addition, the career bureaucracy has been greatly weakened. Under such circumstances, interest groups might well have undue weight in formulating a policy.

The existence of a plan based on a fundamental analysis, which specified how contingencies that might arise would be managed, and around which political support had been rallied, could place policymakers in a position from which they could fend off demands of interest groups that might sink the program. The likelihood is that either a badly constructed plan will be born of crisis and inadequate administrative resources in a presidential administration, or fundamental planning must be achieved before the time it is needed and "elsewhere" than in the high pressure crucible of an Administration preparing to act.

Where is "elsewhere"? That question must be answered by the presidents of foundations and research institutions and by business, labor, and academic statesmen. But they will not consider attempting to institutionalize policy research unless and until the costs of the present quasi-monetarist policy regime begin to be viewed as uncomfortably high and recurring rather than largely behind us.

There is one last point that seems crucial. There are those who believe that it is necessary to wait on an academic breakthrough in the analyses of incentive schemes to provide a fresh reason for a policy experiment. Advances in incentive schemes may well be forthcoming. But perusal of the history of past incomes policies at home and abroad indicates that the construction of a viable and sustainable plan requires the integration of efforts of many different kinds of expertise and experience to solve many different kinds of interrelated problems—political, economic, legal, accounting, and administrative. Any incentive scheme will have compliance problems, and administrative solutions to them will have to stand up in court. A realistic scenario in which such a scheme is adopted and is successful will include a planning process in which testing of different incentive schemes occurs for their fit to dynamic political, economic, legal, and administrative conditions. In the real world of policy anything less will be considered an exercise. It is unlikely that such a multidimensional plan will be produced by individual scholars working in isolation. Given the enormous stakes, one cannot help but wonder whether an institutionalized effort will be undertaken to produce a viable plan.

16 POLITICAL PROBLEMS OF INCENTIVE ANTI-INFLATION PLANS

James K. Galbraith

A hundred years ago, at the urging of the great railroads, the United States undertook a remarkable experiment in social coordination. This was the reform of the system of time: the creation of the four standard time zones and synchronization of watches, clocks, and—most important—timetables. Prior to the reform, each city maintained its own standard, often differing by no more than a few minutes, and travelers, telegraphists, and train switchmen faced nightmares of translation and coordination.

Time reform was perhaps not necessary to the progress of economic life. The computer, though as a practical matter not available for at least another eight decades, could theoretically have kept everything sorted out. But time reform did greatly reduce various inefficiencies involved in running a large national system of railroads. It was a practical measure, virtually without economic cost, and it was put into effect very largely by voluntary action.

Inflation can be seen in today's world as something of the same sort of problem. We ask our price system to convey very large amounts of information. Each actor in the wage and price determination process views the whole from his or her own subjective standpoint, weighting the available information in idiosyncratic ways. Differential wage settlements and benefit indexation atomize popular opinion. Differential contract timing distorts worker perspectives. The result is a pattern of action with a large economic and social cost: misused and misinterpreted economic information, wasted effort based on misguided forecasts, and the erosion of national self-assurance and confidence in political institutions that follows from inflation.

To avoid these threats, we apply macroeconomic instruments whose use vastly amplifies the economic cost and that bring on real human suffering and hardship. It is as though, a hundred years ago, we had attempted to cure the national neurosis over timetables by shutting down the railroads or perhaps requiring the trains to run at a slower speed.

Almost all the authors included in this volume believe that there ought to be a better way. They differ substantially on what that better way is. Many of them believe that TIP and MAP are the better way. I remain unconvinced. To me, the administrative problems discussed by Russell (Chapter 11) and Triplett (Chapter 12) appear compelling.

In this short note, though, I would like to emphasize a different set of problems, stemming from the vulgar realities of the political process. It may be a little unfashionable to remind a scholarly community of the constraints that politics sometimes impose. But they do exist, and it becomes increasingly important to understand them as a proposal moves from the domain of the scholarly exchange toward that of the legislative draftsman.

The political characteristics of TIPs and MAPs, controls and guidelines, and other policies emerge most clearly when each is viewed through the prism of two concepts: The first is the effort expended to *deter* inflationary price/wage behavior at any given time, whether through exhortation, guidelines, controls, or high interest rates and recession, and by whom that effort is expended. Second is the total *time* required for the policy to work.

Deterrence of inflationary behavior is achieved by making continued inflationary wage and price settlements so costly that firms and workers cease to agree to them. *Time* is required for the effects of deterrence to spread through a sufficiently large fraction of the economy, so that enough individual decisions are taken to have the required aggregate effect. The interaction of the locus of deterrence and the time required for each type of deterrence to work sets off the costs of each alternative anti-inflation plan from the others.

DETERRENCE AND THE LOCUS OF RESPONSIBILITY
FOR PRICE-STABILIZING DECISIONS

Every effective price stabilization policy relies on deterrence of inflationary behavior in one form or another. A key difference between these strategies, from a political standpoint, is in the locus of responsibility for deciding the precise terms of deterrence, and hence on the allocation of costs.

With conventional monetary regimes, this locus is "the market." Individuals and companies are left to make their own judgments about appropriate nominal wage and price settlements. This is clearly the ideal solution in the abstract. Monetary anti-inflation regimes are as a rule accompanied by official disclaimer of any intent to enforce an "incomes policy." Yet this advantage carries an offsetting cost: The buffers of slack demand, forgone profit, and forgone employment required so that a sufficient proportion of economic actors arrive at the "right" individual price/wage decisions are forbiddingly large. And, as a rule, the costs fall on those economically least able to bear them.

Expectations-altering regimes—the new fashion in monetary policy—seek to establish a norm for wage/price behavior, but in an oblique way, through the establishment of monetary targets. The central bank thus assumes the mantle of norm-setter. As we have seen, however, this is neither credible nor effective.

Controls and guidelines transfer the onus of responsibility for setting an anti-inflation norm entirely from the private sector to the public. This is the source of the effectiveness of such policies and their Achilles' heel. The costs, being mainly political, fall most heavily on those most capable of resisting them. So long as the government enjoys sufficient legal or moral authority to gain acceptance for the norms it sets, and so long as the practical administration is widely viewed as wise or anyhow exiguous, controls can work. As soon as faith in the government's mandate or its judgment weakens, controls have a tendency to collapse.

Tax-based incomes policies and transferable coupon schemes attempt to combine public and private responsibility: The government sets the norm, but uses economic rather than legal or moral incentives to achieve compliance. TIPs and MAPs thus combine the weaknesses of government intervention with the costs of conventional monetary anti-inflation regimes—although each in attenuated form. The effectiveness of any given incentive will depend on the state of the economy; the stronger the underlying growth of demand, the greater the profit opportunities to be gained from defying the TIP norm and paying the penalty instead. For this reason, some advocates of TIPs and MAPs stress that they can be expected to work only in conjunction with restrictive fiscal and monetary policies and that their purpose is to reduce the costs of monetary disinflation, not to eliminate such costs altogether.

Contrary to some belief, TIPs are vulnerable to political modification much as controls and guidelines are. If faith in the standard-setting authority is not strong, pressure will inevitably be brought to bear to reduce costs of noncompliance. Advocates of TIPs sometimes make the argument that because such schemes work through the market, they will be free of political channels of influence. This is, however, not so.

In particular, such claims ignore the increased administrative and political burden falling on those who write the tax code in the first place. In our day and age, even the most modest effort at rewriting the tax code, such as the 1984 Tax Act, can run to 1,800 pages and take nearly a full legislative year to enact. TIP provisions would not make the tax code simpler. To the contrary, they would certainly fuel endless campaigns for special treatment, leading to massive further complications in the tax code.

In the present political environment, TIPs are infeasible for a reason that stems directly from this fact—the exhaustion of special-interest politics in the tax-writing committees of Congress. It is likely that for the next several years all major debate in the tax area will focus on achievement of a massive, code-simplifying, and at least potentially revenue-raising, tax reform. The position of legislators who might otherwise be sympathetic to a TIP is already taking shape and consists of a generalized assault on special-interest provisions of the tax code in an effort to preserve the income tax as the heart of our revenue system. It is simply inconsistent for such a legislator to advocate, on the one hand, extreme tax simplification and base-broadening and, on the other, a complicated new system of tax incentives and penalties. TIPs will be crowded out, if not precisely by the deficit, then by the political imperative of taking action to correct it.

TIMING AND COSTS OF COMPLIANCE

In making deterrence effective, a single, clear, weighty, morally persuasive signal to workers and businesses is certainly better than a vague, obscure, or insincere one. But the effectiveness of a behavior-modifying policy depends also on the costs of compliance.

Organized labor settles wages through a long-term contract. For those for whom response to a wage signal of the type described above would mean breaking an existing contract, the costs of immediate compliance can be high. Yet if existing contracts are to be respected, and an economy makes key wage decisions, as ours does, on a staggered three-year cycle, then a given behavior-modifying policy must be sustained for three full years before all workers have been affected once. Three years is too long to maintain a single inflation guideline, in the face of rapidly changing world market developments.

None of the alternative anti-inflation policies discussed in this section pays any explicit attention to the timing issue. Each dissipates its force over the existing time pattern of wage settlements and the existing structure of administered prices. And each suffers increased cost and diminished effectiveness as a result. Conventional and expectations-altering monetary regimes find their greatest frustration in the nominal-wage resistance characteristic of U.S. labor compensation. Once a given pattern of nominal settlements has taken hold, it takes a long and difficult effort to break it. And the costs—of forgone output and prolonged unemployment—cumulate over time. Controls and guidelines find that timing frustrates every effort to be fair. One cannot freeze the price/wage action at any point, since in an overlapping game of catch-up someone is always ahead, someone always behind. The inevitable tangle of special cases and hardship exemptions acts corrosively on the prestige and long-term viability of controls. TIPs and MAPs would find these problems present at the creation and complicated by the statutory nature of the governing norm. Requests for special treatment in the name of fairness would clog the tax-writing committees, instead of the administrative courts.

In sum, it is the present author's view that formal anti-inflation policies offered to date have suffered an organic defect. They are politically costly to put into effect. Therefore nothing happens before inflation becomes a serious problem. But when inflation does become a serious problem, it is too serious for these policies effectively to contain. It is the old story of the roof that doesn't need fixing in good weather and is too leaky to fix when it rains.

For this reason, I would urge that attention focus on practical steps first. A practical step may be defined as one that, once put in place, imposes the lowest continuing costs of implementation on the government and the lowest continuing costs of compliance on the people.

Three types of policy measures can be put in place now: (1) measures to raise the trend rate of productivity growth in the expansion; (2) measures to improve the flexibility and effectiveness of national commodity buffer stocks such as the Strategic Petroleum Reserve; and (3) measures to speed the adjustment and stabilization of wage decisions when a relative price shift occurs, such as synchronization of pay settlements and prospective indexation of federal wage and benefit programs. These measures require only small sacrifices. They would improve the price stabilization properties of the economic system. They may or may not prove totally effective. Even with the best rails and switching system, and the most streamlined cars, there is a limit to how fast the train can go.

Thus the small practical steps will not in the end suffice. We will come, in the end, to the need to make a political choice among alternative means of fighting inflation such as those presented in this book. This fundamental political choice, between market-based mechanisms with high economic costs and political mechanisms with lower economic costs, is among the most vital economic choices an enduring democracy must make.

17 IN DEFENSE OF INCENTIVE ANTI-INFLATION PLANS

David C. Colander

Sadists aside, no one would support an incentive anti-inflation plan for its administrative aspects. In fact, if one does not have a healthy fear of administering an incomes policy, incentive or otherwise, he is naive, hasn't read the literature on past incomes policies (Galbraith, the father, excluded), or is bent on the destruction of our economic system. How then can anyone support an incentive anti-inflation plan?

The answer can be seen only in comparison with the alternatives. Here, anti-inflation plan supporters are in agreement. The costs of our current "incomes policy," which consists of periodic recessions and a high average unemployment rate, so far outweigh the administrative costs of the plans that they believe such a policy should be implemented despite the administrative complexity. That judgment is, of course, a benefit/cost judgment and is not shared by all the contributors to this volume or by much of the profession. As both the editor of this volume and a contributor to it, I am well aware that it contains a disproportionate number of papers in support of the plans. Still, I can hardly be accused of stacking the deck. The plans have taken their lumps—the result of good hard shots by Galbraith, Triplett, and Russell (hereafter GTR or TR).

The response of TIP and MAP proponents to GTR might be that these three don't know what they are talking about, but that response would be incorrect. Their papers are well reasoned, solid pieces of research that reflect great administrative and political experience. Their arguments must be taken seriously. This leads to a paradox; Supporters of the plans, too, have serious arguments and similar goals. (Being one such supporter, I would find it hard to hold otherwise.) What accounts for this disagreement among economists who share common values? It is that paradox that I address in this chapter.

The answer is simple. GTR see the costs of incentive anti-inflation plans greater than the benefits; proponents see the benefits greater than the costs. Such disputes are not unheard of; as Russell points out, benefit/cost ratios are inevitably subjective for normal projects; for yet untried projects the benefits and costs are both highly uncertain.

THE COSTS OF THE PLANS

The costs are of three types: political (discussed by Galbraith), administrative (discussed by Triplett and Russell), and efficiency or resource misallocation costs (also discussed by Triplett and Russell).

Political Costs

I agree with Galbraith that the political costs are highest and preclude the plans' early introduction. Nevertheless, we both agree that long-term structural reforms are necessary, and continue to work on them because political costs change suddenly; what is politically impossible at one moment can become politically possible at another. Galbraith quarrels with the political assumptions underlying the design of TIP and MAP, but that is secondary to our agreement on the need for some form of long-term structural change, for an alternative to unemployment as the sole weapon against inflation. Political costs have to be weighed against the alternatives. Moreover, economists are not neutral in determining these costs. Their studies and arguments change the political costs of policies, and thus economists should not take the political argument as decisive. We are hardly the experts on political feasibility, and should not claim to be. (I have discussed the role of economist and politics more specifically in Lerner and Colander 1983). In the past, political costs of implementing incomes policies have changed dramatically. The political constituency for incomes policies dissolves quickly when inflation subsides and rises quickly when inflation reemerges.

Since I strongly believe that inflation will reemerge, I believe that the constituency for incomes policies will return. The question is, What will be done with the constituency? Economists' past role in this political process has been to thwart this constituency, or at least to channel it into temporary controls programs or short-run incomes policies of the type Russell and Triplett worked on in CWPS. They have done so in good faith and without thinking of justifying themselves because they believe that a long-run incomes policy is incompatible with, and would destroy, the market process. Failure, while not desired, was nevertheless preordained. In my view, TR's criticisms are directed at such short-run incomes policies, except they are trying to get a minimal policy to work better than it has in the past. Given their goals for the policy, I am in substantial agreement with them and with the myriad other such assessments (for instance, those by Herbert Stein and others cited in Colander 1979b).

However, incentive anti-inflation plans are not short-run amelioratives. They set forth major institutional changes that alter basic social pricing regimes. I once presented the case for TIP and MAP to Alfred Kahn, who was then President Carter's inflation czar. He commented that what I had in mind was an institutional change as significant as the introduction of the Federal Reserve System. I agreed.

For the short-term objectives of the type TR are considering, they are certainly right that incentive anti-inflation plans are inappropriate. Short-term wages and prices are primarily institutionally set, and the level of incentives we mean when we talk about incentive anti-inflation plans will not significantly influence those decisions. The argument in favor of incentive anti-inflation plans is a long-run argument because it is only in the long run that the anti-inflation incentives can be built into the institutional structure. If the political will that develops in response to inflation is channeled toward a long-run policy, and if economists have developed the plans sufficiently so that they are more than pie-in-the-sky dreams, then such policies will have the political support to be put into effect. Indeed, the political argument for any progressive reform rests on a cognate conviction.

Administrative Costs

The above political argument on administrative costs foreshadows my response to Triplett and Russell. While I agree with their general conclusion—that the plans are not administratively simple—I have numerous quibbles with the specifics and thrust of their arguments. My quibbles have to do with the interpretation of value added and concern issues such as the following:

1. The MAP value-added concept uses financial, not physical, capital. Russell and Triplett criticize the administrative difficulty of determining physical capital. There are some problems with using financial capital, but the arguments Russell and Triplett advance are not relevant to these. (For a discussion of value added measure, see Colander 1981.)[1]

2. The use of a value added per unit input guideline "taxes" only those productivity gains that are not passed on to the consumer (in the same way that competition "taxes" productivity gains); it hurts incentives only to the degree that the input is inappropriately specified. Much of that problem can be eliminated by defining input generously. When inputs are correctly specified, the bias is in favor of, not against, investment and productivity increases because mark-up monopoly is reduced.

3. Contrary to Russell and Triplett, I believe that an input price measure can be just as broad as an output price measure and that an input price measure is preferable to the output price measure since it avoids the productivity gain problem with which the Council on Wage and Price Stability struggled.

The above are quibbles and do not alter the central points that Russell and Triplett make; numerous difficult decisions will have to be made along the way and each of these involves administrative costs and resource allocation costs that might be called microinefficiencies; and these microinefficiencies will be larger for a long-run TIP program than for a short-run voluntary program. These costs are of two types: one-time implementation costs and ongoing costs. GTR group these together, but when the plans are seen as long-run, not short-run plans, the implementation costs (which make up a large percentage of the total) can be amortized over a longer period. Any new proposal has significant administrative problems because it involves change. For a short-run policy, such as TR have in mind, these administrative problems are the ballgame; for a long-run policy such as incentive anti-inflation plans supporters have in mind, they form merely an initial hurdle. For example, if no quality adjustment were made for different quality workers in the labor input, firms would find it in their interest to modify their work forces, replacing skilled with unskilled workers. Over time, such replacement would push up the relative wage of unskilled and push down the relative wage of skilled workers until no more substitution was appropriate. Thereafter there would be no adjustment. The incentives would be built into the system.

Resource Allocation Costs

Resource allocation costs are a separate matter. Different assessments of these costs distinguish proponents from opponents. GTR are judging resource allocation costs in reference to a perfectly competitive system. Proponents of MAP and TIP judge resource allocation costs in reference to a monopolistically competitive system in which the economy deviates toward supplier monopoly, creating continual excess supply. Jobs, sales by existing firms, and entry of new firms must necessarily be rationed by restrictive aggregate policies in order to maintain a competitive fringe—a large enough level of excess supply to prevent accelerating inflation. Incentive anti-inflation plans reduce the amount of necessary rationing and thereby improve, not worsen, the efficiency of the system. The microinefficiencies the plans create are minor compared to the macroefficiencies they resolve.

THE BENEFITS OF THE PLANS

The above discussion of the costs has already led us to the discussion of benefits. TIP and MAP proponents see large macroinefficiencies embedded in the current institutional structure of the economy; they see TIP and MAP helping to eliminate these. Opponents apparently do not. Thus, the key element in supporting the plans is a belief that the economy operates at an excess supply equilibrium. If it does in the absence of an incomes policy, we must rely on unemployment and excess supply to hold down what would otherwise be an accelerating inflation.

In numerical terms supporters are talking about a reduction of one, two, or three percentage points in the average long-run rate of unemployment. Since a 2 percent reduction translates into a net gain to GNP of about $150 billion per year in constant 1985 dollars, the gain is significant. Moreover, because proponents believe the economy is at the NAIRU, not the natural rate, they see little offset to reduced unemployment in lost leisure of the unemployed (the Lucas-Sargent story of unemployment). Since this gain is a steady-state gain, the present value of the flow is the relevant decision variable, and that comes to a gain over $3 trillion at a 3 percent real rate of interest. Comparing these gains to the costs, we see the benefit/cost ratio is enormous.

Fairness

These numbers are impressive, but even if they were smaller, I and many other proponents would still favor the plans' implementation. It is simply *immoral* to have an economic policy where some individuals must be unemployed so that others can have jobs at higher pay than if there were less unemployment. The fact that membership in the unemployment pool is stochastic mitigates the ethical problem, but since different people have very different probabilities of becoming and remaining unemployed, that does not eliminate the ethical problem. Consider a useful analogy: How much should society spend to catch an accused thief? It might cost $100,000 to catch a person who stole $100, but it might still be worthwhile spending the money because stealing is wrong. Because the expected gains so outweigh the expected costs, I do not believe that this argument is necessary to support the plans, but it does play a role in my support.

Another argument against the plans is that they involve compounding government intervention. I believe this argument is incorrect. If implemented, the plans will produce a *large net reduction* of government's role in the economy. Our present system of dealing with unemployment and the inequities that result from monopolization is a Rube Goldberg bureaucratic system. But as the fairness of the system improves under the force of an incentive anti-inflation policy, and unemployment and its resulting poverty fall, there will be ever-decreasing political demand for income redistribution programs to bail out a leaky system. Many of those programs and their associated bureaucracies can be eliminated by this plan. Put simply, the government should do few things, but those few that it does do, it should do right. Creating an economic system in which competition provides people with a fair chance to work is one of those jobs that the government should do right.

A Word of Caution

It should be clear from the above discussion that Triplett, Russell, and I are thinking of quite different programs. I am talking about a long-run institutional change in the system. The Carter program from which they derive their examples was essentially a stopgap measure and could not have had any of the effects I desire, nor could any program other than an incentive program ever be built into the institutional structure of the United States.

Despite my defense of the plans, I am not arguing for immediate implementation. I see the plans as constituting a major institutional change, and I recognize the seriousness with which major institutional changes must be taken. Its newness alone is sufficient to warrant concern. The system we have now works; who knows about another system that exists primarily in the heads of a few economists? And just as there are constitutional fairness issues in favor of the plans, so too are there what might be called constitutional issues against the plans. The tax system is already tremendously complicated and that complication has resulted because attempts have been made to use the tax system to achieve social ends. If a TIP program is the straw that breaks the camel's back, as the Russell and Triplett comments imply it might, then it should not be implemented. That argument, though, is not against incentive anti-inflation plans; it is an argument in favor of using a market-type plan rather than a tax-based plan. Using a market-type plan avoids some problems with the tax system while providing the same incentive gains that the market offers. (These arguments are examined in detail in Lerner and Colander 1980.)

CONCLUSION

The exposition of the issues here does not exhaust my defense of incentive anti-inflation plans, but it does exhaust my space. The arguments are meant to be persuasive, not decisive. To understand incentive anti-inflation plans requires shifting frameworks and analyzing the economy from a quite different perspective than what most economists have been taught to use. My writings about incentive anti-inflation plans have been designed to get people to shift frameworks and to recognize that alternative framework as a useful one in understanding the way an economy works. Russell and Triplett have come further than most critics in thinking in this new framework. As with any idea, all we can ask is that the reader do the same and consider the plans with an open mind.

NOTE TO CHAPTER 17

1. To be fair to Russell and Triplett, the financial measure of capital has not been carefully worked out in print, and they did not have access to the relevant unpublished material.

BIBLIOGRAPHY

Ackley, Gardner. 1958. "A Third Approach to the Analysis and Control of Inflation." In *The Relationship of Prices to Economic Stability and Growth*, papers submitted by panelists appearing before the Joint Economic Committee of the U.S. Congress (March 31): 630 ff.

_____. 1959. "Administered Prices and the Inflationary Process." *American Economic Review* 49, 2 (May): 419–30.

_____. 1975. Comments and Discussion of G. Perry's "Determinants of Wage Inflation." *Brookings Papers on Economic Activity* 2: 436–40. Washington, D.C.: Brookings Institution.

_____. 1978. *Macroeconomics: Theory and Policy.* New York: Macmillan.

"Are Mandatory Wage and Price Controls Needed to Combat Current Inflation?" 1980. Report 80–64 E (March 24). Congressional Research Service.

Arrow, Kenneth. 1959. "Toward a Theory of Price Adjustment." In *The Allocation of Economic Resources: Essays in Honor of Bernard Francis Haley*, edited by Moses Abramovitz et al., pp. 45–50. Stanford: Stanford University Press.

Baily, Martin N. 1976. "Contract Theory and the Moderation of Inflation by Recession and by Controls." *Brookings Papers on Economic Activity* 3: 585–634. Washington, D.C.: Brookings Institution.

Barro, Robert J. 1979. "An Appraisal of the Non-Market Clearing Paradigm." *American Economic Review* 69 (May): 54–59.

_____. 1984. *Macroeconomics.* New York: Wiley.

Barro, Robert J., and H.I. Grossman. 1976. *Money, Employment and Inflation.* New York: Cambridge University Press.

Baumol, William J. 1979. "On Some Microeconomic Issues in Inflation Theory." In *Essays in Post-Keynesian Inflation*, edited by J.H. Gapinski and C.G. Rockwood, pp. 55–78. Cambridge, Mass.: Ballinger.

245

Benassy, Jean-Pascal. 1982. *The Economics of Market Disequilibrium.* New York: Academic Press.

Bergson, Abram. 1942. "Prices, Wages and Incomes Theory." *Econometrica* 10 (July/Oct.): 275-89.

Blackorby, C.; D. Primont; and R. R. Russell. 1978. *Duality, Separability and Functional Structure: Theory and Economic Applications.* Amsterdam: North Holland.

Blinder, Alan S. 1979. *Economic Policy and the Great Stagflation.* New York: Academic Press.

_____ . 1982. "Anatomy of Double-Digit Inflation in the 1970s." In *Inflation: Causes and Effects*, edited by Robert E. Hall, pp. 261-82. Chicago: University of Chicago Press. Also available as NBER reprint 414.

Blinder, Alan S., and William J. Newton. 1981. "The 1971-1974 Controls Program and the Price Level: An Econometric Post-Mortem." *Journal of Monetary Economics* 8, 1 (July): 1-23.

Blyth, C.A. 1979. "The Interaction between Collective Bargaining and Government Policies in Selected Member Countries." *Collective Bargaining and Government Policies.* Paris: OECD.

Bosworth, Barry. 1981. "Re-establishing an Economic Consensus: An Impossible Agenda?" *Brookings General Series Reprint* 362. Washington, D.C.: Brookings Institution.

Bosworth, Barry, and Robert Z. Lawrence. 1982. *Commodity Prices and the New Inflation.* Washington, D.C.: Brookings Institution.

Bronfenbrenner, Martin. 1947. "Price Control under Imperfect Competition." *American Economic Review* 37 (March): 107-20.

Buiter, W.H., and M.H. Miller. 1983a. "Costs amd Benefits of an Anti-Inflationary Policy: Questions and Issues." Working Paper 1252. Cambridge, Mass.: National Bureau of Economic Research.

_____ . 1983b. "Changing the Rules: Economic Consequences of the Thatcher Regime." *Brookings Papers on Economic Activity* 2: 305-65. Washington, D.C.: Brookings Institution.

Bureau of National Affairs. 1979-81. U.S. Government Printing Office. *Federal Controls.* Washington, D.C.

Cagan, Phillip. 1979. "The Economy under Controls, 1971-1973." In *Persistent Inflation*, edited by Phillip Cagan, pp. 157-78. New York: Columbia University Press.

Calvo, G. 1979. "Quasi-Walrasian Theories of Unemployment." *American Economic Review* 69, 2: 102-07.

Canterbery, E. Ray. 1983. "Tax Reform and Incomes Policy: A VATIP Proposal." *Journal of Post Keynesian Economics* 5, 3 (Spring): 430-39.

Carter, Jimmy. 1978 (II). "The President's Anti-Inflation Program." In *Public Papers of the Presidents of the United States.* Washington, D.C.: Office of the Federal Register, National Archives and Records Service.

Chamberlin, Edward H. 1933. *The Theory of Monopolistic Competition.* Cambridge, Mass.: Harvard University Press.

Clark, J.M. 1953. "Basic Problems and Policies." In *Economic Controls and Defense*, edited by Donald H. Wallace, pp. 242-56. New York: Twentieth Century Fund.

Clark, Peter K. 1984. "Productivity and Profits in the 1980s: Are They Really Improving?" *Brookings Papers on Economic Activity* 1: 133–82.

Clower, Robert W. 1965. "The Keynesian Counterrevolution: A Theoretical Reappraisal." In *The Theory of Interest Rates*, edited by Frank H. Hahn and Frank P. Brechling, pp. 103–25. London: MacMillan.

_____. 1967. "A Reconsideration of the Microfoundations of Monetary Theory." *Western Economic Journal* 6: 1–9.

Clymer, Adam. 1983. "The Economic Basis for 'Throwing the Bums Out' in the 1980 and 1982 American Elections." Paper presented at the 1983 Annual Meeting of the American Political Science Association, Chicago, Illinois, Sept. 4.

Colander, David C. 1979a. "Incomes Policies: MIP, WIPP and TIP." *Journal of Post Keynesian Economics* 2 (Spring): 91–100.

_____. 1979b. *Solutions to Inflation.* New York: Harcourt Brace Jovanovich.

_____. 1979c. "A Value Added Tax-Based Incomes Policy." In *Solutions to Inflation*, edited by D. Colander, pp. 188–92. New York: Harcourt Brace Jovanovich.

_____. 1980. "Tax- and Market-Based Incomes Policies: The Interface of Theory and Practice." In *Incomes Policies for the United States: New Approaches*, edited by M. Claudon, pp. 79–97. Boston: Martinus Nijhoff.

_____. 1981. *Incentive Anti-Inflation Plans.* Washington, D.C.: U.S. Government Printing Office.

_____. 1982. "Stagflation and Competition." *Journal of Post Keynesian Economics* 5 (Fall): 17–33.

_____. 1984. "Galbraith and the Theory of Price Control." *Journal of Post Keynesian Economics* 7 (Fall): 30–42.

_____. 1985a. "Why an Incomes Policy Makes an Economy More Efficient." In *Macroeconomic Conflict and Social Institutions*, edited by S. Maital and I. Lipnowski, pp. 97–119. Cambridge, Mass.: Ballinger.

_____. 1985b. "Some Simple Geometry of the Welfare Loss from Competitive Monopolies." *Public Choice* 45: 199–206.

_____. 1986. *Macroeconomic Theory and Policy.* Glenview, Ill.: Scott, Foresman.

Colander, David C., and Kenneth J. Koford. 1984. "Tax and Market Incentive Plans to Fight Inflation." In *Economic Perspectives: An Annual Survey of Economics*, vol. 3, edited by Maurice B. Ballabon, pp. 155–93. New York: Harwood.

Colander, David C., and Mancur Olson. 1984. "Coalitions and Macroeconomics." In *Neoclassical Political Economy*, edited by David Colander, pp. 115–28. Cambridge, Mass.: Ballinger.

Committee on National Statistics. Forthcoming. *Statistical Assessments as Evidence in the Courts.* Washington, D.C.: National Academy of Sciences.

Council on Wage and Price Stability. 1981. *Evaluation of the Pay and Price Standards Program.* Washington, D.C.: U.S. Government Printing Office.

Courthéoux, J.P. 1976. "Perspectives et Limites Du Prélèvement Conjoncturel." *Revue d'Economie Politique* 86, 43: 374–415.

Creamer, Daniel, and others. 1977. *Gross National Product Data Improvement Project Report.* Report of the Advisory Committee on Gross National Prod-

uct Data Improvement. U.S. Department of Commerce, Office of Federal
Statistical Policy and Standards. Washington, D.C.: U.S. Government Printing
Office.

Darby, Michael. 1976a. "Price and Wage Controls: The First Two Years." In
The Economics of Price and Wage Controls, edited by K. Brunner and A.
Meltzer, pp. 253–63. Amsterdam: North Holland.

_____. 1976b. "Price and Wage Controls: Further Evidence." In *The Econom-
ics of Price and Wage Controls*, edited by K. Brunner and A. Meltzer, pp.
269–71. Amsterdam: North Holland.

de Menil, G. 1971. *Bargaining: Monopoly Power versus Union Power.* Cambridge, Mass.: MIT Press.

De Wulf, L. 1976. "The 'Prélèvement Conjoncturel,' or Anti-Inflation Tax in
France: A Theoretical Analysis." *Revista Di Diritto Finanziario E Scienza
Delle Finanze* 35, 1: 42–58.

Diamond, Peter. 1984. "Money in Search of Equilibrium." *Econometrica* 52, 1
(January): 1–20.

Dildine, Larry L., and Emil M. Sunley. 1976. "Administrative Problems of Tax-
Based Incomes Policies." *Brookings Papers on Economic Activity* 2: 363–89.
Washington, D.C.: Brookings Institution.

_____. 1978. "Administrative Problems of Tax-Based Incomes Policies." In
Curing Chronic Inflation, edited by A.M. Okun and G.L. Perry, pp. 127–54.
Washington, D.C.: Brookings Institution.

Eads, George. 1976. *The Commodity Shortages of 1973–74: Case Studies.*
Washington, D.C.: National Commission on Supplies and Shortages.

Eckstein, Otto. 1981. *Core Inflation.* Englewood Cliffs, N.J.: Prentice-Hall.

Economic Report of the President. 1981. Washington, D.C.: U.S. Government
Printing Office.

Economic Report of the President. 1984. Washington, D.C.: U.S. Government
Printing Office.

Eisner, Robert, and Paul Pieper. 1984. "A New View of the Federal Debt and
Budget Deficits." *American Economic Review* 74, 1 (March): 11–29.

Fair, Ray C. 1974. *A Model of Macroeconomic Activity*, vol. 2, *The Empirical
Model.* Cambridge, Mass.: Ballinger.

Feige, Edgar L., and Douglas K. Pearce. 1976. "Inflation and Incomes Policy:
An Application of Time Series Models." In *The Economics of Price and Wage
Controls*, edited by K. Brunner and A. Meltzer, pp. 273–302. Amsterdam:
North Holland.

Fellner, William J. 1981. "Comments on 1981 Paper by Charles Schultze."
Brookings Papers on Economic Activity 2: 577–81. Washington, D.C.:
Brookings Institution.

Fisher, Franklin, and Karl Shell. 1972. *The Economic Theory of Price Indices:
Two Essays on the Effects of Taste, Quality, and Technological Change.*
New York: Academic Press.

Flanagan, R.J. 1984. "Wage Concessions and Long-Term Union Wage Flexibility." *Brookings Papers on Economic Activity* 1: 183–222.

Flanagan, R.J.; D.W. Soskice; and L. Ulman. 1983. *Unionism, Economic Stabilization and Incomes Policy: European Experience.* Washington, D.C.:
Brookings Institution.

Freeman, Richard B. 1983. "Unionism, Price-Cost Margins, and the Return to Capital." National Bureau of Economic Research Working Paper 1164 (July).

Friedman, M. 1968. "The Role of Monetary Policy." *American Economic Review* 58, 1 (March): 1-17.

Frye, Jon, and Robert J. Gordon. 1980. "Variance and Acceleration of Inflation in the 1970s: Alternative Explanatory Models and Methods." National Bureau of Economic Research Working Paper 551 (September).

———. 1981. "Government Intervention in the Inflation Process: The Econometrics of Self-Inflicted Wounds." *American Economic Review* 71, 2 (May): 288-94.

Galbraith, James K. 1983. *The Case for Rapid Growth.* Joint Economic Committee. Washington, D.C.: U.S. Government Printing Office.

Galbraith, John Kenneth. 1952. *A Theory of Price Control.* Cambridge, Mass.: Harvard University Press.

Gordon, Robert J. 1973. "The Response of Wages and Prices to the First Two Years of Controls." *Brookings Papers on Economic Activity* 2: 765-78. Washington, D.C.: Brookings Institution.

———. 1981a. *Macroeconomics.* Boston: Little, Brown.

———. 1981b. "Output Fluctuations and Gradual Price Adjustment." *Journal of Economic Literature* 19 (June): 493-530.

———. 1981c. Discussion of Charles Schultze's "Some Macro Foundations for Micro Theory." *Brookings Papers on Economic Activity* 2: 581-88. Washington, D.C.: Brookings Institution.

———. 1982a. "Inflation, Flexible Exchange Rates, and the Natural Rate of Unemployment." In *Workers, Jobs, and Inflation,* edited by Martin N. Baily, pp. 89-152. Washington, D.C.: Brookings Institution.

———. 1982b. "Price Inertia and Policy Ineffectiveness in the United States, 1890-1980." *Journal of Political Economy* 90, 6 (December): 1087-117.

———. 1983a. Discussion of Jeffrey Sachs' "Real Wages and Unemployment in the OECD Countries." *Brookings Papers on Economic Activity* 1: 290-98. Washington, D.C.: Brookings Institution.

———. 1983b. "A Century of Evidence on Wage and Price Stickiness in the United States, the United Kingdom, and Japan." In *Macroeconomics, Prices and Quantities,* edited by James Tobin, pp. 85-121. Washington, D.C.: Brookings Institution.

Gordon, Robert J., and S.R. King. 1982. "The Output Cost of Disinflation in Traditional and Vector Autoregressive Models." *Brookings Papers on Economic Activity* 1: 205-44. Washington, D.C.: Brookings Institution.

Grandmont, Jean-Michel. 1983. *Money and Value.* New York: Cambridge University Press.

Griliches, Zvi, ed. 1971. *Price Indexes and Quality Change: Studies in New Methods of Measurement.* Cambridge, Mass.: Harvard University Press.

Hagens, John B., and R. Robert Russell. 1985. "Testing for the Effectiveness of Wage/Price Controls: An Application to the Carter Program." *American Economic Review* 75 (March): 191-207.

Hahn, Frank H. 1980. "Memorandum." In *Memoranda on Monetary Policy,* House of Commons, Treasury and Civil Service Committee (July 17): 79-85. London: HMSO.

Hansen, Bent. 1951. *A Study in the Theory of Inflation.* New York: Rinehart.

Hickman, Bert. 1955. "The Korean War and United States Economic Activity, 1950–1952." National Bureau of Economic Research Occasional Paper 49. University Microfilms.

Hicks, J. R. 1969. "Monetary Theory and History: An Attempt at Perspective." In *Monetary Theory*, edited by R. W. Clower, p. 255. Baltimore: Penguin.

Hill, Catherine. 1981. "Monetary and Supply-Side Economics in the United Kingdom." In *Monetary Policy, Selective Credit Policy, and Industrial Policy in France, Britain, West Germany, and Sweden.* Joint Economic Committee (June 26): pp. 36–91. Washington, D.C.: U.S. Government Printing Office.

Isard, Peter. 1973. "The Effectiveness of Using the Tax System to Curb Inflationary Collective Bargains: An Analysis of the Wallich-Weintraub Plan." *Journal of Political Economy* 81: 727–40.

Jackman, Richard, and Richard Layard. 1980. "The Efficiency Case for Long-Run Labour Market Policies." *Economica* 47: 331–49.

———. 1982a. "An Inflation Tax." *Fiscal Studies* 3: 47–59.

———. 1982b. "Trade Unions, the NAIRU and a Wage-Inflation Tax." Appendix to R. Layard, "Is Incomes Policy the Answer to Unemployment?" *Economica* 49: 219–39.

Jackman, Richard; Richard Layard; and Christopher Pissarides. 1983. "On Vacancies." Discussion Paper 165. Centre for Labour Economics, London School of Economics.

———. 1985. "Policies for Reducing the Natural Rate of Unemployment." In *Keynes' Economic Legacy: Contemporary Macroeconomic Theories*, edited by James Butkiewicz. New York: Praeger.

Jacobson, Gary C. 1983. *The Politics of Congressional Elections.* Boston: Little, Brown.

Johnson, G. E. 1980. "The Theory of Labour Market Intervention." *Economica* 47: 309–29.

Johnson, G. E., and R. Layard. 1984. "Long-Run Unemployment and Labor Market Policy." In *Handbook of Labor Economics*, edited by G. Ashenfelter and R. Layard. Amsterdam: North Holland.

Kahn, R. F. 1931. "The Relation of Home Investment to Unemployment." *Economic Journal* 41 (June): 173–98.

Keynes, John Maynard. 1920. *The Economic Consequences of the Peace.* New York: Harcourt, Brace and World.

———. 1936. *The General Theory of Employment, Interest, and Money.* New York: Harcourt, Brace and World.

Kiewiet, D. Roderick. 1983. *Macroeconomics and Micropolitics: The Electoral Effects of Economic Issues.* Chicago: University of Chicago Press.

Klein, L. R., and R. J. Ball. 1959. "Some Econometrics of the Absolute Determination of Prices and Wages." *Economic Journal* 69, 275 (Sept.): 465–82.

Koford, Kenneth J. 1983. "Some Microeconomics of an Incentive Anti-Inflation Plan." Unpublished working paper, University of Delaware.

———. 1984a. "Innovation and Adaptation under Incentive Anti-Inflation Plans." Unpublished. University of Delaware.

———. 1984b. "Do Incentive Anti-inflation Plans Reduce the Natural Rate of Unemployment?" Unpublished. University of Delaware.

Kopits, G.F. 1978. "Wage Subsidies and Employment: An Analysis of the French Experience." *International Monetary Fund Staff Papers* 25, 3 (Sept.): 494–520.

Kosters, Marvin H. 1975. *Controls and Inflation: The Economic Stabilization Program in Retrospect.* Washington, D.C.: American Enterprise Institute.

Kotowitz, Yehuda, and Richard Portes. 1974. "The Tax on Wage Increases: A Theoretical Analysis." *Journal of Public Economics* 3 (May): 113–32.

Krugman, Paul. 1983. "International Aspects of U.S. Monetary and Fiscal Policy." In *The Economics of Large Government Deficits*, Federal Reserve Bank of Boston, proceedings of a conference held at Melvin Village, N.H., October, pp. 112–33.

Kuh, Edwin. 1960. *Profits, Profit Markups, and Productivity: An Examination of Corporate Behavior since 1947.* Study Paper 15 prepared for the Joint Economic Committee of the U.S. Congress in connection with the Study of Employment, Growth, and Price Levels, pp. 61–111. Washington, D.C.: U.S. Government Printing Office.

Lanzillotti, Robert F.; Mary T. Hamilton; and R. Blaine Roberts. 1975. *Phase II in Review: The Price Commission Experience.* Washington, D.C.: Brookings Institution.

Latham, R.W., and D.A. Peel. 1977. "The 'Tax on Wage Increases' When the Firm Is a Monopsonist." *Journal of Public Economics* (October): 247–53.

Layard, R. 1982a. "Is Incomes Policy the Answer to Unemployment?" *Economica* 49 (August): 219–40.

_____. 1982b. *More Jobs, Less Inflation.* London: Grant McIntyre.

Leontief, Wassily W. 1946. "Wages, Profit and Prices." *Quarterly Journal of Economics* 61 (Nov.): 26–39.

Lerner, Abba. 1978. *Curing Chronic Stagflation*, edited by Arthur M. Okun and George L. Perry, pp. 255–69. Washington, D.C.: Brookings Institution.

Lerner, Abba, and David C. Colander. 1980. *MAP: A Market Anti-Inflation Plan.* New York: Harcourt Brace Jovanovich.

_____. 1982. "Anti-Inflation Incentives." *Kyklos* 35: 39–52.

_____. 1983. "Guiding the Invisible Hand." *International Journal of Transport Economics* 10: 25–34.

Liberal/SDP Commission on Unemployment and Industrial Recovery. 1982. *Back to Work.* London: Her Majesty's Stationery Office.

Lucas, Robert E., and Thomas J. Sargent. 1978. "After Keynesian Macroeconomics." In *After the Phillips Curve: Persistence of High Inflation and High Unemployment*, unpublished proceedings of a conference held at the Federal Reserve Bank of Boston.

Malinvaud, E. 1977. *The Theory of Unemployment Reconsidered.* Oxford: Blackwell.

Marion Brick Corporation. Council on Wage and Price Stability Decision of Reconsideration, 15 Nov. 1979.

Mayer, Thomas. 1984. "Fervent Hopes vs. Dismal Reality." *Challenge* (March/April): 49–52.

McDonald, I.M., and R.M. Solow. 1981. "Wage Bargaining and Employment." *American Economic Review* 71, 2 (Dec.): 896–908.

McGuire, Timothy W. 1976. "On Estimating the Effects of Controls." In *The Economics of Price and Wage Controls*, edited by K. Brunner and A. Meltzer, pp. 115–56. Carnegie–Rochester Conference Series 2. Amsterdam: North Holland.

McMenamin, Stuart J., and Robert R. Russell. 1983. "Measuring Labor Compensation in Controls Program." In *The Meausrement of Labor Cost*, edited by Jack E. Triplett, pp. 423–48. Conference on Research in Income and Wealth, Studies in Income and Wealth, Vol. 48. Chicago: University of Chicago Press, for the National Bureau of Economic Research.

Meade, James. 1981. "Fiscal Devices for the Control of Inflation." *Atlantic Economic Journal* 9, 4 (Dec.): 1–11.

_____. 1982. *Wage-Fixing*, vol. 1 of *Stagflation*. London: George Allen and Unwin.

Minford, P. 1983. *Unemployment: Cause and Cure*. Oxford: Martin Robertson.

Mitchell, Daniel J.B. 1981. "Alternatives to Current Anti-Inflation Policy: A Look at Previous Suggestions and a Not-So-Modest Proposal." In *Controlling Inflation: Studies in Wage/Price Policy*. Washington, D.C.: Center for Democratic Policy.

Monroe, Kristen R. 1984. *Presidential Popularity and the Economy*. New York: Praeger.

Nelson, Richard. 1957. "Increased Rents from Increased Costs: A Paradox of Value Theory." *Journal of Political Economy* 65 (Oct.): 387–93.

Nichols, Donald A. 1983. "Wage Measurement Questions Raised by an Incomes Policy." In *The Measurement of Labor Costs*, edited by Jack E. Triplett, pp. 449–62. Conference on Research in Income and Wealth, Studies in Income and Wealth, vol. 48. Chicago: University of Chicago Press, for the National Bureau of Economic Research.

Nickell, S. J., and M. Andrews. 1983. "Trade Unions, Real Wages and Employment in Britain 1951–79." *Oxford Economic Papers* 35 (Supplement): 507–30.

1981 Report of the Council of Economic Advisers. 1981. Washington, D.C.: U.S. Government Printing Office.

Oi, Walter V. 1976. "On Measuring the Impact of Wage-Price Controls: A Critical Appraisal." In *The Economics of Price and Wage Controls*, edited by K. Brunner and A. Meltzer, pp. 7–64. Amsterdam: North Holland.

Okun, A.M. 1977. "The Great Stagflation Swamp." *Challenge* 20 (Nov./Dec.): 6–13.

_____. 1981. *Prices and Quantities: A Macroeconomic Analysis*. Washington, D.C.: Brookings Institution.

Olson, Mancur. 1982. *The Rise and Decline of Nations: Economic Growth, Stagflation, and Social Rigidities*. New Haven: Yale University Press.

Oswald, A. J. 1984a. "Three Theorems on Inflation Taxes and Marginal Employment Subsidies." *Economic Journal* 94 (Sept.): 599–611.

_____. 1984b. "Efficient Bargains Are on the Demand Curve: Theory and Evidence." University of Oxford. Mimeo.

Patinkin, Don, and J. Clark Leith, eds. 1977. *Keynes, Cambridge and the General Theory*. London and Basingstoke: MacMillan.

Pechman, Joseph. 1978. "Comments" in *Curing Chronic Inflation*, edited by Arthur M. Okun and George L. Perry, pp. 154–58. Washington, D.C.: Brookings Institution.

Perry George L. 1975. "Determinants of Wage Inflation around the World." *Brookings Papers on Economic Activity* 2: 403–35. Washington, D.C.: Brookings Institution.

_____. 1983. "What Have We Learned about Disinflation?" *Brookings Papers on Economic Activity* 2: 587–608. Washington, D.C.: Brookings Institution.

Pigou, A.C. 1920. *The Economics of Welfare*. London: MacMillan and Company Limited.

Pissarides, Christopher A. 1985a. "Taxes, Subsidies and Equilibrium Unemployment." *Review of Economic Studies* 52 (January): 121–33.

_____. 1985b. "Short-Run Equilibrium Dynamics of Unemployment, Vacancies and Real Wages." *American Economic Review* 75 (September).

Pittston Company on Behalf of its Compliance Unit, Brink's Incorporated. Council on Wage and Price Stability Decision of Reconsideration, 15 Feb. 1980.

Polak, J.J. 1945. "On the Theory of Price Control." *Review of Economic Statistics* 27 (February): 10–16.

Pollak, Robert A. 1975. "The Intertemporal Costs of Living Index." *Annals of Economic and Social Measurement* 4: 179–95.

Pohlman, Jerry E. 1976. *Inflation under Control?* Reston, Va.: Reston.

Pratt, John W.; David A. Wise; and Richard Zeckhauser. 1979. "Price Differences in Almost Competitive Markets." *Quarterly Journal of Economics* 93, 2 (May): 189–211.

Reder, Melvin W. 1951. "The General Level of Money Wages." *Proceedings of Third Annual Meeting of Industrial Relations Research Association*. Berkeley: Institute of Industrial Relations, pp. 1–17.

Rees, Albert. 1978. "New Policies to Fight Inflation: Sources of Skepticism." In *Curing Chronic Inflation*, edited by Arthur M. Okun and George L. Perry, pp. 217–41. Washington, D.C.: Brookings Institution.

Report of the Joint Economic Committee on the February 1983 Economic Report of the President. 1983. Joint Economic Committee. Washington, D.C.: U.S. Government Printing Office.

Report of the Joint Economic Committee on the February 1984 Economic Report of the President. 1984. Joint Economic Committee. Washington, D.C.: U.S. Government Printing Office.

Robinson, Joan. 1933. *The Economics of Imperfect Competition*. London: MacMillan.

Rutledge, John. 1981. Testimony to the Joint Economic Committee at a Hearing on "Outlook for Recession" (October 21): 32. Washington, D.C.: U.S. Government Printing Office.

Sachs, Jeffrey D. 1979. "Wages, Profits and Macroeconomic Adjustment." *Brookings Papers on Economic Activity* 2: 269–319. Washington, D.C.: Brookings Institution.

_____. 1980. "The Changing Cyclical Behavior of Wages and Prices: 1890–1976." *American Economic Review* 70, 1 (March): 78–90. Also comment by J.E. Price and Sachs's reply. *American Economic Review* 72, 5 (Dec.): 1188–93.

———. 1983. "Real Wages and Unemployment in the OECD Countries." *Brookings Papers on Economic Activity* 1: 255–89. Washington, D.C.: Brookings Institution. Also discussion by Robert J. Gordon and others: 290–304.

Salop, Steven C. 1979. "A Model of the Natural Rate of Unemployment." *American Economic Review* 69, 1 (March): 117–25.

Sato, Kazuo. 1977. "The Meaning and Measurement of the Real Value Added Index." *Review of Economics and Statistics* 58: 434–42.

Schultze, Charles L. 1959. "Recent Inflation in the United States." Study Paper 1 prepared for Joint Economic Committee of Congress in connection with the Study of Employment, Growth, and Price Levels (Sept.). Washington, D.C.: U.S. Government Printing Office.

———. 1975. "Falling Profits, Rising Profit Margins, and the Full-Employment Profit Rate." *Brookings Papers on Economic Activity* 2: 449–69. Washington, D.C.: Brookings Institution.

———. 1980. "Why Controls Don't Work." *Wall Street Journal*, Feb. 27, p. 22.

———. 1981. "Some Macro Foundations for Micro Theory." *Brookings Papers on Economic Activity* 2: 521–75. Washington, D.C.: Brookings Institution.

———. 1983. "Industrial Policy: A Dissent." *Brookings Review* 7 (Fall): 3–12.

Schultze, Charles L., and Joseph L. Tryon. 1960. "Prices and Costs in Manufacturing Industries." Study Paper 17 prepared for Joint Economic Committee of Congress in connection with the Study of Employment, Growth, and Price Levels. Washington, D.C.: U.S. Government Printing Office.

Seidman, L.S. 1978. "Tax-Based Incomes Policies." *Brookings Papers on Economic Activity* 2: 301–48. Washington, D.C.: Brookings Institution. Also in *Curing Chronic Inflation*, edited by Arthur M. Okun and George L. Perry, pp. 65–126. Washington, D.C.: Brookings Institution.

———. 1979. "The Role of Tax-Based Incomes Policy." *American Economic Review* 69 (May): 202–06.

———. 1981. "A Tax-Based Incomes Policy to Reduce Inflation without Recession (and Other Alternatives of Reaganomics)." In *Controlling Inflation: Studies in Wage/Price Policy*, pp. 23–27. Washington, D.C.: Center for Democratic Policy.

Shapiro, C., and J. Stiglitz. 1983. "Equilibrium Unemployment as a Labor Disciplining Device." Princeton University. Mimeo.

Sims, Christopher A. 1969. "Theoretical Basis for a Double-Deflated Index of Real Value Added." *Review of Economics and Statistics* 51: 470–71.

Skånland, H. 1981. *Inntektspolitikkens Dilemma – Kan detloses? (The Dilemma of Incomes Policy – Can It Be Resolved?)* Oslo: Cappelen.

Slitor, Richard E. 1979. "Implementation and Design of Tax-Based Incomes Policies." *American Economic Review* 69 (May): 212–15.

Smith, Bruce. 1983. "Limited Information, Credit Rationing and Optimal Government Lending Policy." *American Economic Review* 73, 3 (June): 305–18.

Solow, Robert. 1966. "The Case Against the Case Against the Guideposts." In *Guidelines, Informal Controls, and the Market Place*, edited by George Shultz and Robert Aliber, pp. 41-54. Chicago: University of Chicago Press.

Stigler, George J., and James J. Kindahl. 1970. *The Behavior of Industrial Prices*. New York: National Bureau of Economic Research.

Stiglitz, Joseph E. 1985. "Theories of Wage Rigidity." *Keynes' Economic Legacy: Contemporary Macroeconomic Theories*. Newark, Delaware: University of Delaware Press.

Triplett, Jack E. 1975. "The Measurement of Inflation: A Survey of Research on the Accuracy of Price Indexes." In *Analysis of Inflation*, edited by Paul H. Earl, pp. 19-82. Lexington, Mass.: Lexington Books.

_____. 1983. "An Essay on Labor Cost." In *The Measurement of Labor Cost*, edited by Jack E. Triplett, pp. 1-60. Conference on Research in Income and Wealth, Studies in Income and Wealth, Vol. 48. Chicago: University of Chicago Press for the National Bureau of Economic Research.

Tufte, Edward R. 1978. *Political Control of the Economy*. Princeton: Princeton University Press.

Usher, Dan, ed. 1980. *The Measurement of Capital*. Conference on Research in Income and Wealth, Studies in Income and Wealth, Vol. 45. Chicago: University of Chicato Press for the National Bureau of Economic Research.

Wallich, H.C., and S. Weintraub. 1971. "A Tax-Based Incomes Policy." *Journal of Economic Issues* 5 (June): 1-19.

Weitzman, Martin. 1983. "Some Macroeconomic Implications of Alternative Compensation Systems." *Economic Journal* 93: 763-83.

_____. 1984. *The Share Economy: Conquering Stagflation*. Cambridge, Mass.: Harvard University Press.

INDEX

257

ABOUT THE CONTRIBUTORS

Sheetal K. Chand, a resident of Norway, was born in Uganda and received a Ph.D. in economics from the University of Western Ontario. At present he holds the rank of a senior economist with the Fiscal Affairs Department of the International Monetary Fund. He has published articles on international finance and on macroeconomics.

James K. Galbraith is visiting associate professor, LBJ School of Public Affairs, University of Texas at Austin. He served as executive director, Joint Economic Committee, U.S. Congress, from 1981–82 and as deputy director 1983–84. He holds a Ph.D. in economics from Yale University, has published numerous articles, and is presently writing a book on the design and conduct of economic policy.

Richard Jackman is currently senior lecturer at the London School of Economics. He has written widely on public finance and monetary policy. A former co-editor of *Economica*, he is currently a member of the editorial board of *Local Government Studies*.

Kenneth Koford is currently associate visiting professor of economics at Washington University, on leave from the University of Delaware. He has written widely on both politics and economics, and on MAP and incentive anti-inflation plans.

Richard Layard is currently professor of economics and head of the Centre for Labour Economics at the London School of Economics. He has written more than ten books and a myriad of articles in journals such as *The Economic Journal, The Journal of Political Economy*, and *Economica.*

Jeffrey B. Miller is an associate professor of economics at the University of Delaware. He has written extensively in the areas of managerial incentives and national planning in market economies. His recent work has focued on incentive policies to reduce inflation.

Christopher Pissarides is currently a lecturer at the London School of Economics. He has visited at Princeton University and worked for the Central Bank of Greece. He has written widely on tax-based incomes policies and is well known in the field of labor economics.

R. Robert Russell is a professor of economics at New York University. He was deputy director, then director, of the Council of Wage and Price Stability in the Carter administration. He has published numerous papers in professional journals and is the co-author of two books on microeconomic theory.

Walter Salant is a senior fellow emeritus in the Economics Studies Program of The Brookings Institution. One of the early Keynesians, he played an important role in introducing Keynesian ideas into government. During World War II he worked on the Price Control Board and had direct experience with the problems of price control. Among his many books are *Worldwide Inflation: Theory and Recent Experience* and *How Has the World Economy Changed since 1929?*

Jerrold E. Schneider is associate professor of political science at the University of Delaware. He is the author of *Ideological Coalitions in Congress.* He has been a research fellow (1969-70) and guest scholar at The Brookings Institution (1976-77; 1980) and was a National Endowment for the Humanities Fellow in 1976.

Laurence S. Seidman, a graduate of Harvard, is currently a professor of economics at the University of Delaware. He has written widely on tax-based incomes policies and on the use of incentives to achieve macroeconomic results. He is also the author of the book entitled *The Design of Federal Employment Programs* and has a macroeconomics book forthcoming.

Jack Triplett is the associate commissioner of the U.S. Office of Research and Evaluation of the U.S. Bureau of Labor Statistics. He is probably the most respected economic theorist specializing in problems of price indices and has written numerous articles and books. He served on the Council of Wage and Price Stability staff in the Carter administration.

William Vickrey is currently McVicker Professor Emeritus of Columbia University. He has written a large number of books and has been a leader in designing abstract schemes in which price incentives are used to achieve a variety of results. Among his books are *Agenda for Progressive Taxation* and *Metastatics.*

ABOUT THE EDITOR

David C. Colander is, together with Abba Lerner, the author of *MAP: A Market Anti-Inflation Plan.* He is one of the early designers of the value-added anti-inflation plan and has recently published a macroeconomics book, *Macroeconomic Theory and Policy.*